Rethinking the Age of Revolution

In the last twenty years, scholars have rushed to re-examine revolutionary experiences across the Atlantic, through the Americas, and, more recently, in imperial and global contexts. While Revolution has been a perennial favourite topic of national historians, a new generation of historians has begun to eschew traditional foundation narratives and embrace the insights of Atlantic and transnational history to re-examine what is increasingly called 'the Age of Revolution'. This volume raises important questions about this new turn, and contributors pay particular attention to the hidden peoples and forces at work in this Revolutionary world. From Indian insurgents in Columbia and the Andes, to the terror exercised on the sailors and soldiers of imperial armies, and from Dutch radicals to Senegalese chiefs, these contributions reveal a new social history of the Age of Revolution that has sometimes been deliberately obscured from view.

This book was originally published as a special issue of *Atlantic Studies*.

Michael A. McDonnell is Associate Professor of History at the University of Sydney, Australia. He is the author of numerous articles, essays, and books on the American Revolution and early American history, including *The Politics of War* (2007), *Remembering the Revolution* (2013), and *Masters of Empire: Great Lakes Indians and the Making of America* (2015).

T0346605

Rethinking the Age of Revolution

Edited by
Michael A. McDonnell

Routledge
Taylor & Francis Group

LONDON AND NEW YORK

First published 2017
by Routledge

2 Park Square, Milton Park, Abingdon, Oxfordshire OX14 4RN
52 Vanderbilt Avenue, New York, NY 10017

Routledge is an imprint of the Taylor & Francis Group, an informa business

First issued in paperback 2018

British Library Cataloguing in Publication Data
A catalogue record for this book is available from the British Library

ISBN 13: 978-1-138-71504-2 (hbk)
ISBN 13: 978-0-367-13912-4 (pbk)

Typeset in Myriad Pro
by RefineCatch Limited, Bungay, Suffolk

Publisher's Note
The publisher accepts responsibility for any inconsistencies that may have
arisen during the conversion of this book from journal articles to book chapters,
namely the possible inclusion of journal terminology.

Disclaimer
Every effort has been made to contact copyright holders for their permission to
reprint material in this book. The publishers would be grateful to hear from any
copyright holder who is not here acknowledged and will undertake to rectify
any errors or omissions in future editions of this book.

Contents

Citation Information   vii
Notes on Contributors   ix

Introduction: Rethinking the Age of Revolution   1
Michael A. McDonnell

1. "The sole owners of the land": Empire, war, and authority in the Guajira
   Peninsula, 1761–1779   15
   Forrest Hylton

2. Militarizing the Atlantic World: Army discipline, coerced labor, and Britain's
   commercial empire   45
   Peter Way

3. "The supreme power of the people": Local autonomy and radical democracy
   in the Batavian revolution (1795–1798)   70
   Pepijn Brandon and Karwan Fatah-Black

4. Rethinking Africa in the Age of Revolution: The evolution of
   Jean-Baptiste-Léonard Durand's *Voyage au Sénégal*   89
   Pernille Røge

5. Sovereignty disavowed: the Tupac Amaru revolution in the Atlantic world   107
   Sinclair Thomson

Index   133

Citation Information

The chapters in this book were originally published in *Atlantic Studies*, volume 13, issue 3 (September 2016). When citing this material, please use the original page numbering for each article, as follows:

Introduction
Rethinking the Age of Revolution
Michael A. McDonnell
Atlantic Studies, volume 13, issue 3 (September 2016), pp. 301–314

Chapter 1
"The sole owners of the land": Empire, war, and authority in the Guajira Peninsula, 1761–1779
Forrest Hylton
Atlantic Studies, volume 13, issue 3 (September 2016), pp. 315–344

Chapter 2
Militarizing the Atlantic World: Army discipline, coerced labor, and Britain's commercial empire
Peter Way
Atlantic Studies, volume 13, issue 3 (September 2016), pp. 345–369

Chapter 3
"The supreme power of the people": Local autonomy and radical democracy in the Batavian revolution (1795–1798)
Pepijn Brandon and Karwan Fatah-Black
Atlantic Studies, volume 13, issue 3 (September 2016), pp. 370–388

Chapter 4
Rethinking Africa in the Age of Revolution: The evolution of Jean-Baptiste-Léonard Durand's Voyage au Sénégal
Pernille Røge
Atlantic Studies, volume 13, issue 3 (September 2016), pp. 389–406

Chapter 5

Sovereignty disavowed: the Tupac Amaru revolution in the Atlantic world
Sinclair Thomson
Atlantic Studies, volume 13, issue 3 (September 2016), pp. 407–431

For any permission-related enquiries please visit:
http://www.tandfonline.com/page/help/permissions

Notes on Contributors

Pepijn Brandon is a Postdoctoral Researcher at the Vrije Universiteit, Amsterdam, and the International Institute of Social History, Amsterdam, the Netherlands. His current projects focus on slavery in the Dutch Atlantic, with specific attention to the relationship between slavery and Dutch capitalism and the interaction between slaves and wage laborers.

Karwan Fatah-Black is Assistant Professor of Social and Economic History at Leiden University, the Netherlands. He is co-editor of the *Journal of Global Slavery*, *Itinerario*, the *Journal of Suriname and Caribbean Studies OSO*, and the Zeven Provinciën book series on the early modern Netherlands.

Forrest Hylton is Visiting Assistant Professor of History at Northwestern University, USA. He is the co-author of *Ya es otro tiempo el presente: Cuatro momentos de insurgencia indígena* (La Paz: Muela del Diablo, 2003), author of *Evil Hour in Colombia* (New York: Verso, 2006), and co-author with Sinclair Thomson of *Revolutionary Horizons: Past and Present in Bolivian Politics* (New York: Verso, 2007).

Michael A. McDonnell is Associate Professor of History at the University of Sydney, Australia. He is the author of numerous articles, essays, and books on the American Revolution and early American history, including *The Politics of War* (2007), *Remembering the Revolution* (2013), and *Masters of Empire: Great Lakes Indians and the Making of America* (2015).

Pernille Røge is Assistant Professor of French Imperial History at the University of Pittsburgh, USA. Her publications include articles on the early modern French, British, and Danish colonial empires.

Sinclair Thomson is Associate Professor of Latin American History at New York University, USA. He is the author of *We Alone Will Rule: Native Andean Politics in the Age of Insurgency* (Madison: University of Wisconsin Press, 2002), and co-author with Forrest Hylton of *Revolutionary Horizons: Past and Present in Bolivian Politics* (New York: Verso, 2007).

Peter Way serves as Professor of American History at the University of Windsor, Canada. The author of *Common Labour: Workers and the Digging of North American Canals, 1780–1860* (winner of the 1994 Frederick Jackson Turner Prize awarded by the Organization of American Historians), he has published widely in the history of laboring peoples in the Anglo-Atlantic World.

Rethinking the Age of Revolution

Michael A. McDonnell

Department of History, University of Sydney, Sydney, Australia

Revolution, it seems, is once again in the air. In the last decade or two, scholars have rushed to re-examine revolutionary experiences across the Atlantic, through the Americas, and more recently in imperial and global contexts. While Revolution has been a perennial favorite topic of national historians, a new generation of historians have begun to eschew traditional foundation narratives and embrace the insights of Atlantic and transnational history to create a new-old field of study – the Age of Revolution – already replete with books, articles, collections, texts, workshops, blogs, conference panels, and even its own genealogy. And the topics are diverse – from analyses of honor to the role of international Protestantism across revolutions – and range ever more broadly – from the revolutionary reverberations of the Wahhabi movement in the Persian Gulf region to Indian and slave Royalists in the northern Andes. Judging by the buzz, many more, and more diverse, studies are in the works. In historiographical terms, we are in the midst of another kind of "age of Revolutions," as Thomas Paine put it in *Age of Reason*, "in which everything may be looked for."[1]

As Sarah Knott recently noted, the revolution in Revolution scholarship has had a curiously long and somewhat halting gestation period. Despite an oft-ignored call to arms by C.L.R. James in 1938, and a more publicized intervention by R.R. Palmer starting in 1959, the historical profession was too mired in nationalist debates and perhaps too wary of international entanglements to revive wholesale an idea of transnational revolution. Arguably, it was not until the publication of Peter Linebaugh and Marcus Rediker's landmark book, *The Many-Headed Hydra: Sailors, Slaves, Commoners, and the Hidden History of the Revolutionary Atlantic* in 2000, that scholars began connecting the concurrent rise in interest in Atlantic history with an Age of Revolution. That connection was cemented with the rediscovery of the importance of the Haitian Revolution starting with Michel-Rolph Trouillot's powerful work *Silencing the Past: Power and the Production of History* in 1995, followed by a spate of new works in the first decade of the twenty-first century, and furthered and extended by contributions from Spanish-American, West African, Indian, British imperial, and global historians.[2]

Given the relative infancy of the field of the Age of Revolution, and the explosion of literature, there are of course many definitional questions yet to be explored let alone agreed upon. Even the umbrella term often gets modified as circumstances dictate. Should we call it an Age of Revolution, Age of Revolutions, Age of Atlantic Revolution, Age of Democratic Revolution, or Age of Imperial Revolution? The reasons for these modifiers often lie in how we define this Revolutionary Age and its scope and whether we believe in a central unifying force behind the era, or a series of disparate ruptures that can be connected in some way. Focusing on the "formal" (read "political") Atlantic Revolutions of the late eighteenth century, scholars often look for the connections or convergences between and among them. Others look for common origins, parallel events, or diverging consequences of these upheavals. Still other scholars are interested in the nature and degree of changes ushered in by successful Revolutions. More flexible definitions return us to an earlier idea of revolution that emphasizes change and transformation caused by major socio-economic disruptions, disorder, or in C.A. Bayly's term, a "world crisis." At the very least, most scholars – though by no means all – can agree that something particularly profound occurred in world history between the years c. 1750 and c. 1848 effectively ushering in the "modern world."[3]

While so much remains ill-defined, and with so much promising research in the works, it would be premature and churlish to mount a critique of the burgeoning scholarship in the field. Yet as we revel in the new worlds revealed, we might at least dwell briefly on what we might lose within these more expansive frameworks. Can the Age of Revolution encompass civil wars as well as revolutionary wars, repression as well as radicalism, slavery as well as abolition, renewed imperial energy as well as colonial wars for independence, and indigenous peoples as well as creole elites? Can and should the Age of Revolution embrace more than just the Atlantic? Are we sufficiently multilingual to write a truly multipolar history of this era? Lynn Hunt has also asked some important questions about whether local, national, or global contexts are best for understanding popular violence and aspirations for popular sovereignty. And as metanarratives of a Revolutionary Age cohere, will they incorporate rather than efface a generation or more of detailed work that has fruitfully and thankfully emerged from local or national studies on topics such as gender, race, class and women, slaves, Native Americans, and the poor.[4]

Even more concerning, perhaps, are the politics behind the emerging Age of Revolution scholarship. While historians have been quick to embrace transnational impulses and to look for global connections and convergences, there seems less of an appetite to embrace a revolutionary or radical politics when trying to make sense of the era. As Jeremy Adelman has noted, it is unlikely a coincidence that R.R. Palmer's work has been revived in the post-Cold War era for a post-nationalist, post-socialist turn in history. The renewed interest in transnational connections and convergences in the Age of Revolution is, in Adelman's view, "in keeping with the temper of the times, which sees the spread of liberal democracy as the dominant tidal process."[5] Sarah Knott has put it more bluntly. Despite the subject matter, she argues, historians even of the Age of Revolution have lost a sense of purpose for history writing (with the exception perhaps of those writing on Haiti). Instead, a renewed empiricism has emerged focused on connections and addressed to "knowledge making in a globalizing present, which appears most often in a socially inclusive but politically quietist narrative form." "This is," Knott concludes, "history writing for neo-liberal times."[6]

At least some of these questions were addressed at a gathering of emerging, mid-career, and established scholars at the University of Pittsburgh in May 2014. Organized by Marcus Rediker and his Atlantic history colleagues, the conference was ambitiously titled "The Future of Atlantic, Transnational, and World History." The goal was to "push the boundaries of boundary-less history and to imagine new ways to explore perennial subjects of historical investigation."[7] The organizers were especially interested in original approaches that linked the local with the regional and global and that proposed innovative ways to think about those connections. From across the widely ranging themes of "Labor," "Race," "Empire," and "Resistance," a discussion emerged about who and what were included or excluded from narratives of Atlantic history, and especially of the Age of Revolution, and why this was so. Out of this came the current collection of essays, which cohere around the silences and omissions – the still hidden histories – and the politics that often obscure our view of the Age of Revolution.

Taken together, the essays give us a sense of what a purposeful and politically engaged Age of Revolution literature could look like, however imperfect a project that might be at this moment in time. Certainly, the essays by Forrest Hylton, Pernille Røge, and Sinclair Thomson all draw inspiration from an anti-colonial impulse dating back to the Age of Revolution and running through C.L.R. James to more recent postcolonial critiques of the new nations that arose in place of empires. In the case of the indigenous peoples that each of these authors write about, that anti-colonial movement predated the Age of Revolution and is still a source of conflict – another challenge to our periodization.[8]

Yet all of the authors also either explicitly or implicitly follow the struggles of different peoples to engage with or resist the spread of capitalism. As Peter Way's essay reminds us, the same imperial ambitions that ultimately led to the Age of Revolution were also deeply implicated in the successful spread of globalizing capitalism. The competitive and conflict-ridden race to acquire new territories, to plant them with produce commodities for profits, using slaves, indentured servants, and laborers, and to create the social hierarchies needed to sustain them, gave this era a central unifying force. Though the nature and outcomes of these engagements with and struggles against imperialism and the spread of capitalism varied, the conflicts themselves connected and gave animating force to the Age of Revolution.[9]

Moreover, in probing the silences and hidden histories of this era, the essays trace their lineage not just from C.L.R. James and Linebaugh and Rediker in their commitment to understanding the dynamic energy of ordinary people and the way they shaped revolution but also Michel-Rolph Trouillot's call to overcome the many erasures, silences, and disavowals in the archives and our historical work. The two political projects are not unrelated, of course. Trouillot argued that historical silencing began with the lived inequalities of the time that gave rise to inequalities in the sources produced, and the ways in which narratives were initially spun. In turn, this initial silencing skewed the preservation and retrieval of surviving archival material and the narratives they seemed to justify, and the subsequent retrospective significance assigned to peoples and events. In this formulation, "lived inequalities yield unequal historical power."[10] Historians working within local and national frameworks have struggled, and still struggle, to overcome those silences. As we zoom out to Atlantic, imperial, and global contexts, those silences can become deafening.[11]

Nowhere is this silencing more evident than in the absence of indigenous peoples in the literature on Atlantic history and now the Age of Revolution. Whether you take your cue from the Haitian radicals of C.L.R. James' *Black Jacobins*, the liberal democrats of R.R. Palmer's *Age of the Democratic Revolution*, the industrial workers and capitalists of Hobsbawm's *Age of Revolution*, the motley crew of Rediker and Linebaugh's *Many-Headed Hydra*, or more recent iterations of a revolutionary world, one would struggle to find indigenous peoples at all, let alone indigenous peoples as driving part of the story themselves. They sometimes appear at the margins of revolutionary struggles, such as in North America, where they are typically depicted as being compelled by Europeans to make the best of a number of bad choices in choosing a side. In Latin America, they often appear only as a specter that delayed or limited independence movements across much of the continent. And of course, we know and sometimes acknowledge that dispossessed Indian lands were used to provide much of the fuel – in the form of cultivating new crops – that drove the industrial revolution. In these studies, indigenous peoples are victims, and objects of study, passive players or pawns in a game in which they could only lose.[12]

Yet as Forrest Hylton's essays suggest, there is much more to the story of many indigenous peoples in the Age of Revolution. When we do take into account indigenous peoples, at the very least we gain a new perspective on the origins, nature, and consequences of European and American Revolutions. Hylton takes the insights of a new generation of historians of Native Americans and through careful attention to the historical-anthropological dynamics underlying Guajiro–Spanish relations in eighteenth-century New Granada (now Columbia, and eastern Venezuela), overturns conventional images of Native peoples reacting to imperial initiatives. Instead, Hylton shows that we cannot understand Spanish imperial reform efforts in the late eighteenth century without understanding the long history of indigenous ethnogenesis, resistance, and adaptation to new Atlantic realities. By the mid-eighteenth century, Guajiro power, politics, law, and kinship patterns set the parameters within which Spanish colonial officials acted in the region. Initiating a cycle of insurgency and counter-insurgency in the 1760s and 1770s involving tens of thousands of armed Indians, the Guajiro helped undermine Spanish efforts to rule the region for decades or more, added immensely to the costs of empire, diverted and reshaped capitalism in the region, and contributed to a growing sense of crisis in the Spanish imperial world.[13]

Hylton uses this history of the Guajiro to link the local and global through the lens of a region not often included in our ideas of a Revolutionary Age. In doing so, he reminds us of the rich rewards of looking locally, and rethinking the Atlantic from the so-called peripheries outward; it also reminds us of the fragilities of empire – the cracks in the edifice, and the sometimes paper thin veneer of empire at the margins, which help explain the faultlines that ruptured in the Age of Revolution. Yet his essay also points to Atlantic connections and the rippling political and economic turbulence regional events precipitated – a turbulence that C.A. Bayly might incorporate as part of his description of the world crisis that underpinned the Age of Revolution. But as new studies of the Middle East and South Asia would suggest, we need to look carefully at the roots of such disruptions outside Europe, even among and between indigenous communities. Radical shifts in power between autonomous groups in the Americas, the Cape, West Africa, and the Indian and Pacific Ocean predated and sometimes unfolded simultaneously with new European initiatives in the West and new encounters in the East, and often shaped the nature of European enmeshment in native affairs.[14]

Few studies of Asian–European relations begin at the waterfront, or point of meeting; nor should they for indigenous–European relations. We need deep histories of indigenous peoples that force us to rethink colonial encounter and enmeshment, and to discern longer term patterns amid the sometimes revolutionary changes ushered in by it. Indigenous peoples had long forged important strategies and tactics to deal with newcomers and applied them to Europeans, often leaving an indelible mark – on Europeans and the trajectory of European history. Whether they affected the course of independence movements, or redirected exploration, settlement, and economic relationships, indigenous peoples changed the nature and purpose of European empires at this critical juncture in subtle, and sometimes not so subtle, ways. Hylton's essay thus shows the promise of taking a new and oft-ignored perspective on the Age of Revolution, as well as the need to pay attention to the long histories of indigenous peoples in this era.[15]

Hylton points to the often hidden levers driving the Age of Revolution. In the same vein but from an entirely different perspective, Peter Way's essay on the coerced labor at the heart of imperial expansion in this period lays bare the violence and discipline that were a vital precondition for the Age of Revolution. Though Hylton's findings show that it had uneven results in different quarters, the mid-eighteenth century saw a marked uptick in the use of military force to police and expand European empires in all quarters of the globe. Way argues that while some Atlantic historians have paid too little attention to the central instruments of the expansion of capitalism and imperialism – the army and navy – far more have neglected such important subaltern subjects as soldiers and sailors. As a result, he maintains we have missed the crucial ingredient in the spread of capitalism alongside that of empires – the forced labor and horrific discipline inherent to the success of the growing imperial armies and navies of the day. The rapid colonial expansion of the late eighteenth and early nineteenth centuries was facilitated by the rise of the fiscal-military state, but it was sustained by the raw violence of military service. The story has been silenced, in Trouillot's terms, by the historic narratives and conventions we use, and the retrospective significance assigned to it. We have reduced this violence and terror to the banal.[16]

In contrast, Way documents the day-to-day lawful terror and dominion exercised upon and over common soldiers by their officers in gripping detail. Imperial agents beat, whipped, humiliated, shot, and hanged the men who were in turn tasked with the appropriation of lands and the creation of new regimes of coerced labor on colonial plantations. Rarely mentioned in the pamphlet literature of the era, and oft-neglected within sweeping studies of connections, convergences, and parallels across the oceans, this violence permeated the Age of Revolution. It was also only marginally ameliorated in the armies of Revolution that fought against imperial forces. And in turn, that brutal discipline was replicated in the armed forces of the new and often imperial nations created by Revolution. The cycle of violence continued across and through the revolutionary era.[17]

Moreover, the violence at the heart of imperial expansion gave rise to different forms of resistance within the armed forces that ranged from noncompliance, to disobedience, and through to desertion and mutiny. The extremes that common soldiers and sailors endured could thus not only inspire the radicalism of Linebaugh and Rediker's motley crew in the revolutionary Atlantic, but also the more formal instances of revolutions within revolutionary moments, such as the massive transnational naval strikes that spread across the North Atlantic between 1780 and 1805, about which Niklas Frykman has written. Of course, the sailors who were struck, and who in turn struck, left few traceable records of their own that might explain their movements or their conversations and give shape to and legitimate their own revolution against often despotic and arbitrary force. National and imperial archives have exacerbated this silence rendering less visible the system-wide transnational forces connecting soldiers and especially sailors and driving these mutinies. Within national narratives, stories about desertion and mutinies and have been quarantined, contained, and marginalized.[18]

Pepijn Brandon and Karwan Fatah-Black shift our attention to another quarter of the revolutionary Atlantic, and another kind of silencing – brought about by local contests over the narration of events at the time. The authors look inside the Batavian Revolution of 1795 and explore a revealing moment in which provincial moderates arrested five well-known radical democrats in Leiden. Their crime was to call for a nation-wide assembly of neighborhood councils. Moderates believed they wanted to make an end-run around the moderate-dominated National Convention and push the Revolution in a more radical direction. They hoped to use the power of locally elected councils to pursue a more democratic agenda, including universal male suffrage, more political representation, the purging of Orangist sympathizers from the National Convention, and greater local autonomy. The arrests threatened to precipitate a revolutionary stand-off between Provincial Authorities and popular radicals. Yet moderates at the municipal level managed to regain control over the situation by condemning the arrests as an infringement of local jurisdiction, but also criticizing the call for an Assembly of Neighbourhood Councils. In doing so, they avoided a direct conflict with popular radicals and managed to steal their thunder by emphasizing local jurisdiction as the main principle at stake. Subsequently, in the face of determined conservative resistance, radicals themselves could not rally and unify beyond the local, and were forced to reframe their struggles in terms of a defense of ancient local rights. Their more far-reaching and revolutionary aims gave way to a rear-guard action against a vision of a strong, rational, and unified state among revolutionary elites.[19]

As Brandon and Fatah-Black note, the clash between national ideals and highly localized realities played out in a distinctive way in the Batavian Revolution. But the tensions between programs for the rationalization of state bureaucracy along nationalizing lines and popular support for far-reaching local autonomy was common to each of the Atlantic Revolutions. As the authors note of Pierre Serna's recent work, all the Atlantic revolutions contained elements of a "War of Independence," yet at the national level these Revolutions increasingly evolved into wars of subjugation of the regions to the center. At the same time, the center reconfigured the narrative and stole the mantle of radicalism. R.R. Palmer, for example, noted that the process of people becoming a constituent power was one of the key defining features of his Age of Democratic Revolution. Yet Palmer never defined the people, and they only ever seemed to constitute themselves in his work at the national level. That the anti-democratic creators of the Federal Constitution in the USA are now seen as the champions of American radicalism during the revolutionary era is testimony to the silencing power inherent in appropriating contemporary narratives.[20]

In her essay on Jean-Baptiste-Léonard Durand, director of the French *Compagnie de la gomme du Sénégal* in the 1780s and author of a later account of these experiences called *Voyage au Sénégal*, Pernille Røge demonstrates just how some of those new narratives were created. While the decolonization of the Americas and the abolition of the slave trade might be counted as achievements of the Age of Revolution, they also have to be put alongside a new European imperial commitment to colonization and the spread of commerce and capitalism elsewhere in the world, particularly in Africa. By studying Durand's activities in Senegal in the mid-1780s and comparing this with his published account of those experiences in 1802, Røge shows that Durand's belief in the idea of

Africans as "savage" and in need of civilization through colonization arose from his deep frustration with powerful gum and slave merchants along the Senegal River, and their unwillingness to negotiate new trade deals that worked against their own interests. European colonial agents' inability to dominate and control commercial expansion in this region was increasingly interpreted as the result of African flaws. Durand later argued that powerful groups such as the Trarza, Brakna, and Darmankour Moor, the Wolofs, who dominated trade in Senegal were savage barbarians from which other ethnic groups needed rescuing.[21]

In tracing the evolution of Durand's experiences and thinking about the region, Røge reveals the elisions and subtle ways in which the currents of the revolutionary Atlantic formed and reformed ideas of "others" in this era of transformation. And, echoing Linebaugh and Rediker, she demonstrates the ways in which imperialists reconceived and rejustified new ventures in the face of indigenous intransigence. For the Age of Revolution was equally complicit in this reconfiguration, altering the parameters of acceptable colonial expansion. The French and Haitian Revolutions simultaneously made centuries-old forms of human exploitation unacceptable, including the enslavement of Africans. For a colonial agent such as Durand, desperate to see France advance its interests in Africa over the claims of other European powers, illustrating how those ethnic groups formerly used in the slave trade were not only in need but also desirous of Europe's "civilizing" influence was "politically and economically expedient." Like the Guajiro in Hylton's essay, indigenous peoples in West Africa played a powerful role in frustrating and reshaping imperial ambitions. Both essays thus bring us closer to understanding how seemingly local contests over trade, autonomy, and sovereignty could help trigger the Age of Revolution.[22]

Many of the themes in the foregoing essays come together in the final essay by Sinclair Thomson. His contribution confronts the silences inherent in our notion of the Age of Revolution most directly. Thomson, a historian of the extraordinary events that should be labelled the Andean Revolution of the early 1780s, asks why it has been generally ignored in the Atlantic historiography of the Age of Revolution. Drawing on Trouillot's notion of silencing and Sibylle Fischer's idea of "disavowal," Thomson traces the neglect back to contemporary Spanish responses to the Revolution. While knowledge of the events in the Andes circulated widely throughout the Atlantic World in the early 1780s, desperate Spanish attempts to prevent circulation of the news of the insurrection limited its reach. Yet more importantly, the Spanish were quick to revise reports of the conflict as merely an ugly and brutal expression of racial violence – a race war. In doing so, the Spanish disavowed the radical principle at the heart of the Andean Revolution – indigenous political sovereignty.[23]

Thomson pushes us to take these findings further. Rather than trying to fit the Andean Revolution into an existing paradigm of Atlantic Revolutions, Thomson argues, with Trouillot, that we need to rethink our ideas of the Age of Revolution in light of movements to claim or reclaim indigenous lands and political authority that challenged European and creole sovereignty in the Americas. A nation under Indian rule was a revolutionary goal from which even the most enlightened European dissidents and revolutionary dreamers ultimately drew back. The silencing and disavowals of the movement reflect a contemporary awareness of the profound implications of this goal. And the repudiation of Indigenous sovereignty that marked the period would later shape the historical narratives about the era. While those narratives emphasized self-determination, representative democracy, and liberal individualism and citizenship, they often positioned themselves against, Thomson argues, native claims. In the Andean case: "an anticolonial emancipation movement in the Americas that drew upon alternative conceptions of self-determination, communal democracy, and native territorial rights, and that envisioned a society in which Indians ruled rather than served." Moreover, rather than a "backward" or "un-modern" movement, the Andean Revolution arguably prefigured the contests over land and sovereignty that shaped much of the history of the new American nations in the nineteenth and twentieth centuries – and were arguably one of the most lasting legacies of the Age of Revolution. Yet, in turn, the losses sustained by indigenous peoples in the Age of Revolution and beyond also gave rise to the lived inequalities that contributed further to the silencing of their voices, and histories.[24]

Taken collectively, the essays that follow all compel us to think carefully about the underlying forces as well as the silences that shaped the Age of Revolution. As we rush to explore this historiographic field, the essays demonstrate the need to think about the lived inequalities and the imbalances and omissions that resulted in a skewed archival record and distorted contemporary narrations of events. But we must also question our own narratives of the period and the retrospective significance we assign to peoples, places, processes, and events in this era. And in doing so, as Way argues, we would do well not to abjure "the trenchant empiricism of good social history." We must be attuned to the local as much as the regional, national, and global – attuned to the depth and dynamism of those local histories as much as the pervasive nature of imperial expansion and the spread of capitalism. We must also be open-minded enough, as Sinclair Thomson urges, to take these events we uncover seriously enough to "reevaluate our notions of the Age of Revolution and of revolutionary Atlantic geography, and to reimagine that period in history and that world in new ways." Such was the promise of the Atlantic history at one time. Such was the promise of Revolution at one time. We are, we might hope, in another moment in which "everything may be looked for."[25]

Finally, for a truly global history of the Age of Revolution to emerge, we also have to expand our vision. In May 2013, Nicholas Guyatt and Luke Clossey drew our attention to the fact that in Canada, the USA, and the UK, 80% of historical scholarship is about the "Global North," which comprises about 20% of the world's population.[26] Less than 20% of historical scholarship is about the rest of the world, or the Global South. When we write about "the few" in the Age of Revolution, we usually mean liberal elites. Today, at least in terms of historical scholarship, those in the Global North are the few. And we historians are still only writing about the few. Guyatt and Clossey, along with Røge, Hylton, and Thomson at least, remind us that there are many histories still unread; many histories still untold. The future of global history will invariably emerge far from our current purview. The "rest of the world" had a long history before the rise of the Atlantic empires, or "the West," and will arguably have a much longer history after its inevitable decline. Historians of all people ought to have some appreciation of their future irrelevancy in a globalizing world if we continue to study only western history. As Michel Trouillot reminded us over twenty years ago now, non-western peoples will always remain only a part of the history of the global domination of the West if we do not retell stories that bring forward the perspective of the world. In the meantime, and at the very least, we need to recognize that our histories may already perpetuate and reinforce the many lived inequalities of the past, and present.[27]

Notes

1. Knott, "Narrative the Age of Revolution," 3–36; Klooster, *Revolutions in the Atlantic World*; Armitage and Subrahmanyam, *The Age of Revolutions in Global Context*; "Age of Revolutions"; Compeau, "Dishonoured Loyalists"; Engel, "'The Cause of True Religion'"; Bayly, "Revolutionary Age"; Echeverri, *Indian and Slave Royalists*; Paine, *Rights of Man*, 162.
2. Knott, "Narrating the Age of Revolution," esp. 12–24; James, *The Black Jacobins*; Palmer, *The Age of the Democratic Revolution*; Linebaugh and Rediker, *The Many-Headed Hydra*; Trouillot, *Silencing the Past*. Latin American scholars could also lay claim to the recent revival, though via a different genealogy. See, for example, Guerra, *Modernidad e independencias* or Rodríguez O, *Mexico in the Age of Democratic Revolutions*. The bicentennial celebrations of Latin America's independence movements starting in 2009 also contributed to an explosion of new literature. Trouillot's work was followed by an outpouring of works on Haiti and the Caribbean more generally that continue to lead, rather than follow, the field. See, for example, Fischer, *Modernity Disavowed*; Dubois, *Colony of Citizens*; Ferrer, *Freedom's Mirror*.
3. Adelman, "An Age of Imperial Revolutions"; Linebaugh and Rediker, *Many-Headed Hydra*; Armitage and Subrahmanyam, *The Age of Revolutions in Global Context*, xii–xxxii; Bayly, *Imperial Meridian*, esp. 164–192; Bayly, *Birth of the Modern World*, 86–120. Knott argues that we now echo a pre-Age of Revolution Lockean definition of revolution as a general sense of changes and disorders, or transformational disruptions, rather than a collective and unfolding transformative act that might suggest a hope for a better future. The latter sense may have prevailed among cosmopolitans in the late eighteenth century and historians in the twentieth. See Knott, "Narrating the Age of Revolution," 34–35.
4. Hunt, "The French Revolution in Global Context," 22.
5. Adelman, "An Age of Imperial Revolutions," 320–321.
6. Knott, "Narrating the Age of Revolution," 21.
7. See the CFP: http://events.history.ac.uk/event/show/9182.
8. Hylton, "'The Sole Owners of the Land'"; Røge, "Rethinking Africa in the Age of Revolution"; Thomson, "Sovereignty Disavowed."
9. Way, "Militarizing the Atlantic World." While many historians are disillusioned with Palmer's unifying idea of the spread of liberal democracy, few have come up with an alternate organizing concept for the era; instead, they often fall back on the idea of looking for connections or convergences between events and/or peoples. Though historians can agree about the central role of imperial expansion in shaping the Age of Revolution, most seem reluctant to link this to the spread of capitalism and the many struggles that resulted over land, labor, and the creation of social formations in new colonies and the metropoles to facilitate commercial expansion.
10. Trouillot, *Silencing the Past*, 47; Thomson, "Sovereignty Disavowed"; Ferrer, "Talk about Haiti"; Fischer, *Modernity Disavowed*. See also Scott, "The Common Wind"; Barcia, "'A Not-so-Common Wind'," 169–193.
11. For an earlier meditation on the theme of local versus transnational frameworks, especially with regard to Atlantic history, see McDonnell, "Paths Not Yet Taken," 46–62.
12. Nor have indigenous peoples made much of an impression in the literature on the Atlantic history more generally. See McDonnell, "Paths Not Yet Taken," 46–62; Cohen, "Was There an Amerindian Atlantic?," 388–410; Bushnell, "Indigenous America," 191–222. See, for example, the lack of Native American perspectives or topics in the pioneering collection by Armitage and Braddick, eds. *The British Atlantic World, 1500–1800*, and compare with the same in the more recent volume Bailyn and Denault, eds., *Soundings in Atlantic History*. Weaver, in *The Red Atlantic*, has made some progress in this direction, but the literature on the Age of Revolution – particularly for the North Atlantic – continues to ignore indigenous perspectives. See, for example, Armitage and Subrahmanyan, eds., *The Age of Revolutions in Global Context*, as well as a forthcoming collection of essays entitled *Facing Empire: Indigenous Histories of a Revolutionary Age* edited by Fullagar and McDonnell, which aims to redress this absence. For earlier essays on indigeneity and indigenous influences on empire see Wood, "North America in the

Era of Captain Cook," 484–501; Bayly, "British and Indigenous Peoples," 19–42; Morgan, "Encounters between British and 'Indigenous' peoples," 42–78.

13. Hylton, "The Sole Owners of the Land."

14. Ibid.

15. There is now a rich and growing body of literature on the history and influence on indigenous peoples and their relations with Europeans. For a sample of this work see, for North America, Richter, *Facing East*; Richter, *Before the Revolutio*; DuVal, *The Native Ground*; Blackhawk, *Violence over the Land*; Hämäläinen, *The Comanche Empire*; and McDonnell, *Masters of Empire*. For Latin America, see Thomson, *We Alone Will Rule*; Weber, *The Spanish Frontier in North America*; Van Young, *The Other Rebellion*; and Walker, *The Tupac Amaru Rebellion*. For the Cape, see Price, *Making Empire*; Lester, *Imperial Networks*; Newton-King, *Masters and Servants on the Cape Eastern Frontier*; and Peires, *The House of Phalo*. For the Pacific and Indian Oceans, see, for example, Thomas, *Islanders*; Reynolds, *Frontier*; Goodall, *From Invasion to Embassy*; Karskens, *The Colony*; and Banivanua Mar, *Decolonisation and the Pacific*.

16. Way, "Militarizing the Atlantic World." While some historians such as Brewer, *The Sinews of Power*, have argued for the importance of the army and navy to the rise of the fiscal-military state they have rarely dwelt upon the violence needed to sustain this expansion.

17. Way, "Militarizing the Atlantic World."

18. Frykman, "The Mutiny on the Hermione," 159–187; Anderson et al., eds., *Mutiny and Maritime Radicalism in the Age of Revolution*; Frykman, *The Marine Republic*.

19. Brandon and Fatah-Black, "The Supreme Power of the People."

20. Ibid.; Serna, "Every Revolution is a War of Independence," 165–182. See Nash, *The Unknown American Revolution*, and compare with Wood, *The Radicalism of the American Revolution*. See also the contributions and critiques in the ensuing "Forum: How Revolutionary Was the Revolution?" and Taylor, *American Revolutions*.

21. Røge, "Rethinking Africa in the Age of Revolution."

22. Ibid.

23. Thomson, "Sovereignty Disavowed"; Trouillot, *Silencing the Past*; Fischer, *Modernity Disavowed*.

24. Thomson, "Sovereignty Disavowed." Scholars of the American Revolution have now firmly established that that uprising was a Janus-faced event, as much an anti-colonial war for independence in the East as it was a neo-imperial war in the west. See Hinderaker, *Elusive Empires*; Sadosky, *Revolutionary Negotiations*; Gould, *Among the Powers of the Earth*; and Edling, *A Revolution in Favor of Government*. There is now a rich literature on the postcolonial legacy of the Age of Empire, as well as a burgeoning scholarship on settler colonialism and its pervasive, ongoing, and debilitating influence in the modern world. For a pioneering and classic statement of this thesis see especially Wolfe, "Land, Labor, and Difference," 866–905 and Wolfe, *Traces of History*.

25. Thomson, "Sovereignty Disavowed"; Paine, *Rights of Man*, 162. Others have made similar points. See, for example, Miller, "The Dynamics of History," 101–124.

26. Clossey and Guyatt, "It's a Small World After All."

27. Trouillot, *Silencing the Past*.

Acknowledgements

The author would like to thank Forrest Hylton, Pernille Røge, Pepijn Brandon, Fatah Karwan-Black, and Sinclair Thomson for their comments on a draft of the introduction, and their good humor, patience, and intellectual engagement with the purpose of this collection of essays and the revisions of their own essays. He would also like to thank the participants of the conference on *The Future of Atlantic, Transnational, and World History* held at the University of Pittsburgh in May 2014 for their original insights and stimulating discussion, and especially Marcus Rediker and Nicholas Frykman for their support and encouragement in putting this selection together. Kate Fullagar also read a draft of this introduction and helped clarify its argument. Many thanks, too, go to Manuel Barcia and Dorothea Fischer-Hornung for their patience and hard work in bringing this project to fruition.

Disclosure statement

No potential conflict of interest was reported by the author.

References

Adelman, Jeremy. "An Age of Imperial Revolutions." *American Historical Review* 113, no. 2 (April 2008): 319–340.

"Age of Revolutions: A HistorioBLOG." Accessed June 8, 2016. https://ageofrevolutions.com/

Anderson, Clare, Niklas Frykman, Lex Heerma van Voss, and Marcus Rediker, eds. *Mutiny and Maritime Radicalism in the Age of Revolution: A Global Survey*. Cambridge: Cambridge University Press, 2014.

Armitage, David, and Michael J. Braddick, eds. *The British Atlantic World, 1500–1800*. Houndmills: Palgrave Macmillan, 2002.

Armitage, David, and Sanjay Subrahmanyam, eds. *The Age of Revolutions in Global Context, c. 1760–1840*. Basingstoke: Palgrave Macmillan, 2010.

Bailyn, Bernard, and Patricia L. Denault, eds. *Soundings in Atlantic History: Latent Structures and Intellectual Currents, 1500–1830*. Cambridge, MA: Harvard University Press, 2009.

Banivanua Mar, Tracey. *Decolonisation and the Pacific: Indigenous Globalisation and the Ends of Empire*. Cambridge: Cambridge University Press, 2016.

Barcia, Manuel. "'A Not-so-Common Wind': Slave Revolts in the Age of Revolutions in Cuba and Brazil." *Review (Fernand Braudel Center)* 31, no. 2 (2008): 169–193.

Bayly, C. A. "The British and Indigenous Peoples, 1760–1860: Power, Perception, and Identity." In *Empire and Others: British Encounters with Indigenous Peoples, 1600–1850*, edited by M. J. Daunton and Rick Halpern, 19–41. London: University College Press, 1999.

Bayly, C. A. *Imperial Meridian: The British Empire and the World, 1780–1830*. London: Longman, 1989.

Bayly, C. A. *The Birth of the Modern World, 1780–1914: Global Connection and Comparisons*. Malden, MA: Blackwell Publishers, 2004.

Bayly, C. A. "The Revolutionary Age in the Wider World, c.1790–1830." In *War, Empire and Slavery, 1770–1830*, edited by Richard Bessel, Nicholas Guyatt, and Jane Rendall, 21–43. Basingstoke: Palgrave Macmillan, 2010.

Blackhawk, Ned. *Violence over the Land: Indians and Empires in the Early American West*. Cambridge, MA: Harvard University Press, 2006.

Brandon, Pepijn, and Karwan Fatah-Black. "'The Supreme Power of the People': Local Autonomy and Radical Democracy in the Batavian Revolution (1795–1798)." *Atlantic Studies* 13, no. 3 (September 2016): 370–388. doi:10.1080/14788810.2016.1190634.

Brewer, John. *The Sinews of Power: War, Money and the English State, 1688–1783*. Orig. ed. 1989; rpt. ed. London: Routledge, 1994.

Bushnell, Amy Turner. "Indigenous America and the Limits of the Atlantic World, 1493–1825." In *Atlantic History: A Critical Appraisal*, edited by Jack Greene and Phillip Morgan, 191–222. New York: Oxford University Press, 2009.

Clossey, Luke, and Nicholas Guyatt. "It's a Small World After All: The Wider World in Historians' Peripheral Vision." *Perspectives on History* 51, no. 5 (May 2013). https://www.historians.org/publications-and-directories/perspectives-on-history/may-2013/its-a-small-world-after-all

Cohen, Paul. "Was There an Amerindian Atlantic? Reflections on the Limits of a Historiographical Concept." *History of European Ideas* 34, no. 4 (2008): 388–410.

Compeau, Timothy J. "Dishonoured Americans: Loyalist Manhood and Political Death in Revolutionary America." PhD diss., University of Western Ontario, 2015.

Dubois, Laurent. *A Colony of Citizens: Revolution and Slave Emancipation in the French Caribbean, 1787–1804*. Chapel Hill: University of North Carolina Press, 2004.

DuVal, Kathleen. *The Native Ground: Indians and Colonists in the Heart of the Continent*. Philadelphia, PA: University of Pennsylvania Press, 2006.

Echeverri, Marcela. *Indian and Slave Royalists in the Age of Revolution: Reform, Revolution and Royalism in the Northern Andes, 1780–1825*. New York: Cambridge University Press, 2016.

Edling, Max. *A Revolution in Favor of Government: Origins of the U.S. Constitution and the Making of the American State*. New York: Oxford University Press, 2003.

Engel, Kate Carté. "The Cause of True Religion': International Protestantism and the American Revolution." Paper presented at the WMQ & EMSI Workshop: The Age of Revolutions, The Huntington Library, May 30–31, 2014.

Ferrer, Ada. "Talk about Haiti: The Archive and the Atlantic's Haitian Revolution." In *Tree of Liberty: Cultural Legacies of the Haitian Revolution in the Atlantic World*, edited by Doris Garraway, 21–37. Charlottesville: University of Virginia Press, 2008.

Ferrer, Ada. *Freedom's Mirror: Cuba and Haiti in the Age of Revolution*. New York: Cambridge University Press, 2014.

Fischer, Sibylle. *Modernity Disavowed: Haiti and the Cultures of Slavery in the Age of Revolution*. Durham, NC: Duke University Press, 2004.

"Forum: How Revolutionary Was the Revolution? A Discussion of Gordon S. Wood's *The Radicalism of the American Revolution*." *William and Mary Quarterly* 3rd ser. 51, no. 4 (1994): 677–716.

Frykman, Niklas. "The Mutiny on the Hermione: Warfare, Revolution, and Treason in the Royal Navy." *Journal of Social History* 44, no. 1 (2010): 159–187.

Frykman, Niklas. *The Marine Republic: Maritime Radicalism and the Revolutionary Atlantic* (forthcoming).

Goodall, Heather. *From Invasion to Embassy: Land in Aboriginal Politics in NSW from 1770–1972*. Sydney: Black Books, 1996.

Gould, Eliga H. *Among the Powers of the Earth: The American Revolution and the Making of a New World Empire*. Cambridge, MA: Harvard University Press, 2012.

Guerra, François-Xavier. *Modernidad e independencies. Ensayos sobre las revoluciones hispánicas*. Madrid: Editorial MAPFRE, 1992.

Hämäläinen, Pekka. *The Comanche Empire*. New Haven, CT: Yale University Press, 2008.

Hinderaker, Eric. *Elusive Empires: Constructing Colonialism in the Ohio Valley, 1673–1800*. New York: Cambridge University Press, 1997.

Hunt, Lynn. "The French Revolution in Global Context." In *The Age of Revolutions in Global Contexts, c. 1760-1840*, edited by David Armitage and Sanjay Subrahmanyam, 20–36. Basingstoke: Palgrave Macmillan, 2010.

Hylton, Forrest. "The Sole Owners of the Land': Empire, War, and Authority in the Guajira Peninsula, 1761–1779." *Atlantic Studies* 13, no. 3 (September 2016): 315–344. doi:10.1080/14788810.2016.1192797.

James, C. L. R. *The Black Jacobins: Toussaint L'Ouverture and the San Domingo Revolution*. 2nd ed. New York: Vintage Books, 1963.

Karskens, Grace. *The Colony: A History of Early Sydney*. Sydney: Allen & Unwin, 2009.

Klooster, Wim. *Revolutions in the Atlantic World: A Comparative History*. New York: New York University Press, 2009.

Knott, Sarah. "Narrative the Age of Revolution." *William and Mary Quarterly*. 3rd. ser. 73, no. 1 (January 2016): 3–36.

Lester, Alan. *Imperial Networks: Creating Identities in Nineteenth-Century South Africa and Britain.* London: Routledge, 2001.

Linebaugh, Peter, and Marcus Rediker. *The Many-Headed Hydra: Sailors, Slaves, Commoners, and the Hidden History of the Revolutionary Atlantic.* Boston, MA: Beacon Press, 2000.

McDonnell, Michael A. "Paths Not Yet Taken, Voices Not Yet Heard: Rethinking Atlantic History." In *Connected Worlds: History in Transnational Perspective*, edited by Anne Curthoys and Marilyn Lake, 46–62. Canberra: Australian National University Press, 2005.

McDonnell, Michael A. *Masters of Empire: Great Lakes Indians and the Making of America.* New York: Hill and Wang, 2015.

Miller, Joseph C. "The Dynamics of History in Africa and the Atlantic 'Age of Revolutions.'" In *The Age of Revolutions in Global Context, c. 1760–1840*, edited by David Armitage and Sanjay Subrahmanyam, 101–124. Basingstoke: Palgrave Macmillan, 2010.

Morgan, Philip D. "Encounters between British and 'Indigenous' Peoples, c. 1500–1800." In *Empire and Others: British Encounters with Indigenous Peoples, 1600–1850*, edited by M. J. Daunton and Rick Halpern, 42–78. London: University College Press, 1999.

Nash, Gary B. *The Unknown American Revolution: The Unruly Birth of Democracy and the Struggle to Create America.* New York: Viking, 2005.

Newton-King, Susan. *Masters and Servants on the Cape Eastern Frontier.* Cambridge: Cambridge University Press, 1999.

Paine, Thomas. *The Rights of Man: Being an Answer to Mr. Burke's Attack on the French Revolution.* London: J.S. Jordan, 1791.

Palmer, R. R. *The Age of the Democratic Revolution: A Political History of Europe and America, 1760–1800.* Princeton, NJ: Princeton University Press, 1959, 1964.

Peires, J. B. *The House of Phalo: A History of the Xhosa People in the Days of their Independence.* Berkeley: University of California Press, 1982.

Price, Richard. *Making Empire: Colonial Encounters and the Creation of Imperial Rule in Nineteenth-Century Africa.* Cambridge: Cambridge University Press, 2008.

Reynolds, Henry. *Frontier: Aborigines, Settlers and Land.* Sydney: Allen & Unwin, 1987.

Richter, Daniel. *Facing East from Indian Country: A Native History of Early America.* Cambridge, MA: Harvard University Press, 2001.

Richter, Daniel. *Before the Revolution: America's Ancient Pasts.* Cambridge, MA: Belknap Press of Harvard University Press, 2011.

Rodríguez O, Jaime E. *Mexico in the Age of Democratic Revolutions, 1750–1850.* Lynne Rienner: Boulder, 1994.

Røge, Pernille. "Rethinking Africa in the Age of Revolution: the Evolution of Jean-Baptiste-Léonard Durand's Voyage au Sénégal." *Atlantic Studies* 13, no. 3 (September 2016): 389–406. doi:10.1080/14788810.2016.1181519.

Sadosky, Leonard J. *Revolutionary Negotiations: Indians, Empires, and Diplomats in the Founding of America.* Charlottesville: University of Virginia Press, 2010.

Scott III, Julius S. "The Common Wind: Currents of Afro-American Communication in the Era of the Haitian Revolution." PhD diss., Duke University, 1986.

Serna, Pierre. "Every Revolution is a War of Independence." In *The French Revolution in Global Perspective*, edited by Suzanne Desan, Lynn Hunt, and William Max Nelson, 165–182. Ithaca, NY: Cornell University Press, 2013.

Taylor, Alan. *American Revolutions: A Continental History, 1750–1804.* New York: W.W. Norton & Company, 2016.

Thomas, Nicholas. *Islanders: The Pacific in the Age of Empire.* New Haven, CT: Yale University Press, 2010.

Thomson, Sinclair. "Sovereignty Disavowed: The Tupac Amaru Revolution in the Atlantic World." *Atlantic Studies* 13, no. 3 (September 2016): 407–431. doi:10.1080/14788810.2016.1181537.

Thomson, Sinclair. *We Alone Will Rule: Native Andean Politics in the Age of Insurgency.* Madison: University of Wisconsin Press, 2002.

Trouillot, Michel-Rolph. *Silencing the Past: Power and the Production of History.* Boston, MA: Beacon Press, 1995.

Van Young, Eric. *The Other Rebellion: Popular Violence, Ideology, and the Mexican Struggle for Independence*. Durham, NC: Duke University Press, 2001.

Walker, Charles. *The Tupac Amaru Rebellion*. Cambridge, MA: Belknap Press, 2014.

Way, Peter. "Militarizing the Atlantic World: Army Discipline, Coerced Labor, and Britain's Commercial Empire." *Atlantic Studies* 13, no. 3 (September 2016): 345–369. doi:10.1080/14788810.2016.1188257.

Weaver, Jace. *The Red Atlantic: American Indigenes and the Making of the Modern World, 1000–1927*. Chapel Hill: University of North Carolina Press, 2014.

Weber, David. *The Spanish Frontier in North America*. New Haven, CT: Yale University Press, 1994.

Wolfe, Patrick. "Land, Labor, and Difference: Elementary Structures of Race." *American Historical Review* 106, no. 3 (June 2001): 866–905.

Wolfe, Patrick. *Traces of History: Elementary Structures of Race*. London: Verso, 2016.

Wood, Gordon S. *The Radicalism of the American Revolution*. New York: Vintage Books, 1993.

Wood, Peter H. "North America in the Era of Captain Cook: Three Glimpses of Indian-European Contact in the Age of the American Revolution." In *Implicit Understandings: Observing, Reporting, and Reflecting on the Encounters between Europeans and Other Peoples in the Early Modern Era*, edited by Stuart B. Schwartz, 484–501. Cambridge: Cambridge University Press, 1994.

"The sole owners of the land": Empire, war, and authority in the Guajira Peninsula, 1761–1779

Forrest Hylton

Department of History, Northwestern University, Evanston, IL, USA

ABSTRACT

This essay reverses conventional images of the colonial Atlantic world by showing how Native power and politics set the parameters within which Spanish colonial officials acted. It charts shifting alliances between the latter and Guajiro *alaulayus* (leaders) – who were related by blood or marriage – in the 1760s and 1770s, and between *alaulayus* and the captains of non-Spanish ships. It argues that conflict and competition among *alaulayus* determined the contours and limits of such alliances. Conflict and competition among *alaulayus*, in turn, was fueled by perceived violations of Guajiro law concerning property rights, principally cattle rustling, as well as by conflicts over access to key Atlantic ports. Thus Guajiro kinship, law, property relations, trade, and politics dictated the terms, extent, and success of Spanish engagement, missionary as well as martial. Spanish presence was contingent on the goodwill of one or more Guajiro *alaulayus*, whose power derived in part from the broader Atlantic trade networks in which they participated, and constrained Spanish imperialism. This view rejects conflict and competition among European imperial agents as the chief determinants of indigenous autonomy. Native peoples such as the Guajiros shaped the course of European empires as much as they were shaped by them.

The Age of Revolution ushered in a general crisis of sovereignty in the Atlantic world, and the continental Caribbean, known as Tierra Firme, was the weakest link in the Spanish imperial chain. Spanish claims to sovereignty were guided by mercantilist ideas about trade monopolies, which made Spain's vulnerability two-sided: first, vis-à-vis unconquered indigenous peoples like the Kuna, the Moskitu, and the Guajiros, and second, vis-à-vis the captains of French, British, and Dutch ships who traded with them.[1] Native peoples, born out of processes of ethno-genesis, shaped colonial markets and Atlantic commodity circuits, and through trade networks, helped the rise of the Holland, France, and especially Great Britain. War and trade were two intertwined aspects of the Atlantic world, and during the Age of Revolution, Spain devoted most of its increased revenues to strengthening military defenses. After the British occupied Havana and nearly took Cartagena in 1762, Spanish policy dictated constant vigilance.

Beginning in the 1760s, through military campaigns and garrison frontier settlements from Alta California to Patagonia, Spain aimed to block trade between agents of competing European empires and unconquered indigenous peoples – who occupied half the land, and made up one fifth of the population, that Spain claimed to rule.[2] One of Spain's earliest moves to build fortified settlements unfolded in the Guajira, the northernmost coastal peninsula of New Granada, in what is today Colombia and Venezuela, during the 1760s and 1770, and it provoked an anti-colonial insurgency. Armed with rifles as well as bows and arrows, beginning on 2 May 1769, some 7000–10,000 Guajiro warriors burned and looted seven Capuchin mission towns in the Lower Peninsula, killing hundreds of colonial settlers, and taking dozens captive.[3]

The uprising surprised no one. Leading citizens of Riohacha, the port town of 4000 Spanish, creole, and mixed-race people east of Santa Marta and west of Maracaibo, warned Governor Gerónimo de Mendoza that a revolt was coming. They knew this because their Guajiro *compadres* – fictive kin – told them so. Authorized by Mendoza in late 1768, and led by Spaniards and creoles, mixed-race settlers carried out assaults on Guajiro persons, settlements, and cattle that constituted a grave violation of Guajiro law, which led Guajiro authorities (*alaulayus*) Antonio Paredes and Juan Jacinto to seek payment for damages, as stipulated by Guajir law, under which crimes were collective rather than individual, so that all settler colonists were held responsible for the crimes committed by those acting on Mendoza's authority.[4] In 1771, with Riohacha still besieged and the rest of the peninsula entirely in Guajiro hands, one Spanish military official asserted, "They say they intend to continue their hostilities and to be the sole owners of the land."[5]

By showing how Native power and politics set the parameters within which Spanish colonial officials acted, this essay reverses conventional images of the colonial Atlantic world, which stress European action and Native reaction, as well as European strategies of divide and rule. The essay charts shifting alliances between Spanish officials, and Guajiro *alaulayus* (leaders) – who were related by blood or marriage – in the 1760s and 1770s, and between *alaulayus* and the captains of British, French, and Dutch ships. It argues that conflict and competition among *alaulayus* determined the contours and limits of such alliances. Conflict and competition among *alaulayus*, in turn, was fueled by perceived violations of Guajiro law, principally property rights in cattle, as well as conflict over access to key Atlantic ports. Thus Guajiro kinship, law, property relations, trade, and politics dictated the terms, extent, and success of Spanish engagement, missionary as well as martial. Spanish presence was contingent on the goodwill of one or more Guajiro *alaulayus*, whose power derived in part from the broader Atlantic trade networks in which they participated, and which constrained Spanish imperialism. This view rejects conflict and competition among European imperial agents as the chief determinants of indigenous autonomy. Indigenous peoples such as the Guajiros shaped the course of European empires as much as they were shaped by them.[6]

How did the cycle of insurgency and counterinsurgency develop in the Guajira in the 1760s and 1770s? Part of the answer lies in the militarization of Spanish frontier policy in the Americas after 1759 under Charles III, achieved through the construction of garrison settlements. But there were more contingent, local causes as well. In 1765, Cecilio López Sierra, whom the Spanish appointed "General Cacique of the Guajira Nation" in 1735, stepped down due to old age and illness.[7] López Sierra, whose father was Spanish and mother was Guajiro, began his service to the Spanish Crown in the early eighteenth century, along with other members of his lineage. Though the results were ephemeral and ambiguous at best for Spain, when López Sierra resigned, there were seven Capuchin mission settlements in the Lower Guajira, composed mostly of mixed-race people – *mulatos*, *zambos*, and *mestizos* – rather than Spanish or creoles (*criollos*-people of Spanish descent born in the Americas). This new population grew rapidly in the second half of the eighteenth century, and embraced the Spanish colonial project by converting to Catholicism and settling in missions and garrisons.[8] Yet it was dwarfed by Guajiro predominance.

Without López Sierra as a mediator between Guajiro *alaulayus*, to whom he was related by blood – through his mother – and marriage, relations between *alaulayus* and Spanish colonial officials and settler colonists deteriorated. López Sierra appointed his son to succeed him as General Cacique, and his son led a group of settlers on a murderous rampage, first in 1766, then again in May 1769, against a backdrop of escalating conflict between mixed-race colonial settlers and Guajiro leaders.[9] In this López Sierra's son had the support, financial as well as military, of the Governor of Reiohacha, Gerónimo de Mendoza.

We might have expected the breakdown of Spanish-Guajiro mediation in the mid-1760s, followed by state-sanctioned settler colonial violence in the late 1760s, to have united Guajiro *alaulayus* against settlers, especially given close kinship ties among the Guajiro leaders. When these events are remembered and discussed among clan authorities descended from colonial-era *alaulayus*, they are taken as proof of the Guajiro capacity for unity across clan divisions when faced with outside threats.[10] However, following the eclipse of Cecilio López Sierra and the success of the 1769 uprising against Spanish missions in the Lower Guajira, competition between López Sierra's Guajiro brother and brother-in-law – Antonio Paredes and Juan Jacinto, respectively – for control of the port of Bahía Honda, and the market in pearls, and conflict over property rights in cattle, determined what the Spanish could and could not do to colonize the Upper Guajira.

These findings have important methodological consequences, namely that in this part of the revolutionary Atlantic, and perhaps elsewhere, we cannot explain conflict, competition, or cooperation using ethnic and national identities as a theoretical baseline. Instead, this essay examines changing relationships between specific Guajiro leaders, specific captains of non-Spanish ships, and specific Spanish colonial officials in a context in which Guajiros were far more powerful than Europeans, and in which Guajiro law provided a normative framework for Guajiro actions and expectations. A micro-history of Guajiro law, kinship, trade, and property relations helps link the local and the global through the lens of the region. Where possible, emic categories are used to explain the processes and outcomes detailed below.[11] They help us read the "prose of counter-insurgency" authored by Spanish military officials and clergy.[12]

Like the Guajira Peninsula itself, this essay serves as a point of confluence and convergence of diverse and seemingly disconnected perspectives. Atlantic history and ethnohistory have "passed like ships in the night,"[13] and with two important exceptions, literature on North American and South American borderlands fails to intersect.[14] Studies of the Age of Revolution focus mainly on the North Atlantic, while literature on the revolutionary South Atlantic concentrates on people of African descent, the indigenous heartlands of Spanish colonialism, or creole elites.[15] For New Granada, scholarly attention has been concentrated mainly on the Bourbon Reforms, popular patriotism, and popular royalism during the Wars of Independence.[16]

The first section of this essay sets the scene of interaction between humans and nature in a place where European political and social power was weak to non-existent, and colonial Atlantic trade networks provided the basis of indigenous wealth, prestige, and political power. The second section narrates the history of Capuchin missions and describes the rise of Cecilio López Sierra as a mediator between Spanish power in the Lower Guajira and the *alaulayus* of the Upper Guajira. The third section analyzes Guajiro insurgency in the Lower Peninsula in the late 1760s and early 1770s, the basis of peace agreements with the Spanish in 1773, and the unraveling of those agreements during the failed counterinsurgency campaigns in the Upper Guajira from 1775 to 1777, and concludes with the aftermath in the 1780s.

Ecology and ethno-genesis

Led by Amerigo Vespucci and Alonso de Ojeda, Spanish explorers sailed around the Guajira in 1499 in a quest for pearl beds like the ones they would soon exhaust further east in Venezuela. They established their first settlement, Santa Cruz, at what became known as Bahía Honda, the Guajira's most important port, under Ojeda's direction in 1502, which lasted less than a season. Under Rodrigo de Bastidas, the Spanish made the first permanent settlement in Tierra Firme to the west, in nearby Santa Marta, in 1525, but never exercised sovereignty in the Guajira. In 1545, the Spanish founded Rio del Hacha, on the site of the region's lone river, the Calancala, introducing cattle, disease, and miscegenation with Guajiro women. The Calancala River and the fertile plains that surrounded it were the center of what Guajiros called the Lower Guajira (*Wopu'-müin*). The Calancala was the only source of fresh water on the western side of the Guajira, and along the plains stretching east and west from its banks south of Riohacha, the Spanish pastured herds of cattle and horses. It was in this area where contact, conflict, and cooperation between Guajiros and colonial settlers loyal to the Spanish crown were most sustained and intense.

For the Spanish, the greatest prize in the region were the pearl fisheries located north of Riohacha at Carrizal and Cabo de la Vela, which, after an initial golden age that lasted from 1540 to 1550, underwent a decline from 1570 to 1600 in part because of endemic Guajiro resistance to Spanish efforts to enslave them as divers.[17] At least as early as 1578, again in 1616, and yet again in 1649, the Spanish waged counterinsurgency campaigns against the Guajiros. None succeeded.[18] Guajiro *alaulayus* in Bahía Honda and Carrizal took control of the pearl fisheries in the seventeenth century and sold pearls to colonial settlers, who did not pay taxes to the Crown, as well as to captains of non-Spanish ships.

Riohacha became a booming market town for pearls and cattle, but was vulnerable to attack from the sea, and Guajiros staged constant raids on Spanish herds. The most salient aspect of everyday life there was fear of foreign invasion: Francis Drake burned and looted it twice, in 1567 and 1590, and corsairs and privateers plundered it five times between 1655 and 1671.[19] The other threat that shaped daily life in Riohacha was the fear of Guajiro invasion. The town was not a promising place from which to extend Spanish dominion, and depended on contraband trade with non-Spanish merchants and ships' captains for profit and subsistence.

Outside Riohacha, there were no Spaniards or colonial settlers closer than Santa Marta or Maracaibo, but through their cattle, the Spanish extended their presence along the Calancala River. The Lower Guajira was linked to the Upper Guajira (*Wüinpumüin*) through Guajiro kinship structures, as well as by the circulation of goods like pearls, slaves, cattle, horses, guns, ammunition, liquor, and textiles. Yet the Spanish were unable to gain a foothold in the Upper Guajira, most of which lacked fresh water for most of the year. Without water, the Spanish could neither establish settlements nor pasture their herds. Thus the Lower Guajira felt the impact of Spanish colonial projects much more directly than the Upper Guajira.

Like the Kuna in the Darién or the Moskito in Nicaragua, the Guajiros did not exist as a separate ethnic group prior to contact with Europeans, and following the impact of epidemics in the sixteenth century, fused multiple ethnicities and runaway slaves into one people. As a result of disease, the Guajiros appear to have been born out of a shatter zone similar to the one that gave rise to the Choctaw, the Chickasaw, and the Creek in the southeastern US – groups which also absorbed runaway slaves at the moment of their emergence.[20]

The largest unconquered indigenous group in the Americas after the Mapuche, by the late eighteenth century the Guajiros numbered between 30,000 and 40,000.[21] They lived in a matrilineal kinship structure that was non-capitalist but organized in relation to the Atlantic capitalist economy. Guajiro society was composed of dozens of decentralized clans (*eirrukus*) composed of extended maternal families (*apüshis*) that inhabited *píichipalas*, settlements that included an ancestral cemetery (*amóuyú*) and territory (*womain*). Clans could number in the hundreds or well over one thousand. Smaller clans were generally poorer and larger clans richer, but within clans, vast gulfs separated elites from commoners. The de-centralized nature of power and authority, which was built into Guajiro kinship structures, led to a patchwork of micro-territories and micro-sovereignties. This meant that factionalism was rife, due to power struggles between *apüshis* and between clans over territory and leadership, and economic competition between clans and between *apüshis* of the same clan in the Atlantic captialist economy.

Conflicts among the Guajiro *alaulayus* were endemic, and during the second half of the eighteenth century, they may have been most intense between *apüshis* of the same *eirruku* during the dry season, when water was scarce. Trusted nephews of leading *alaulayus* acted as "men of the word" (*pútchipút*), or in Spanish parlance, "ambassadors" (*pútchejeechi*), mediating disputes according to Guajiro law, which depended on precedent for the reparation of damages with a just settlement. When mediation failed, brothers and brothers-in-law, as well as cousins, fought one another over property rights in herds and territory. Family membership, status and rank, wealth and property in cattle and livestock, as well as political authority, passed through the mother's line, and the mother's brothers or uncles were the leading clan authorities of an *apüshi*. There was no political representation above the level of the clan (*eirruku*), and clan leadership was not hereditary. Thus competition among young men for power, wealth, and prestige was particularly intense, and the need for adjudication of conflict to regulate disputes was correspondingly important.[22]

Like the Comanche and the Apache, through participation in trade networks with Europeans, the Guajiros became equestrian pastoralists.[23] This made them difficult for the Spanish to conquer, since Guajiros had mobility and martial capacities far beyond those of their neighbors, the Chimila and the Motilón. The latter two groups did not have trade relations with Europeans, and were successfully conquered by the Spanish in the 1760s and 1770s.[24] Yet equestrian pastoralism also contributed to conflict among Guajiro *alaulayus*, whose power, wealth, and authority depended on the size of their herds of cattle, the extent of their kinship networks, the number of guns and amount of ammunition they could marshal, and access to ports, pastures, watering holes, and pearls.

Various Guajiro clans had adopted equestrian pastoralism as well as European firearms when they first appeared in colonial Spanish sources in the 1550s, but both the archaeology and ethno-history of the region are in their infancy, particularly for the Upper Guajira.[25] Based on Spanish sources, recognizable elements of Guajiro kinship structure, law and jurisprudence, mythology, transhumance, property rights, and territorial claims appear to have emerged between 1540 and 1590. They accompanied the transition from hunting and gathering to a pastoral economy based on the export of Cocina slaves, salt, pearls, mules, horses, and cattle and the import of arms, munitions, gunpowder, textiles, liquor, tobacco, foodstuffs, and African slaves.[26]

Pastoralism differentiated the Guajiros from their hunter-gatherer neighbors, the Cocina, whom they enslaved and sold to captains of non-Spanish ships. The Cocina lived near Cerro de la Teta mountain (*Epits*), and controlled the road running southwest from Riohacha to Maracaibo. They spoke the same language as the Guajiros, *Wayuunaiki*, but stole cattle and other livestock from Guajiros and Spaniards to sell in Cojoro, the port they controlled on the eastern shore of the peninsula on the Gulf of Venezuela.[27] Cocinas used their strategic position along the road from Maracaibo to Riohacha to specialize in banditry. Yet the Cocina also did business with Guajiros, and some Cocina factions even allied with the Spanish against enemy factions. In total, they numbered from 4000 to 5000 at the end of the eighteenth century.[28]

Despite the distance of the Guajira from the Spanish slave markets at Cartagena and the cacao plantations which ran on slave labor in Coro, Venezuela, the slave trade was central to the Atlantic economy during the Age of Revolution. Hence the power and authority of Guajiro *alaulayus* depended on it, since slaves were among the Atlantic world's most valuabe commodities. But the slave trade cut both ways.[29] While Guajiro leaders relied on trade networks with captains of British, Dutch, and to a lesser extent, French ships, these relationships were also marked by conflict. In addition to official slave markets in Kingston and Cartagena, Atlantic commodity circuits and colonial markets featured a thriving, largely unregulated traffic in indigenous people. Non-Spanish ship captains kidnapped family members of leading Guajiro authorities and sold them into slavery, and Guajiro chiefs held African slaves for ransom in order to get them back.[30]

Spanish presence, legal codes, and colonization efforts, including mission settlements, did not lead to Spanish cultural influence, much less political, military, or economic predominance. But particularly in the second half of the eighteenth century, they did incite antagonism between Guajiros and people with non-Guajiro mothers. Those with Guajiro mothers were incorporated into matrilineal clans, as were domestic slaves of both genders. *Mestizaje*, or race mixture, between Guajira women and "Spanish" men, including creoles, *negros* (the offspring of Africans), *mulatos* (the offspring of Spanish or creole men and African women), and *zambos* (descendants of African men and Guajiro women), led to the spread of Guajiro, rather than Spanish or African, language, law, customs, and culture.[31] Those with non-Guajiro mothers, very few of whom were light skinned, incubated a new settler colonial culture in Riohacha and the Spanish mission settlements, which were nominally regulated by Spanish law. Unlike the rest of the Colombian Caribbean, where free people of color and frontier settlers formed the majority of the population, in the Guajira, they were a distinct minority, increasingly at loggerheads with the Guajiro majority.[32]

Guajiro trade and kinship networks were inseparable from topography and climate. Temperatures between 80°F and 100°F, and strong, steady winds made for minimal rainfall for nine months each year. Grasses grew in the flooded lowlands during the rainy season, from September to November (*juyapu*), making for excellent pasture, but quickly disappeared, since there were no streams or lakes in which the water could be stored. The hardest months came between May and October (*jóutaleulu*), when clans would move with herds of cattle, mules, and horses in search of water, a voyage called *Oonowa*, which could lead to clashes with other clans or between *apüshis* of the same clan.[33]

The history of the peninsula, like kinship and property relations within it, is bound to the winds and tides that shaped Atlantic trade routes and networks. Bucking the counterclockwise trend that prevails close to shore throughout the Caribbean basin, ocean currents in the Guajira moved west, along with the northeastern trade winds blowing in from the Windward Islands and Venezuela, thereby isolating Riohacha from Cartagena de Indias, the seat of Spanish power in Tierra Firme. In most seasons, it took a well-fitted Spanish sloop at least 20 days to reach Riohacha from Cartagena during the eighteenth century, whereas to reach Cádiz from Cartagena took just 20 more.[34] The condition for the possibility of Guajiro long-distance trade networks was the Dutch occupation of Curaçao, Bonaire, and Aruba beginning in 1634; the British occupation of Jamaica beginning in 1655; and the French occupation of St. Domingue in 1697.[35] It took just days to get to the former and back, and several weeks at most, depending on the season, to get to the latter two and back.

The Guajira's more than 30 coves provided ideal cover for smuggling, and in the course of the eighteenth century, the Guajira became a smuggler's paradise. Shallow water, abundant reefs, and offshore rocks made it impossible for Spanish coast guard sloops to pursue small craft. Furthermore, the Spanish coast guard did not patrol the eastern shores of the peninsula, which featured some of the best ports. Smuggling took place on a diminished scale, with individual consignments and small cargoes; there were no massive shipments nor centralized authority coordinating them.[36] This strengthened the wealth and prestige of the leading *alaulayas*: Cecilio López Sierra in the Lower Peninsula, and his father-in-law, Toribio Caporinche, brothers Pablo Majusare and Antonio Paredes, and brother-in-law Juan Jacinto, all in the Upper Peninsula.

Aside from Riohacha, the Guajira had a number of natural ports through which Guajiro *alaulayus* conducted long-distance trade with captains of European ships. Heading north by boat from Riohacha, moving against the current, past the mouth of the Calancala River, sailors would first have encountered La Cruz and El Pájaro, then Carrizal and Rincón del Carpintero. This area, still part of the Lower Guajira, held the peninsula's pearl fisheries. Next came Cabo de la Vela, which marked the beginning of the Upper Guajira, where the Spanish established their first fleeting settlement in the region, and where Guajiro souls (*wanülu*) went to rest after death at *Jepira*, a hill made of stone. To the north and east of Cabo de la Vela lay Bahía Portete, which featured minimal winds, making it optimal for loading and unloading cargo. Next came Bahía Honda, which had a wider mouth and fiercer winds, as well as deeper water than Portete, and Bahía Hondita, which was smaller than either of the other two. Then, still moving north and east in the Upper Guajira, came Chimare, facing due north, followed by Puerto Estrella to the east. Sailors then moved south and west past Punta Espada to Apiesi and Sabana del Valle, and further south and west to Cojoro and Simamaica – the last of these located at the mouth of the Sucuy River and Lake Maracaibo.[37]

Though the Guajira had once been a damp forest extending some 150 miles (241 km) to the northeast of the Sierra Nevada de Santa Marta, which rises out of the Caribbean to a height of 18,700 feet (5700 m), when the first Spanish explorers caught sight of it in 1499, it was roughly 5000 square miles (8000 km) – the size of Massachusetts – of semi-arid savannahs dense with cacti, low, spiny leguminous trees such as brazil wood (*Caesalpinia*) and divi-divi trees (*Libidibia*), and volcanic hills. Several mountain ranges crisscross the Upper Guajira (*Wüinpumüin*) – the Sierra de Jerara and the Sierra de Cocina – and broad plains run from coast to coast between them.[38] At 800 m, the highest point of the Guajira, the Sierra de Macuira in the Upper Peninsula faces northeast out onto the Caribbean Sea, and is the region's most ecologically diverse area, with a variety of microclimates suited to agriculture, and abundant sources of fresh water.

The Macuira is the heart of the Upper Guajira, since that is where Maleiwa, the Creator God, brought Guajiros into the world, before they spread south into the rest of the peninsula with Maleiwa's blessings.[39] Guajiro mythology testifies to the importance of colonial ethno-genesis: Maleiwa made branding irons to distinguish each Guajiro clan, then distributed cattle, and gave them knives and machetes: "The weapons are for killing people; this is for cutting up and preparing your food."[40] Maleiwa also created rich and poor:

> The rich people got cheese, cattle, and a branding iron. But poor people were given nothing but a long stick, and were made to go somewhere else. With the stick they were able to eat *yosu* fruit and *aitpia* fruit, and that way they did not starve.[41]

Thus ostensibly Spanish elements, particularly domestic animals and implements, became central to the Guajiro vision of their own identity as a distinctive people.[42] So did divisions of wealth and status in terms of those *apüshis* and clans that owned cattle – from which both chattel and capital are derived, etymologically – and those that hunted and gathered or fished.

Missionary positions

For much of the eighteenth century, the Spanish sought to conquer the Lower Guajira south of Riohacha through the mediation of a Spanish-Guajiro lineage, the López Sierras. Cecilio López Sierra's father was one of three Spanish brothers who served as Regidores in Riohacha beginning in 1692, and his grandmother was Luisa de Velasco de Amoscótegui. She and her husband, Juan de Amoscótegui, were the first two Guajiros that Capuchin friars baptized in 1696.[43] Cecilio began his relationship with the Spanish in 1702 when King Phillip V named him Infantry Captain and Sergeant Major, and became Cacique of the Guajiro Nation in 1735. In 1755, Viceroy José Solis Folch de Cardona named him Field Marshal.[44]

Before attempting conquest by military means in the 1760s and 1770s, with the help of the López Sierras, the Spanish sought to extend their power though missions and evangelization, mixed with occasional counterinsurgency operations. Though the Capuchin friars made repeated attempts to evangelize and establish mission settlements, they failed to gain a foothold before the 1750s.[45] The López Sierras monopolized evangelization efforts and access to Spanish officials, and this, together with ties to Spanish and creole merchants in Riohacha, was the key to their growing wealth and power in the 1750s and 1760s. Jesuit priest Antonio Julián wrote a detailed account of his time in Riohacha and his relations with Cecilio López Sierra and his half-brother, Father Joseph López Sierra, with whom he shared a Spanish father. According to Joseph, who spoke with Julián in January 1751, the time for Spanish conquest had come, because in the future it would be impossible for two reasons: first, the Guajiros were increasingly well armed; and second, domestic slaves were swelling Guajiro ranks in the Lower Guajira, where Africans were adopted into Guajiro families, which, López feared, would lead mixed-race settlers in the mission towns – a majority of their residents – to unite with Guajiros against the Spanish.[46] Father Joseph's fears were unfounded, since Spanish colonial projects of missions and garrisons enlisted people with non-Guajiro mothers as soldiers and settlers, thus dividing them from the Guajiros rather than uniting them. Julián also spoke with Cecilio López Sierra, and learned that in the late 1740s and early 1750s, accompanied by two African slaves wearing striped uniforms with European insignias, López Sierra traveled to Spain to lobby the Royal Court, then to Santa Fe de Bogotá to speak with Viceroy Solíz de Fochs, then back to Spain again, hoping to gain permission to conquer the Guajira on behalf of Carlos III and the Catholic faith.[47]

Although Spain gained a precarious place in the Lower Guajira through the López Sierra lineage, the Upper Guajira remained beyond reach. Where Cecilio López Sierra, anchored in the Lower Guajira, gravitated to Spain and Bogotá, his brother Pablo Majusare, and father-in-law Toribio Caporinche, both traveled from the Upper Guajira to Curaçao to meet with trading partners.[48] Their power depended in part on their access to merchants and ship captains operating under the Dutch flag, rather than Spanish missionaries or officials. In 1753, Lt. Governor Joseph Xavier de Pestaña y Chumacero wrote to his superior asking him to write Cecilio López Sierra and order him to subdue Caporinche and Majusare, whom Pestaña y Chumacero called "Indian magnates."[49] Pestaña y Chumacero also related that Caporinche and Majusare were rivals, and that it might be possible for the Spanish to ally with one against the other.[50] Pestaña y Chumacero considered the two chieftains to be the wealthiest and most powerful in the Upper Peninsula, and saw that the Spanish could only reach them through López Sierra, who monopolized communication and translation, but in spite of Pestaña y Chumacero's observations, the Spanish were unable to craft a viable strategy of divide and rule.

Thanks to the López Sierras, Capuchin friars did not encounter a blanket rejection of their presence or doctrines, and redoubled their missionary effort when seven of them arrived in 1759, followed by eight more in 1761, including Father Antonio de Alcoy. Alcoy traveled from mission to mission and met with Guajiro leaders like Cecilio López Sierra's brother-in-law, Juan Jacinto, in Bahía Honda, who claimed – in Spanish, no less – to have always wanted to have a priest in order to know God and obey the King.[51] Juan Jacinto likely traded with Spanish contraband merchants through Bahía Honda, the Upper Guajira's largest port, and with Spanish and creole merchants in Riohacha. Along with his wives and sisters and their children, as well as some 700 members of his clan (eirruku), Juan Jacinto celebrated a mass that Alcoy conducted, and prayed with Alcoy nightly during April 1761.[52] Juan Jacinto may have sought an alliance with the

Spanish because he was competing with his in-laws for authority, and likely saw the Spanish as potential trading and diplomatic partners who could bolster his spiritual power.

Though Spanish missionaries hoped to augment their flock, they fully supported efforts to suppress Guajiro trade, and blamed foreigners for the unwillingness of Guajiros to obey the Spanish. Alcoy warned Juan Jacinto and his cousin that if they continued to trade with foreigners, they would be considered traitors and punished accordingly, but Alcoy promised to send a priest to minister to Bahía Honda and Bahía Hondita, which featured abundant water and fertile pastures, even in the dry summer months. Alcoy came down with a fever soon after his visit to Bahía Honda, and decided to leave the missions in Macuira and Chimare for the following year, exchanging messages with Caporinche and Majusare to that effect. Although those missions were never built, and Alcoy did not return, there were nevertheless eleven missions in the Lower Peninsula, as well as one in Bahía Honda and one in Bahía Hondita in the Upper Peninsula, in 1762.[53] Thus the missionary strategy appeared to be succeeding after more than half a century of failure.

Guajiro *alaulayus* in the Upper Peninsula accepted Catholic missions on the condition that they would not include colonial settlers, and insisted on compliance with Guajiro law concerning property rights in cattle – rustling would not be tolerated. Initially, Spain was unwilling to invest government resources in the conquest or colonization of the Guajira, and in 1760, Charles III granted the merchant Bernardo Ruíz de Noriega permission to do so at his own expense. Ruíz de Noriega then sealed his partnership with López Sierra by acting as godparent to one of López Sierra's children. The powers the Crown gave Ruíz de Noriega were extensive, amounting to a virtual monopoly on trade – including the official slave trade – and the use of armed force, in exchange for 5000 pesos annually for 10 years and the pacification of the Guajiros.[54] In January 1761, together with Cecilio López Sierra, who translated for him, and Father Joseph López Sierra, Ruíz de Noriega obtained signed, 15-point capitulations from Toribio Caporinche, Pablo Majusare, and Antonio Paredes. All three pledged their fealty to God and King in exchange for guarantees that no settlers would try to colonize their territory. By April 1761, however, because some of Ruíz de Noriega's troops stole his livestock and failed to pay damages, thus violating Guajiro law concerning property rights, Majusare broke with the Spanish.[55] Further, Ruíz de Noriega turned the local elite in Riohacha against him by trying to cut local notables as well as corrupt Spanish officials out of the contraband trade with Guajiros. Charles III soon removed him.[56] In 1762, as if to emphasize Spanish failure, Paredes, Majusare, and Caporinche provided the British navy with 600 head of cattle to provision British troops for the successful siege of Havana.[57]

Yet Cecilio López Sierra's powers of mediation remained considerable even after disillusion with Ruíz de Noriega set in among López Sierra's kin, and he helped implement measures designed to help Spain increase taxation and tribute. With the collaboration of his non-Guajiro half-brother, Father Joseph López Sierra, and Guajiro half-brothers Antonio Paredes and Pablo Majusare with whom he shared a mother, as well as his father-in-law, Caporinche, in 1763 López Sierra carried out a census that listed the number of men in arms, as well as the general population.[58] The openness of *alaulayus* in the Upper Guajira to dealing with the Spanish is surprising, but they likely considered the Spanish as potential commercial and diplomatic partners who could enhance Guajiro spiritual and ritual power.

From cross to sword

The militarization of Spanish frontier policy under Charles III encouraged and supported settler colonial violence against Guajiro persons, property, and settlements. Viceroy Pedro Messía de la Cerda and Governor Gerónimo de Mendoza – the former appointed the latter in 1766 – considered the Capuchin missionary efforts to convert Guajiros into sedentary, tribute-paying, Catholic subjects of the Crown a failure. In order to conquer and colonize them, Governor Mendoza deliberately aimed to impoverish the Guajiros whom Spanish officials characterized as "magnates" by cutting off trade with captains of British, French, and above all, Dutch ships.[59] Settler colonial attacks duly escalated. First, one of Cecilio López Sierra's non-Guajiro half-brothers, Félix Sierra, carried out a raid in which he found himself badly outnumbered and miraculously escaped after killing several Guajiros. Then López Sierra's Guajiro son, Joseph Antonio, led settlers on violent raids in 1766. In 1767, fearing an attack on Riohacha, townspeople in the cabildo voted to carry out punitive campaigns in Guajiro territory in response to Guajiro cattle and horse rustling, and in order to wrest control of the pearl trade from the hands of Guajiro *alaulayus* in Carrizal and Bahía Honda.[60] Backed by Messía de la Cerda, the arrival of an arms shipment from Cartagena led Governor Mendoza to authorize Riohacha's townspeople to bear arms.[61] In December 1768, he instructed them to burn Guajiro settlements, take their cattle, horses, and weapons, settle them in mission towns, and evangelize their children. The same month, Mendoza dispatched a military mission composed of 171 "Spaniards" – mostly *mestizos*, *mulatos*, *zambos*, and *negros*, together with a handful of Spanish and creole leaders – along with 30 Guajiros from nearby mission towns in the Lower Guajira, led by Diego López Sierra, one of Cecilio López Sierra's Guajiro nephews. They were to punish and capture a group of Cocina Indian cattle and horse rustlers on the eastern side of the peninsula, north of Maracaibo.[62]

Rather than attacking the Cocina, however, the war party opted to pursue two of the leading Guajiro *alaulayus* in the Upper Guajira. Having marched north to Bahía Honda, instead of continuing around the peninsula to the eastern shores of Cojoro in pursuit of the Cocina, the war party decided it would make overtures to Antonio Paredes and his brother-in-law, Juan Jacinto. Unable to locate Juan Jacinto in Bahía Honda, the party set out to find Paredes in Chimare, and demanded that he turn over his weapons, give up his livestock, and submit to the authority of the Catholic Church and Carlos III. When Paredes refused, the war party retreated, kidnapping a number of his family members and stealing his livestock, along with livestock from Paredes's brother, Pablo Majusare, and his brother-in-law, Juan Jacinto. Governor Mendoza then authorized a second expedition to the Upper Peninsula in which 283 settlers and 30 Guajiro Indians participated, but they were met by 3000 of Paredes's warriors, and wisely retreated. Juan Jacinto wanted to negotiate with Spanish officials before conflict escalated further, while Paredes claimed he would await Spanish soldiers with "guns and gunpowder." Any priest would receive an arrow.[63]

Despite the offenses committed against Paredes, the uprising that began on 2 May 1769, took place in the Lower Peninsula, where Spanish colonization efforts were concentrated, rather than the Upper Peninsula, which had been largely free of Spanish presence before the raid of December 1768. Once townspeople in Riohacha caught word of what the war party had done, a number of them followed its example, stealing livestock and taking prisoners from the very mission settlements – Rincón and Moreno – that provided troops for the raid against Paredes in the Upper Peninsula. In response, Paredes provided a steady flow of arms, munitions, and gunpowder to *alaulayus* in the Lower Guajira – including 200 British weapons in a single shipment – which he exchanged for livestock that Guajiros stole from colonial settlers and Spanish officials.[64] Far from disrupting Guajiro trade with foreigners, settler colonial depredations provided incentives to engage in it, and strengthened ties between the Lower and the Upper Guajira.

In the course of May 1769, insurgent Guajiros cleared Spanish missions out of the Lower Peninsula. According to an eyewitness, Capuchin Father Pedro de Altea, Guajiro warriors from the mission town of Rincón del Carpintero killed Joseph Antonio López Sierra, Cecilio's son and successor, and two Spaniards, inside the mission's church, "profaning the sacred cups, drinking their liquor in chalices," and then burned the Capuchin archives. They killed 19 townspeople the following day.[65] On 4 May Guajiro warriors took over the plains along the peninsula's only waterway, the Calancala River, and two days later, killed 15 men, women, and children. On 9 May, they burned nearby Cayuz, and from 11 to 15 May, they took over Soledad and La Cruz, whose residents fled to Riohacha. On 16 May, 100 townspeople fanned out from Riohacha to recover their stolen livestock, but insurgents burned another settlement nearby on 20 May, appropriating all cattle and livestock outside Riohacha town limits. Guajiro insurgents burned an additional five settlements before the month was out, and rumors that they would take Riohacha, where colonial settlers had fled, persisted into 1770.[66]

This came as no surprise to leading townspeople of Riohacha, who had warned Mendoza that a revolt against Spanish colonial power was inevitable if he sent several dozen Guajiro prisoners to Cartagena as slaves to build fortifications against a possible British invasion.[67] This perception was based on what townspeople heard from their Guajiro *compadres* – fictive kin, and presumably smuggling partners – about the consequences of Spanish violations of Guajiro law. By this measure, the "Spaniards" – most of whom, as we have seen, were in fact mixed-race people – owed Guajiros for lives and livestock they had taken. Settler colonialists showed no intention of paying damages, so Guajiro *alaulayus* enforced their law through warfare.[68]

In sanctioning settler colonial rampages against Guajiro persons and property in 1768–1769, Governor Mendoza opened the floodgates to revolt against Spanish pretentions to sovereignty in the Lower Peninsula. Although Mendoza received 100 regular troops from Cartagena's fixed garrison in November 1769, with another 100 arriving in June 1770, plus militia reinforcements from Maracaibo to the east and Santa Marta to the west, giving Mendoza 600 militia men in total, he was barely able to hold Riohacha, much less recover lost ground.[69]

Spanish military initiatives were slow to materialize, and at once massive and underwhelming when they did. In June 1771, Messía de la Cerda authorized 400 troops from the Savoy Battalion to help Mendoza, but they were held up in Cartagena for a month due to rumors of war with the British. Led by Colonel Benito Encío, they arrived in mid-November 1771, accompanied by another 100 regulars from Cartagena's fixed garrison. By this time, there were already 200 regulars from Cartagena there along with 340 militiamen from Valledupar to the south, as well as militiamen from Santa Marta and Maracaibo.[70] Perhaps on the advice of Cecilio López Sierra, Encío decided to stay put, squandering the crown's resources on provisions, to the tune of 34,000 pesos by February

1772, arguing that it was pointless to take on the Guajiros on their own territory without another 2000 troops, at a cost of an additional 100,000 pesos.[71] Even then, Encío argued, unless the Spanish could cut off the mountain fastness of the Sierra Nevada to the west and the Sierra de Perijá to the south, there was little to be accomplished by setting out into the desert.

Ironically, the costs of Spanish military buildup limited Spanish ability to wage military campaigns: Messía de la Cerda advised his successor, Viceroy Manuel Guiror, that the Crown lacked the requisite resources for retaking the Guajira. Between 1772 and 1775, Guiror nevertheless spent 248,000 pesos on counterinsurgency, amounting to one quarter of New Granada's entire budget during the 1770s, but failed to pay, provision, or adequately discipline the military forces he hoped to deploy.[72] Replacing Colonel Encío was Colonel Antonio Arébalo, an engineer who mapped Cartagena, where he oversaw the construction of San Felipe de Castillo, a fortification built to defend against British attack after 1762. He arrived in Riohacha on 26 November 1772, and on the instructions of Viceroy Guiror, posted a general amnesty on 28 November; he also began planning the construction of fortified garrison settlements in the Upper Guajira. These were to be manned by small contingents of regulars and militiamen, as well as families of creole and mixed-race settler colonists, in order to block Guajiro trade with captains of European ships. They would be situated at the strategic ports of Bahía Honda to the north and Sabana del Valle to the east, and on the road from Riohacha to Maracaibo.[73] Arébalo's two-pronged approach all but guaranteed further conflict, but Arébalo established contact with Antonio Paredes in Chimare, and through him, with the other leaders of the Upper Peninsula. According to Arébalo, settler colonial raids sanctioned by Mendoza provoked Paredes, a man of "wealth and reputation" who had no prior history of conflict with the Spanish. Arébalo considered him the "most outstanding member of his nation," and noted that Paredes "concedes neither superiority nor even equality to anyone, because he thinks he is the only king on earth."[74]

Arébalo may have viewed Paredes's understanding of power, authority, and autonomy as a threat to Spanish absolutism, but he knew Paredes wished to trade with the Spanish and hoped to enjoy peaceful relations with them. Arébalo stressed that Mendoza and the townspeople of Riohacha – whom two Guajiros called "conquerors and enemies of the Indians" – were, in the words of one Guajiro, "greedy," and had violated Guajiro law, which Arébalo understood as follows: "they do not know how to pardon insults: when one of them is killed, they take everything their enemies own."[75] Arébalo exonerated Paredes, and planned to visit him, but one third of Arébalo's troops were either sick or convalescent, so he had to wait before leaving Riohacha.[76]

When Arébalo arrived in Riohacha, a generational shift in leadership marked the Upper Peninsula as well as the Lower, with Antonio Paredes's power waxing. On 9 December 1772, Cecilio López Sierra died without sacraments, since Capuchin friars had not returned to Boronata. His eldest Guajiro son, Joseph Francisco López Sierra, replaced him as Cacique General, but proved ineffectual, although Paredes trusted him enough to use him as a go-between with Arébalo.[77] Around the same time, Cecilio López Sierra's father-in-law, Toribio Caporinche, died in the Macuira; one of Paredes's brothers, Pablo Majusare, died in Chimare in 1771.[78]

In the wake of the deaths of two of the most powerful, venerated authorities in the Upper Peninsula, Paredes controlled Chimare, Apiesi, Macuira, Sabana del Valle, and

Cojoro – most of the north, northeast, and southeast. These ports and their hinterlands had direct year-round access to the best pastures, the largest herds, the widest variety of microclimates and foodstuffs, as well as the best sources of fresh water. Cojoro, located on the eastern shore north of Maracaibo, was known as the Cocina port, but Paredes had good relations with the Cocina leader there. He nominated Caporinche's brother-in-law and his nephew to command the Macuira, where a new church would be built, and nominated other relatives to be in charge in Bahía Honda.[79] Such nominations demonstrate the efforts Paredes made to extend his domain and his control of political representation through alliance with the Spanish.

In allying with Arébalo, Paredes hoped to consolidate his power and authority beyond the *womain* that corresponded to his *apüshi* in Chimare and to enforce Guajiro law concerning property rights and human life, which Juan Jacinto had violated. Arébalo pledged to favor Paredes in his war against Juan Jacinto, the success of which would provide Paredes with direct access to the Upper Peninsula's most important port, Bahía Honda, and the pearl trade, which Juan Jacinto controlled through his nephew, as well as the other main ports in the Upper Guajira. After what must have been difficult negotiations, Juan Jacinto agreed to be sent to the other side of the peninsula. In January 1773, through one of his nephews, Paredes asked Arébalo to charge Juan Jacinto – whose ear Paredes had recently cut off – for damages suffered by another of Paredes's nephews, whom Juan Jacinto killed.[80] Paredes discussed brother-in-law Caporinche and brother Majusare. Although he did not mention the cause of their deaths, had their lives been taken by Spanish officials or colonial settlers, Paredes would have asked Arébalo to help him enforce Guajiro law by charging damages for stolen property and loss of human life, just as he did in his dispute with Juan Jacinto.

Like Paredes, Juan Jacinto also sought an alliance with Spanish officials, but unlike Paredes, he appealed to previous alliances in writing – the preferred means of Spanish communication. Along with a detachment of cavalry troops, Juan Jacinto and his wife arrived in Bahía Honda in April 1773 to speak with Arébalo. The following month, Juan Jacinto returned with a letter, written in Spanish by Father Alcoy in 1762, nominating him as Mayor (Alcalde Mayor) of Bahía Honda, as well as lists in English with the names of ship captains and the prices of imports and exports. Thus Juan Jacinto was keen to establish his authority and credentials with Arébalo. Rather than hide his business relations with British merchants, he foregrounded them, using written documents as proof of his stature.[81] Like Paredes, Juan Jacinto welcomed Spanish missionaries in order to bolster his own power vis-à-vis his rivals, but Arébalo appeared to favor Paredes, perhaps based on his estimation of the relative power of each.

Paredes wished to do business with the Spanish on his own terms and according to Guajiro law regulating property rights, and Arébalo may have realized that an alliance with Paredes in the Upper Peninsula could compensate for the loss of mediation that resulted from Cecilio Lopez Sierra's resignation and subsequent death in the Lower Peninsula. In effect, Arébalo would try to repair the damage López Sierra's half-brother and son had caused. Such an alliance could also serve as the lynchpin for the construction of the fortified garrison settlements. In March 1773, Arébalo set off on a reconnaissance mission to Bahía Portete and Bahía Honda, both of which he mapped with the idea of building fortified settlements to cut off trade with Europeans, which Arébalo thought would put an end to clashes among Guajiros themselves.[82]

Hence Arébalo correctly understood the Atlantic capitalist economy to be the source of competition and conflict between men with strong kinship ties, and that Guajiro unity might have created an opening for more effective Spanish control. He was impressed by Paredes's wealth and stature. At 10 AM on 24 May 1772, Paredes, his wife, four of his nephews (the sons of Pablo Majusare), two daughters, and eight grown children arrived at Paredes's settlement (*píichipala*) to greet Arébalo. The settlement was composed of 50 open-air huts divided into clusters of three to six; most were made exclusively of wood and thatch, but three had mud walls, and some people camped underneath trees. Paredes had many corrals, and so many cattle that Arébalo could not count them. Arébalo was surprised at the corpulence of some of Paredes's relatives, and noticed that not only the cattle were abundant and well fed: so were the chickens, roosters, goats, horses, burros, and mules, which were equally numerous. Neither mosquitoes nor wild animals bothered people or livestock, which had access to verdant pastures and abundant water.[83]

Paredes received Arébalo as an honored guest and potential associate, not as his superior, and at no point did he or any other Guajiro leader acknowledge Spanish law as valid during the 1770s. Like Native leaders throughout the Americas, Paredes ritualized diplomatic affairs through smoking tobacco. Along with shamans (*piaches*), "Indian magnates" (wealthy and powerful *alaulayus*) and other leading authorities from Chimare, Paredes and Arébalo held a meeting at an open-air hut set aside for politics and diplomacy. Such meetings were accompanied by rituals: above all, smoking tobacco rolled in corn husks, "their oracle and infallible director," in Arébalo's words, which *piaches* interpreted in terms of which way the wind blew the smoke.[84] He explained relations with rivals, and reassured Arébalo regarding his attitude toward the Spanish. While smoking, Paredes said that he had nothing against Spanish merchants and officials, and traded ecumenically with them as he did with captains of ships from other European countries. He said that he never would have agreed to sign Ruíz de Noriega's capitulation in 1761 if it had not been for Cecilio López Sierra, and that he had a number of enemies among the Guajiros, including Juan Jacinto and López Sierra. Though Paredes did not specify the nature of his dispute with López Sierra, it is probable that like Spanish, creole, *zambo*, *negro*, and *mulato* settlers from the Lower Peninsula – which he explicitly named as enemies – Paredes held López Sierra responsible for violations of Guajiro law committed in the Upper Peninsula after 1761. After a long day of diplomatic business concluded, at 9 PM on 24 May, Paredes and his *apüshi* organized a party with music and dancing, and urged the Spanish troops to join in, which Arébalo considered "the best proof that he no longer mistrusts the Spanish."[85]

One of Paredes's principal objectives in meeting with Arébalo was to enlist Arébalo's compliance in enforcing Guajiro law. Paredes said he had heard that Arébalo was settling claims and paying damages, and informed Arébalo that if so, he could count on Paredes's friendship. Then Paredes enumerated the violations of Guajiro law he wished to address: Juan de Armas had burned Caporinche's settlement and stolen his cattle; and Juan Jacinto had stolen cattle from Paredes, his sons, his nephews, and Caporinche, who died soon after Juan de Armas's incursion in December 1768. Juan Jacinto was married to two of Caporinche's daughters, and to avenge the offense against Caporinche, Paredes, who was married to at least one of Caporinche's sisters, retrieved his cattle and killed and burned six of Juan Jacinto's warriors.[86]

Paredes was keen to have Arébalo help him collect for damages, but also to recover relatives kidnapped into slavery in Jamaica years before, as well as several sons recently stolen by captains of British, Dutch, and French ships. Kidnapping and ransom were common in the Guajira: Atlantic commerce led by non-Spanish ship captains was based on conflict as well as cooperation, and coercion as well as consent. It commodified Native subjects. When the captain of a French ship kidnapped one of his sons, Paredes took one of the ship's rowboats and a sailor as ransom, and got his son back. To get his oldest son back from a captain named Santiago Piche, "a Christian from Curaçao," Paredes had to give Piche 10 burros, 6 mules, 3 hammocks, 17 cattle, and 3 Indian children (presumably Cocinas), in October 1772. In June 1772, a "Dutch mulatto" ship captain based in Curaçao stole Paredes' herdsman at Apiesi. One of Paredes's brothers had a family member stolen by a British ship captain, and Paredes held four escaped African slaves captive in order to ransom them. A captain of a British ship had stolen Paredes's nephew's wife, and the nephew tried to ransom her with two Cocina captives.[87] Paredes explained the precedents for this violation of Guajiro law, and enlisted Arébalo's help in recovering those family members still at large.

Insofar as peace was subordinate to war, Spanish strategy was not internally consistent. Arébalo came away from his diplomatic meeting with an exaggerated sense of Spanish power and sovereignty. Having reached an agreement with Paredes, as well as the sons of Pablo Majusare, Arébalo returned to Cartagena in May 1773, leaving Captain of the Royal Artillery Corps, Joseph Galluzo, as Governor of Riohacha. In June 1773, Arébalo filed his report to Viceroy Guiror about the causes of insurgency that began in 1769, arguing that Guajiros were neither tough nor warriors, and that 700 Spanish regulars and 321 militiamen would have been more than enough to defeat them. Arébalo suggested that in the event it was necessary to try again, the Spanish should mount "search and destroy" missions without hesitation, and punish the Guajiros so that they would remember it. Arébalo stressed that if the campaigns were carried out in the summer months between January and April, when fresh water and pasture were scarce, it might be possible to starve Guajiros by cutting off trade.[88]

Unsurprisingly, given Arébalo's counterinsurgent commitments, peace with Paredes scarcely outlasted Arébalo's visit. In November 1773, the Lieutenant of Apiesi and the Captain of Sabana del Valle, whom Paredes appointed, told Governor Galluzo that for the past month, Paredes had been holding meetings and telling them to burn down any new settlement that the Spanish tried to establish; Paredes then threatened the Lieutenant of Apiesi "for being a friend of the Spanish."[89] Paredes sold Cocina Indians, cattle, and horses in exchange for guns, powder, and rum, and then allegedly re-sold guns to insurgents led by the *zambo* José Antonio Pérez, a native of Boronata, Cecilio López Sierra's mission settlement in the Lower Guajira. Pérez, whose mother was Guajiro, was trying to impede the construction of Pedraza, a fortified settlement located on the road running southwest from Riohacha to Maracaibo.[90]

Although Galluzo appeared to be losing control, he was satisfied that he had things firmly in hand. Galluzo's false sense of security and superiority rested on his willingness to mediate between Paredes's sons and nephews after Paredes's death in mid-1774 – presumably of natural causes, since there is no mention of claims for payment of damages. Paredes's sons came to seek protection from their uncles, who tried to gain control of Paredes's herds on behalf of Paredes's nephews – the rightful heirs according to Guajiro law.

Paredes's nephews asked Galluzo to mediate their dispute with their cousins over the inheritance of Paredes's herds. Unsurprisingly, Galluzo failed to broker a settlement.[91]

Atlantic trading partners proved crucial to determining how Guajiro leaders understood Galluzo's intentions. Although Galluzo and Arébalo had little reason to fear Guajiro unity, Guajiro *alaulayus* were unwilling to accept fortified Spanish garrison towns. In 1774, one ship's captain from Curaçao, alias "the One who Knows," told Guajiros that Galluzo had written the Governor of Curaçao to tell him that he would remove the Guajiros a few at a time; another captain said the letter was a request to have the Governor of Curaçao prevent merchants from supplying guns and powder to Guajiros.[92] In September 1775, Paredes's sons told Galluzo that their Dutch business partners advised them not to let Galluzo found a settlement at Apiesi, near the Macuira, because it would cut off trade. Juan Jacinto also received word from Dutch and British partners that by building Apiesi, the Spanish would end Guajiro trade, especially in weapons and munitions, and would sell goods at higher prices as well as disarm Guajiros.[93]

Captains of non-Spanish ships occasionally posed a direct threat to Spanish claims to rule. In October 1775, Guajiros from Paredes's former territory, Chimare, told Galluzo that "Constantino the Pirate" said that if the Spanish built their garrison settlement at Apiesi, they would then disarm the Guajiros, end their trade, and Guajiros would no longer be able to get guns, gunpowder, and ammunition, and would therefore be at the mercy of the Spanish. Allegedly banned from Jamaica, Curaçao, and St. Domingue, Constantino operated offshore from Kingston, and bought Cocinas, mules, horses, and cattle in exchange for heavy artillery. He gave out staffs of authority to Guajiro "captains," that is, *alaulayus* with whom he traded.[94]

With the mediaton of Paredes's nephews, Galluzo met with Guajiro leaders and confirmed what their non-Spanish business partners had told them. On 3 December 1775, Galluzo set out from Bahía Honda to Apiesi with a massive entourage numbering in the hundreds, and arrived the next day in Chimare, where Paredes's nephews offered their sons and nephews as guides. After a marathon march overland, followed by a full day of rest, Galluzo and his troops continued up steep, forested hillsides toward the Sierra de Macuira, only to find their path blocked by felled trees, as thousands of warriors massed on the highest mountaintops, near *Itojolu*, the mountain where Maleiwa created the Guajiros out of clay. At dawn on 7 December, Galluzo met with the Guajiro *alaulayus* of Macuira and Apiesi, who explained their opposition to the construction of a garrison settlement at Apiesi – again, based on what their British and Dutch associates told them. Unmoved, Galluzo told the Guajiro leaders that he would build the fort in spite of them.[95]

Galluzo expected to obtain capitulation with threats of violence. While this appeared to work initially, it soon backfired. At dawn on 8 December, Galluzo told the Guajiros that they would be on the losing end of any war because they did not own ships, and could therefore be hunted down; and because their supply of ammunition would be enough for several days, whereas the Spanish had enough for several years. By 10 AM, the two Guajiro *alaulayus* from Apiesi and Macuira appeared to back down, and the following day, 9 December, one of their uncles arrived and pledged fealty to Galluzo, saying he would insure that Guajiros would not harm the Spanish. On 10 December, Galluzo handed out coca leaves and liquor as gifts, and three days later, Guajiros began to build a church. One of their leaders helped Galluzo find the best place to build a settlement.

On 16 December, Galluzo returned to Bahía Honda, and soon after, Guajiros massacred those who remained: of the 90 soldiers and one missionary left behind, only 23 soldiers survived.[96]

Galluzo sought revenge through raids, but his Guajiro allies were reluctant to participate in reprisals; since Galluzo's mother was not Guajiro, Guajiro law did not oblige them to do so. In April 1776, Galluzo set out to punish those responsible for the massacre at Apiesi, and took one of the relatives of the Guajiro *alaulayus* prisoner, then used him as a guide. Galluzo sent word to one of Paredes's nephews to see if he could count on his support, but both nephews declared their neutrality. Juan Jacinto also declined to join Galluzo, feigning illness. Galluzo worried that because of Guajiro law regulating kinship and mobilization in times of war, his allies would be obliged to unite with kin from Apiesi, Macuira, and Sabana del Valle against him.[97] When the leader of Apiesi sent word in favor of making peace, Galluzo demanded that Guajiros return 200 cattle, 300 horses, as well as the guns and munitions they had taken from the Apiesi garrison.[98]

Thus Galluzo was preparing for war, not looking for peace, and with Arébalo's consent, Galluzo's campaigns turned homicidal, featuring exemplary cruelty. At the end of May 1776, Galluzo and his men killed at least 80 Guajiros, including the nephew of the leader of Apiesi, as well as many members of Juan Jacinto's *apüshi*. Galluzo carried out another massacre of 25 Guajiros in June 1776, with the assistance of one of Paredes's nephews, who gave Galluzo horses and guides, and whom Galluzo called his "compadre."[99]

Due to endemic factionalism, Guajiro unity remained a mirage, and Galluzo and his troops continued the carnage they had begun. At the end of June 1776, one of Paredes's nephews sent word to Galluzo that Juan Jacinto had united with leaders from Macuira, Apiesi, and Sabana del Valle to attack Sabana del Valle. Galluzo, who noted, "News from the Indians, especially if it is about their enemies, is usually true," responded by vowing to hunt down Juan Jacinto, whom he considered "the cause of all the disorder experienced in the province."[100] At the same time, in the Lower Guajira, José Antonio Perez, the *zambo* from Boronata previously allied with Antonio Paredes, was conspiring with the Cocina to steal Spanish cattle, and allegedly working with Juan Jacinto to drive them from Pedraza, the fort located on the road from Riohacha to Maracaibo. Along with many others, Galluzo's troops killed Juan Jacinto in November, and then exhibited his head on a pike in a metal box. Eighty-nine Guajiro prisoners, including some "magnates," were taken to jail in Riohacha to await death.

Yet wanton brutality was no substitute for economic, military, or political power. Even as Galluzo assured Arébalo that he had secured all the garrison settlements, troops and settlers deserted because of the scarcity of cattle, gunpowder, and foodstuffs.[101] In 1777, dozens of colonists in Sabana del Valle and Bahía Honda died after suffering several days of agonizing stomach pain – Guajiros had poisoned the water supply using a root from the Macuira – while conflicts between Guajiros and settlers occurred daily.[102] Before the Spanish were through, however, in March 1777 they killed another 180 Guajiros and Cocinas in the Upper and Lower Peninsula, and took 35 prisoner.[103]

In addition to the balance of power, which favored Guajiros in spite of their disunity, Spanish counterinsurgency operations were hamstrung by the realities of climate and the geo-politics of the revolutionary Atlantic. Because of a bad harvest in Pennsylvania and Ohio and the outbreak of the War of Independence, flour was scarce in Kingston, hence in Curaçao, and hence in the Guajira, such that Galluzo could not provision the settlement at Sabana del Valle, on the eastern shore near Maracaibo, and Cocinas killed troops who deserted it.[104] Galluzo was unable to marshal more than 200 regulars at any time between 1776 and 1779, and all but forty regulars returned to Cartagena when Spain entered the American War of Independence against Britain in 1779.[105]

Although diplomacy proved more effective and less costly than war, Spanish officials were convinced that only fortified garrison colonies could end Guajiro participation in Atlantic trade with non-Spanish ships' captains. After issuing a general amnesty in 1772, Colonel Antonio Arébalo momentarily achieved peace through diplomacy with *alaulayus* Antonio Paredes and Juan Jacinto in 1773, and returned to Cartagena, leaving artillery captain Josef Galluzo as Governor and Commander of Riohacha. When Paredes and Juan Jacinto died in the mid-1770s, Galluzo's attempts to build garrison settlements provoked Guajiro resistance, and his ability to respond depended on rivalries between Paredes's sons and nephews over Paredes's legacy. Looking to vanquish their cousins, Paredes's nephews remained Galluzo's allies even as Spanish counterinsurgent massacres against Guajiros escalated to historic proportions in the mid-1770s. This did not lead to the durable Spanish occupation of Guajiro territory in the Upper Peninsula, however, but rather its opposite: in the 1780s and 1790s, Spanish authorities were forced to recognize Guajiro law and tolerate free trade.

Conclusion

Following the failed counterinsurgent campaigns in the Guajira during the 1760s and 1770s, and the entry of Spain into the American War of Independence in 1779, the Spanish shifted their attention to the Moskito Coast and the Darién during the 1780s, where they met with similar results. In 1780, Spanish troops destroyed Sabana del Valle and Bahía Honda, and abandoned the Upper Guajira. In 1789, some 600 Guajiros, representing less than two percent of the Guajiro population, had been settled in rebuilt mission towns near Riohacha. In 1790, the Spanish abandoned Pedraza, their only remaining fortified settlement in the Lower Guajira. Several thousand creole and settlers, many with commercial and kinship ties to Guajiros, remained in Riohacha. The rest of the peninsula was ruled by Guajiro *alaulayus*, as it had been since the sixteenth century.

Conflict and competition among Guajiro leaders exploded during overlapping succession crises in the Upper and Lower Guajira during the 1760s and 1770s, which allowed Spanish officials to forge alliances and wage settler colonial counterinsurgency operations, without thereby conquering the Guajira. Ironically, just as the colonial system of indirect rule through Native lords the Spanish had established in the Andes and New Spain unraveled during the Age of Revolution, in the Guajira, the Spanish sought to create the figure of a central, hierarchical authority among indigenous people in order to turn them into tribute-paying subjects of the Spanish crown. But the Guajira was a radically decentralized environment, made up of a complex patchwork of micro-territories and micro-sovereignties, which foiled Spanish strategies that were themselves inconsistent and contradictory, oscilating wildly between war and diplomacy.

The history of Guajiro insurgency shows that the Spanish mission towns and their residents were only there as long as Guajiro authorities tolerated them, and that Guajiro law, rather than Spanish law, governed all interactions outside of Riohacha. *alaulayus* in the

Upper Peninsula like Paredes, Majusare, and Caporinche, who pledged fealty to the Spanish Crown and promised to support missions in the early 1760s, most likely expected to incorporate the Spanish as trading partners. Guajiros would treat them as they treated non-Spanish ship captains on whom they depended for wealth and prosperity. The difference, of course, was that Spaniards left their boats and tried to live among the Guajiros by founding garrison towns and missions peopled with settlers. Futher, for the most part, Spaniards were clergy or military men, not merchants.[106] Since the Spanish could not effectively police Atlantic trade networks, and since settlers were badly outmatched, they never represented a long-term military or political threat, especially not in the Upper Peninsula, which lacked mission towns altogether. But as the debacle at Apiesi showed, Spanish insistence on building and settling against the will of leading *alaulayus* guaranteed disaster.

First and foremost, the Spanish wanted to eliminate trade between unconquered indigenous peoples and non-Spanish ships in order to monopolize it for the Spanish Crown. Once Charles III ascended the throne in 1759, Spain militarized its frontier policies with counterinsurgency campaigns that won neither hearts nor minds. Spanish efforts to conquer the Guajira reflected an unwavering ideological commitment to mercantilism, even as the Bourbon Reforms turned Venezuela and Río de la Plata into laboratories of free trade. Spanish officials like Arébalo aimed to promote and protect economic development on the Spain's imperial frontiers through increased revenue, tighter taxation, and administrative centralization. But the commitment to mercantilism was material as well, since Britain posed an insuperable military and commercial threat to Spanish sovereignty and fortunes, dramatized first during the War of Jenkins's Ear, when Britain almost took Cartagena. Spain shifted away from Europe to the Indies, especially following the siege of Havana in 1762. Thereafter, Spanish policy prioritized security, and the increased revenue it attained through centralization and modernization went principally into military coffers.[107]

In spite of Spanish backing, then, Cecilio López Sierra never became the undisputed leader of the de-centralized Guajiro clans, which were themselves internally divided. But insofar as López Sierra maintained peaceful relations with his relatives in the Upper Peninsula until the mid-1760s, he gave the Spanish a place in the region, however tenuous, and enlarged his own networks of trade, patronage, and diplomacy to the point where he had no challenger in the Lower Peninsula. Once López Sierra stepped down in 1765, his non-Guajiro half-brother and Guajiro son helped draw the Spanish into violent conflicts with his other Guajiro brothers, and the Spanish lost control of the Lower Peninsula without having established a base in the Upper Peninsula.

Thus the uprising that began on 2 May 1769, resulted from a succession crisis in the Lower Guajira and state-backed settler colonial raids in the Upper Guajira. For all practical purposes, the only lineage through which the Spanish had established relations with the Guajiros of the Upper Peninsula had reached its end. Once López Sierra retired, in line with the broader drift of Spanish imperial frontier policy, the Spanish overcompensated with militarized responses to this limited system of mediation. López Sierra's relatives and descendants helped lead the shift. Although we might have expected settler colonial aggression to lead to Guajiro unity, and perhaps even ethno-national consciousness, Guajiro *alaulayus* did not unite to confront the Spanish, except momentarily, and on a small scale. The extent of trade with non-Spanish merchants, their own military strength, and the limits of Spanish finances and military discipline guaranteed their supremacy nonetheless. Disunity and factionalism may have favored Guajiro autonomy.

Spaniards could be pulled into conflicts among Guajiro authorities because individual *alaulayas* in the Upper Peninsula – first Cecilio López Sierra, then Pablo Majusare, Toribio Caporinche, Antonio Paredes, and Juan Jacinto – actively sought alliances with them to augment their own power and authority.[108] This suggests an extremely fluid field of power within the Guajira, coinciding with a generalized crisis of sovereignty in the Atlantic world in the Age of Revolution. This crisis did not threaten the material basis of Guajiro wealth and power, and may have favored Guajiro autonomy, but it appears to have exacerbated conflicts among *alaulayas*, as well as between these and settler colonial shock troops. The latter group, though growing, was a tiny minority of the peninsula's population, and the Spanish colonial project of missions and settlements put it on a collision course with the Guajiros.

Generalizations about Guajiros, Spaniards, Dutch, British, and French are difficult to sustain, and categories of ethno-national identity were not the most salient in this part of the revolutionary Atlantic. The Upper Guajira Peninsula was not a borderlands region, nor a frontier, but rather the Guajiro homeland. Unlike the Caribbean Sea, the peninsula was native ground rather than middle ground.[109] Though the Lower Guajira might have become a middle ground or a borderlands had the Spanish institutionalized the position of General Cacique after the resignation and death of Cecilio López Sierra, they did not.

While the Venezuelan and Colombian nation-states have attempted to exercise sovereignty over the Guajira since the late nineteenth century – with increasing violence since the late twentieth century – the results so far have been inconclusive. Especially in the Upper Guajira, in accordance with the 1991 Colombian Constitution's provisions regarding indigenous autonomy and jurisdiction, Guajiro clans continue to be the sole owners of the land, and in the face of a crisis of social reproduction brought on by drought, famine, and environmental deterioration, strive to govern themselves according to their law.[110]

Notes

1. Kuethe and Andrien, *The Spanish Atlantic World*, 346–348. See also, García, "Interaccón étnica y diplomacia de fronteras," 95–121; Rogers, "Caribbean Borderland," 117–138; Rodríguez, "El imperio contraataca," 201–223. A note on ethnic terminology: Like the terms Aymara and Quechua in Bolivia, the word Wayúu comes from nineteenth-century ethnology, and has been used for the purposes of self-identification since the 1970s. Following the most common colonial usage, I refer to Guajiros, while acknowledging that Spanish colonial officials imposed the term on people who would not have used it to identify themselves. Neither term is fully adequate to the realities of the eighteenth century.
2. Weber, *Bárbaros*, 12.
3. Kuethe, "Pacification Campaign," 467–481; Kuethe, *Military Reform and Society*, 130–137; García, "Los levantamientos goajiros," 110–118; Barrera Monroy, *Mestizaje, comercio y resistencia*, 197–210; Polo Acuña, *Indígenas, poderes y mediaciones*, 183–230.
4. For a Spanish understanding of Guajiro law in the eighteenth century, see de la Rosa, *Floresta de la Santa Iglesia*, 280–281. For an ethnography of Guajiro law, see Guerra, *La disputa y la palabra*. See also, Bolinder, *Indians on Horseback*, 91–102; Weston, *The Cactus Eaters*, 159–

169; Camacho and Segura, "La institución jurídica," 89–114; Goulet, "Guajiro Social Organization and Religion"; Barrera Monroy, *Mestizaje, comercio y resistencia*, 45–50.

5. Francisco Baraya y de la Campa to Don Pedro Messía de la Cerda, Riohacha, 12 May 1771, Archivo General de la Nación, Milicias y Marina 119, ffs. 253–255, quoted in Barrera Monroy, *Mestizaje, comercio y resistencia*, 201.

6. See Adelman and Aron, "From Borderlands to Borders," 814–841.

7. Cecilio López Sierra to Don Pedro Messía de la Cerda, Boronata, 29 September 1766, Archivo General de la Nación (Hereafter AGN): Bogotá, Sección Colonia, Milicias y Marina (Hereafter MM), 114, ffs. 210–213, in Moreno and Tarazona eds., *Materiales*, 121–123; Restrepo Olano, "Un ejemplo," 187–189.

8. For inter-ethnic conflict, as well as cooperation and ethno-genesis, among Natives and Africans in Latin America, see Restall, ed., *Beyond Black and Red*; Restall, *The Black Middle*; and Bryant, *Rivers of Gold*.

9. Geronimo de Mendoza to Don Pedro Messía de la Cerda. Riohacha, 19 August 1766. AGN: MM, 114, ffs. 654–657, Moreno and Tarazona, eds., *Materiales*, 131–133.

10. Britto and Hylton, *Espíritus Guerreros*.

11. For studies that use emic categories, see Price, *First-Time*; Price, *Alabi's World*; Nabakov, *A Forest of Time*; Whitehead, *Histories and Historicities*.

12. Guha, "The Prose of Counter-Insurgency," 45–84.

13. Quoted in Bahar, "People of the Dawn," 411. See also, Saunt, "Our Indians," 77–89; McDonnell, "Paths Not Yet Taken, Voices Not Yet Heard," 46–62; Cohen, "Was There an Amerindian Atlantic?" 388–410. Bushnell, "Indigenous America," 191–222; Sidbury and Jorge Cañizares-Esguerra, "Mapping Ethnogenesis," 181–208.

14. Weber, *Bárbaros*, and Radding, *Landscapes of Power*, are exceptions. See Hennessy, *The Frontier*; Weber, *Spanish Frontier*; Hämäläinen and Truett, "On Borderlands"; DeLay, ed., *North American Borderlands*. See also, Bryant, Radding, and Readman, eds., *Borderlands in World History*.

15. For calls that sounds similar notes, see Millett, "Borderlands in the Atlantic World," 268–295; and Bassi Arébalo, "Beyond Compartmentalized Atlantics," 704–716. For a synthesis of North and South Atlantic, see Klooster, *Revolutions*. For the South Atlantic, see McFarlane and Eduardo Posada Carbó, *Independence and Revolution*; Adelman, *Sovereignty and Revolution*; Adelman, "Iberian Passages," 59–82; McFarlane, *War and Independence*. For the Caribbean, see Geggus, ed., *Impact of the Haitian Revolution*; Garaway, ed., *Tree of Liberty*; Geggus, "The Caribbean," 83–100; Ferrer, *Freedom's Mirror*. For creole nationalism, see Brading, *First America*; Earle, *Return of the Native*; Lynch, *Simón Bolívar*; Lynch, *San Martín*. For the indigenous heartlands, see Van Young, *The Other Rebellion*; Thomson, *We Alone Will Rule*; Guardino, *Time of Liberty*; Serulnikov, *Revolution in the Andes*; Walker, *Tupac Amaru Rebellion*.

16. See Jane M. Loy, "The Forgotten Comuneros," 235–257; Earle, "Indian Rebellion," 99–124; Saether, "Independence and the Re-Definition of Indianness," 55–80. See also, Leddy Phelan, *The People and the King*; McFarlane, *Colombia before Independence*; Helg, *Liberty and Equality*; Saether, *Identidades e independencia*; Lasso, *Myths of Harmony*; Múnera, *El fracaso de la nación*; Echeverri "Popular Royalists," 237–269; Pérez Morales, *El gran diablo*; Bassi Arébalo, "Turning South," 107–132.

17. Barrera Monroy, *Historia de la Guajira*, 37, 46–63; Barrera Monroy, "Los esclavos de las perlas," 3–33; Cwik, "Curazao y Riohacha," 281–311; Warsh,"A Political Ecology," 541–543.

18. Grahn, *Political Economy of Smuggling*, 40; Picon, *Pasteurs du Noveau Monde*, 217–252; "Alzamiento de indios guajiros en Santa Marta y Riohacha." Archivo General de Indias (hereafter AGI): Santo Domingo 869, L.6, ffs. 151v–152v; "Cartas de gobernadores solicitando licencia para someter a los indios guajiros." AGI: Santa Fe 49, R. 16, N. 119; "Prevenciones contra los indios guajiros." AGI: Panama 234, L.4, ffs. 78v–79v.

19. Grahan, *Political Economy*, 17–18.

20. Weber, *Bárbaros*, 249. See also, Hill, ed., *History, Power, and Identity*; Schwartz and Salomon, "New Peoples," 443–501.

21. For Native population figures in the late eighteenth century, see Weber, *Bárbaros*, 61, 72–75. For Guajiro figures, see Barrera Monroy, *Mestizaje, comercio y resistencia*, 235–237, based on sources from AGN: MM, 119, ffs. 375-378; AGN: MM, 124, ffs. 532–585; AGN: MM, 138, f. 860; Narvaez de la Torre, *Escritos de dos economistas*, 35–36; Silvestre, *Descripción*, 83.

22. Barrera Monroy, *Mestizaje, comercio y resistencia*, 40–45.

23. Weber, *Bárbaros*, 71–75, 86.

24. Helg, *Liberty and Equality*, 19–31; Herrera, "La geografía de la guerra," 141–192. See also, Grahn, "Indian Pacification," 88–144; Douglas, "Patterns of Indian Warfare," 78–125.

25. See Wilbert, *Survivors of El Dorado*, 163– 205; Picon, *Pasteurs du Nouveau Monde*, 183–202; Ardila, "La historia prehispánica," 59–77; Oliver, "Reflexiones," 81–127; Ardila, *Los tiempos*; Barrera Monroy, *Historia de la Guajira*; Ardila, "Cambio y permanencia," 41–72.

26. Barrera Monroy, *Historia de la Guajira*, 38–45.

27. Moreno, "Guajiros-Cocinas."

28. AGN: Sección Colonia, Caciques e Indios (Hereafter CI), Vol. 47, f. 343.

29. For the importance of Indian slavery in North America and the Caribbean, see Brooks, *Captives and Cousins*; Gallay, *Indian Slave Trade*; Snyder, *Slavery in Indian Country*; Rushforth, *Bonds of Alliance*.

30. Barrera Monroy, *Mestizaje, resistencia y comercio*, 154–158.

31. Gutierrez de Pineda, "Organización social," 89–114; Triana Varón, "El Mestizaje," in ibid., 115–120; Picon, *Pasteurs*, 65–121; Polo Acuña, *Indígenas, poderes y mediaciones*, 231–274; Polo Acuña and Carmona Nobles, "El mestizaje," 130–155.

32. For the preponderance of free people of color in the Colombian Caribbean, see Helg, *Liberty and Equality*; Lasso, *Myths of Harmony*; and Múnera, *Fracaso de la nación*.

33. Barrera Monroy, *Mestizaje, resistencia y comercio*, 38–40.

34. Grahn, *Political Economy*, 44.

35. For the Dutch, see Araúz Mofante, *El contrabando holandes*; Klooster, *Illicit Riches*; Rupert, *Creolization and Contraband*. For the British, see Pearce, *British Trade with Spanish America*. For contraband in the second half of the eighteenth century, see Gutiérrez, "Prácticas sociales," 39–65. On trade relations with the French West Indies, see Durango Loaiza, "Contagiando la insurrección."

36. De la Rosa, *Floresta de la Santa Iglesia*, 278–279.

37. Pichon, *Geografía*; Guhl, "Geografía," 13–28. See also, Polo Acuña, *Indígenas, poderes y mediaciones*, 25–64.

38. Armstrong and Métraux, "The Goajiro," 369; Grahn, *Political Economy*, 32–33. See also, Simons, "An Exploration," 781–796.

39. Pineda Giraldo, "Mareiwa y Wanurú," 139–150.

40. Epieyuu, "Clans and the First Ancestors," 116.

41. Gonzalez Epieyuu, "Birth of Maleiwa," 115.

42. Grahn, "Guajiro Culture," 152.

43. De la Rosa, *Floresta*, 233–234; Alcacer, *Las misiones capuchinas*, 41–60, 62–63; AGI: Santa Fe, 162, N.26–27; ibid., 163, N.1.

44. AGN: CI, 48 bis, D.4, ffs. 354–356. Ibid., 27, D.18, fols. 556–566; AGN: Colonia, Historia Eclesiástica SC.30, 15, D.14.

45. AGN, CI 4, ffs. 997–1002, Moreno and Tarazona, eds., *Materiales*, 126–127; AGN: CI, 59, D.8, fols. 284–285; Ibid., 71, D.23, ffs. 888–897; AGN: MM, 124, ffs. 210–213, Moreno and Tarazona, eds., *Materiales*, 121–123.

46. Julián, *La perla de América*, 196.

47. Ibid., 210–212.

48. AGN: MM, 119, fols. 375–378; AGN: CI, 4, D.78, ffs. 647–647v.

49. Joseph Xavier de Pestaña y Chumacero to Marquez de Villar. Riohacha, 17 February 1753, AGN: MM, 124, f. 218v; Joseph Xavier de Pestaña y Chumacero to Marquez de Villar. Riohacha, 26 April 1753, AGN: MM, 124, ffs. 203–204, Moreno and Tarazona, eds., *Materiales*, 42, 44.

50. Joseph Xavier Pestaña y Chumacero to Marques de Villar. Riohacha, 21 October 1753. AGN: MM, 118, f. 835v, in ibid., 50.

51. Alcacer, *Las misiones capuchinas*, 158.
52. Ibid., 154.
53. Ibid., 156–157.
54. Ibid., 142.
55. Don Bernardo Ruiz to Don Francisco Piñero. Riohacha, 7 April 1761. AGN: MM, 124, fols. 177–184, 274, P. Moreno and Tarazona, eds., *Materiales*, 63–68. Franco Piñero to Viceroy Messía de la Cerda. Riohacha, 6 April 1761. AGN: MM, 124, ffs. 670–74, in ibid., 70–72. Barrera Monroy, *Mestizaje, comercio y resistencia*, 186–187.
56. Dr. Antonio de Lascano y Naiza to Viceroy Pedro Messía de la Cerda, Riohacha, July–August 1761, AGN: Colonia, Miscelanea, ffs. 1–68, in ibid., 75–111. Cabildo of Riohacha to Pedro Messía de la Cerda. Riohacha, 13 July 1762, AGN: MM, 126, ffs. 403–404, in ibid., 117.
57. Barrera Monroy, *Mestizaje, resistencia, y comercio*, 180; Polo Acuña, *Indígenas, mediaciones, y poderes*, 128. Though not cited, the source for this estimate appears to be Arébalo, "Plan de operaciones," 187.
58. Barrera Monroy, *Mestizaje, resistencia y comercio*, 232–324.
59. Alcacer, *Las misiones capuchinas*, 166.
60. Barrera Monroy, *Mestizaje, resistencia y comercio*, 77–80.
61. AGN: CI, 71, ffs. 128–139v. Gerónimo de Mendoza to Pedro Messía de la Cerda. Riohacha, 9 March 1769.
62. Antonio Arébalo to Viceroy Manuel Guiror, "Informe sobre la situación." Riohacha, 11 July 1773. AGN: MM, 119, ffs. 453–468, in *La pacificación*, edited by Sourdis, 38–39.
63. AGN: CI, 71, ffs. 59–66. Gerónimo de Mendoza to Pedro Messía de la Cerda. Riohacha, 5 January 1769.
64. Arébalo, "Informe sobre la situación," 36.
65. Alcacer, *Las misiones capuchinas*, 167.
66. Manuel Herra Leyva to Pedro Messía de la Cerda. Riohacha, 5 June 1769. AGN: MM, 138, fols., 857–862, Moreno and Tarazona, *Materiales*, 135–141.
67. Arébalo, "Informe sobre la situación," 40.
68. Ibid., 42.
69. Kuethe, "Pacification Campaign," 471–472.
70. Kuethe, "Pacification Campaign," 472.
71. Ibid., 473.
72. Restrepo Tirado, *Historia de la provincia*, vol. II, 227.
73. Arébalo, "Diario de operaciones Número 1," November–December 1772. AGN: Colonia, Historia Civil (Hereafter HC), 20, ffs. 409–411, in Arébalo, *La pacificación*, 62.
74. Arébalo, "Informe," in ibid., 56.
75. Arébalo, "Diario de operaciones Número 3," December 1772, in ibid., 81.
76. Barrera Monroy, *Mestizaje, resistencia y comercio*, 204.
77. Arébalo, "Diario de operaciones Número 2," December 1772, in Arébalo, *La pacificación*, 75.
78. Arébalo, "Diario de operaciones Número 14," May 1773, in ibid., 213, 218–219, 224.
79. Ibid., 215.
80. Arébalo, "Diario de operaciones Número 5," January 1773, in ibid., 99–106.
81. Arébalo, "Diario de operaciones Número 12," April 1773, in ibid., 188; Arébalo, "Diario de operaciones Número 13," Bahía Honda, May 22, 1773. AGN: HC, 20, ffs. 510–519, in ibid., 201.
82. Arébalo, "Diario de operaciones Número 8," February 1773. AGN: HC, 20, ffs. 461–474, in ibid., 151.
83. Ibid.
84. Arébalo, "Diario de operaciones Número 14," 12 June 1773. AGN: HC, 20, fols. 520–539, in ibid., 213.
85. Ibid., 214.
86. Ibid.
87. Ibid., 216.
88. Arébalo, "Informe sobre la situación," in ibid., 58.
89. Joseph Galluzo, "Diario de operaciones," November–December 1773. AGN: MM, 142, fols. 524–530, in ibid., 238–239, 242.

90. Ibid., 246.
91. Antonio Arébalo to Don Pedro de Ureta, "Carta remisoria y diario de operaciones Número 36," Cartagena, 11 October 1775. AGN: MM, 124, ffs., 234–238, in ibid., 282.
92. Ibid., 244.
93. Joseph Galluzo, "Diario de operaciones Número 38." AGN: MM, 2, ffs. 892–895, in ibid., 306–307.
94. Ibid.
95. Antonio Arébalo to Don Pedro Ureta, "Carta remisoria y diario de operaciones Número 40." Cartagena, 11 January 1776. AGN: MM, 140, ffs. 402–411, in ibid., 321–324.
96. Barrera Monroy, *Mestizaje, resistencia y comercio*, 212.
97. Antonio Arébalo to Viceroy Manuel Antonio Flores, "Carta remisoria y diario de operaciones Número 47." 4 May 1776. AGN: MM, 140, ffs. 543–555, in ibid., 354–355.
98. Joseph Galluzo, "Continuación de diario de Apiesi." AGN: MM, 140, ffs. 571–581, in ibid., 361–362.
99. Ibid., 363. Antonio Arébalo, "Diario de operaciones Número 50." Riohacha, 9 June 1776, in ibid., 378.
100. Joseph Galluzo to Antonio Arébalo, "Carta remisoria y diario de operaciones Número 56." Riohacha, 8 November 1776. AGN: MM, 140, ffs. 612–618, in ibid., 405, 408.
101. Galluzo to Arébalo, "Carta remisoria y diario de operaciones Número 57," Riohacha, 26 November 1776. AGN: MM, 140, ffs. 536–541, in ibid., 410–411.
102. Galluzo, "Diario de operaciones Número 60," January–February 1777. AGN: HC, 20, ffs. 593–599, in ibid., 429.
103. Galluzo, "Diario de operaciones Número 64." AGN: HC, 20, ffs. 605–607, in ibid., 440–441.
104. Arébalo, "Diario de operaciones Número 50," Riohacha, 9 June 1776. AGN: MM, 140, ffs. 536–541, in ibid., 384.
105. Kuethe, "Pacifaction," 479–480; Grahan, *Political Economy*, 57–63; Araúz Mofante, *Contrabando holandés*, Vol. II, 87. Cited in Polo Acuña, *Indígenas*, 128. See also, Kamau Brathwaite, *Development of Creole Society*, 63–101; Hunter, "Wheat, War," 505–526.
106. Barrera Monroy, *Mestizaje*, 139.
107. Kuethe and Andrien, *Spanish Atlantic World*, 352–353.
108. See Matthew and Oudjik, eds., *Indian Conquistadors*.
109. DuVal, *Native* Ground; Deloria, "What Is the Middle Ground," 15–22; White, *The Middle Ground*.
110. Hylton and Britto, *Espíritus guerreros*.

Acknowledgements

The author would like to thank the participants in conferences and seminars at the University of Pittsburgh, Rutgers University, Northwestern University, the New School, Vanderbilt University, and New York University, as well as Michael A. McDonnell, Sinclair Thomson, and two anonymous readers.

Disclosure statement

No potential conflict of interest was reported by the author.

References

Adelman, Jeremy. *Sovereignty and Revolution in the Iberian Atlantic*. Princeton, NJ: Princeton University Press, 2009.

Adelman, Jeremy. "Iberian Passages: Continuity and Change in the South Atlantic." In *The Age of Revolutions in Global Context*, edited by David Armitage and Sanjay Subrahmanyam, 59–82. New York: Palgrave Macmillan, 2010.

Adelman, Jeremy, and Stephen Aron. "From Borderlands to Borders: Empires, Nation-States, and the Peoples in between in North American History." *American Historical Review* 104, no. 3 (1999): 814–841.

Alcacer, Fray Antonio. *Las misiones capuchinas en el Nuevo Reino de Granada, hoy Colombia*. Bogotá: Seminario Seráfico Misional Capuchino, 1959.

Andrien, Kenneth, and Allan Kuethe. *The Spanish Atlantic World in the Eighteenth Century: War and the Bourbon Reforms, 1713–1796*. Cambridge: Cambridge University Press, 2014.

Araúz Mofante, Celestino Andrés. *El contrabando holandes en la primera mitad del siglo XVIII*. Caracas: Academia Nacional de Historia, 1984.

Ardila, Gerardo. "Cambio y permanencia en el Caribe colombiano tras el contacto con Europa: Una mirada desde la Guajira." In *Cartagena de Indias en el siglo XVI*, edited by Heraldo Calvo Stevenson and Adolfo Meisel Roca, 41–72. Cartagena: Banco de la República, 2009.

Ardila, Gerardo. *Los tiempos de las conchas: Investigaciones Arqueológicas en la costa de la peninsula de la Guajira*. Bogotá: Editorial Universidad Nacional de Colombia, 1996.

Ardila, Gerardo. "La historia prehispánica de la Guajira." In *La Guajira: de la memoria al provenir. Una vision antropológica*, edited by Gerardo Ardila, 59–77. Bogotá: Universidad Nacional de Colombia, 1990.

Arébalo, Antonio. *La pacificación de la provincia de Río del Hacha, 1770–1776*, edited by Adelaida Sourdis. Bogotá: El Áncora, 2004.

Arébalo, Antonio. "Plan de operaciones, 26 de julio 1776." In *La Goajira*, edited by Maria Teresa Oliveros de Castro, 177–197. Mérida: Universidad de los Andes, 1975.

Armstrong, John M., and Alfred Métraux. "The Goajiro." In *Handbook of South American Indians: The Circum-Caribbean Tribes*, Vol. 4, edited by Julian Steward, 369–380. Washington, DC: Smithsonian Institution, 1948.

Bahar, Matthew R. "People of the Dawn, People of the Door: Indian Pirates and the Violent Theft of an Atlantic World." *Journal of American History* 101, no. 2 (2014): 401–426.

Barrera Monroy, Eduardo. "Los esclavos de las perlas. Voces y rostros indígenas en la granjería de perlas del Cabo de la Vela (1540–1570)." *Revista Boletín Cultural y Bibliográfico* 39, no. 61 (2002): 3–33.

Barrera Monroy, Eduardo. *Historia de la Guajira durante los Siglos XVI–XVII*. Bogotá: Ministerio de Cultura, 1998.

Barrera Monroy, Eduardo. *Mestizaje, comercio y resistencia: La Guajira durante la segunda mitad del Siglo XVIII*. Bogotá: ICANH, 2001.

Bassi Arébalo, Ernesto. "Beyond Compartmentalized Atlantics: A Case for Embracing the Atlantic from Spanish American Shores." *History Compass* 12, no. 9 (2014): 704–716.

Bassi Arébalo, Ernesto. "Turning South before Swinging East: Geopolitics and Geopolitical Imagination in the Southwestern Caribbean after the American Revolution." *Itinerario* 36, no. 3 (2012): 107–132.

Bolinder, Gustaf. *Indians on Horseback*. London: Dennis Dobson, 1957.

Brading, D.A. *The First America: The Spanish Monarchy, Creole Patriots, and the Liberal State, 1492–1867*. Cambridge: Cambridge University Press, 1993.

Brathwaite, Kamau. *The Development of Creole Society in Jamaica, 1770–1820*. Kingston: Ian Randall, 2005 [1978].

Britto, Lina, and Forrest Hylton. *Espíritus Guerreros: La presencia de las luchas indígenas del siglo XVIII*, directed by Lina Britto. Bogotá: UniAndes/Northwestern University, 2012/2014.

Brooks, James F. *Captives and Cousins: Slavery, Kinship, and Community in the Southwest Borderlands*. Chapel Hill: University of North Carolina Press, 2002.

Bryant, Chad, Cynthia Radding, and Paul Readman, eds. *Borderlands in World History, 1700–1914*. New York: Palgrave Macmillan, 2014.

Bryant, Sherwin. *Rivers of Gold, Lives of Bondage: Governing through Slavery in Colonial Quito*. Chapel Hill: University of North Carolina Press, 2014.

Bushnell, Amy Turner. "Indigenous America and the Limits of the Atlantic World, 1493–1825." In *Atlantic History: A Critical Appraisal*, edited by Jack Greene and Phillip Morgan, 191–222. New York: Oxford University Press, 2009.

Camacho, Álvaro, and Nora Segura. "La institución jurídica." In *Indios y blancos en la Guajira*, edited by Ernesto Guhl, A. I. Staffe, Álvaro Camacho, Nora Segura, Virginia Gutierrez de Pineda, Gloria Triana Varon, Gregorio Hernandez de Alba, José Agustín de Barranquilla, Roberto Pineda Giraldo, Alvaro Guzman Cortes, and Antonio López Epieyu, 89–114. Bogotá: Tercer Mundo, 1963.

Cañizares-Esguerra, Jorge, and James Sidbury. "Mapping Ethnogenesis in the Early Modern Atlantic." *William and Mary Quarterly* 68, no. 2 (2011): 181–208.

Cohen, Paul. "Was There an Amerindian Atlantic? Reflections on the limits of a historiographical concept." *History of European Ideas* 34, no. 4 (2008): 388–410.

Cwik, Christian. "Curazao y Riohacha: Dos puertos caribeños en el marco del contrabando Judío: 1650–1750." In *Ciudades portuarias en la gran Cuenca del Caribe: Historia, cultura, economía, y sociedad*, edited by Jorge Enrique Elías Caro and Antonio Vidal Ortega, 281–311. Barranqulla: Universidad de Magdalena-Universidad del Norte, 2009.

DeLay, Brian, ed. *North American Borderlands*. New York: Routledge, 2013.

Deloria, Phillip J. "What is the Middle Ground, Anyway?" *William and Mary Quarterly* 63, no. 1 (2006): 15–22.

Douglas, W. Clark. "Patterns of Indian Warfare in the Province of Santa Marta." PhD diss., University of Wisconsin, 1974.

Durango Loaiza, Eiver Miguel. "Contagiando la insurrección: Los indios guajiros y los revolucionarios franceses, 1769–1804." MA thesis, Universidad de los Andes (Bogotá), 2013.

DuVal, Kathleen. *The Native Ground: Indians and Colonists in the Heart of the Continent*. Philadelphia: University of Pennsylvania Press, 2006.

Earle, Rebecca. "Indian Rebellion and Bourbon Reform in New Granada: Riots in Pasto, 1780–1800." *Hispanic American Historical Review* 73, no. 1 (1993): 99–124.

Earle, Rebecca. *The Return of the Native: Indians and Myth-Making in Spanish America, 1810–1930*. Durham, NC: Duke University Press, 2007.

Echeverri, Marcela. "Popular Royalists, Empire, and Politics in Southwestern New Granada, 1809–1819." *Hispanic American Historical Review* 91, no. 2 (2011): 237–269.

Epieyuu, Josefana Gonzalez. "The Birth of Maleiwa and the Origin of the Clans." In *Folk Literature of the Guajiro Indians*, edited by Karin Simoneau and Johannes Wilbert, 115. Los Angeles: UCLA Latin American, 1987.

Epieyuu, "Simon." In *Folk Literature of the Guajiro Indians*, edited by Karin Simoneau and Johannes Wilbert, 116. Los Angeles: UCLA Latin American, 1987.

Ferrer, Ada. *Freedom's Mirror: Cuba and Haiti in the Age of Revolution*. Cambridge: Cambridge University Press, 2014.

Gallay, Allan. *The Indian Slave Trade: The Rise of the English Empire in the American South, 1670–1717*. New Haven, CT: Yale University Press, 2002.

Garaway, Doris, ed. *Tree of Liberty: Cultural Legacies of the Haitian Revolution in the Atlantic World*. Charlottesville: University of Virginia Press, 2008.

García, Antonio. "Los levantamientos goajiros y el ordenamiento capitalista del Caribe." In *Los comuneros en la pre-revolucion de independencia*, edited by Antonio García, 110–118. Bogotá: Plazas y Hanes, 1986.

García, Claudia. "Interaccón étnica y diplomacia de fronteras en el reino miskitu a fines del siglo XVIII." *Anuario de Estudios Americanos* 56, no. 1 (1999): 95–121.

Geggus, David, ed. *The Impact of the Haitian Revolution in the Atlantic World*. Columbia: University of South Carolina Press, 2001.

Geggus, David. "The Caribbean in the Age of Revolution." In *The Age of Revolutions in Global Context*, edited by David Armitage and Sanjay Subrahmanyam, 59–82. New York: Palgrave Macmillan, 2010.

Giraldo, Roberto Pineda. "Mareiwa y Wanurú." In *Indios y blancos en la Guajira*, edited by Ernesto Guhl, A. I. Staffe, Álvaro Camacho, Nora Segura, Virginia Gutierrez de Pineda, Gloria Triana Varon, Gregorio Hernandez de Alba, José Agustín de Barranquilla, Roberto Pineda Giraldo, Alvaro Guzman Cortes, and Antonio López Epieyu, 139–150. Bogotá: Tercer Mundo, 1963.

Goulet, Jean. "Guajiro Social Organization and Religion." PhD diss, Yale University, 1978.

Grahn, Lance. "Guajiro Culture and Capuchin Evangelization." In *The New Latin American Mission History*, edited by Erick Langer and Robert H. Jackson, 130–156. Lincoln: University of Nebraska Press, 1995.

Grahn, Lance. "Indian Pacification in the Viceroyalty of New Granada, 1740–1803." MA thesis, Texas Tech University, 1979.

Grahn, Lance. *The Political Economy of Smuggling: Regional Informal Economies in Early Bourbon New Granada*. Boulder, CO: Westview Press, 1997.

Guardino, Peter. *The Time of Liberty: Popular Political Culture in Oaxaca, 1750–1850*. Durham, NC: Duke University Press, 2005.

Guerra, Wilder. *La disputa y la palabra: La ley en la sociedad wayúu*. Bogotá: Ministerio de la Cultura, 2002.

Guha, Ranajit. "The Prose of Counter-Insurgency." In *Selected Subaltern Studies*, edited by Ranajit Guha and Gayatry Chakravorty Spivak, 45–84. Oxford: Oxford University Press, 1988.

Guhl, Ernesto. "Geografía." In *Indios y blancos en la Guajira*, edited by Ernesto Guhl, A. I. Staffe, Álvaro Camacho, Nora Segura, Virginia Gutierrez de Pineda, Gloria Triana Varon, Gregorio Hernandez de Alba, José Agustín de Barranquilla, Roberto Pineda Giraldo, Alvaro Guzman Cortes, and Antonio López Epieyu, 15–28. Bogotá: Tercer Mundo, 1963.

Gutierrez de Pineda, Virginia. "Organización social." In *Indios y blancos en la Guajira*, edited by Ernesto Guhl, A. I. Staffe, Álvaro Camacho, Nora Segura, Virginia Gutierrez de Pineda, Gloria Triana Varon, Gregorio Hernandez de Alba, José Agustín de Barranquilla, Roberto Pineda Giraldo, Alvaro Guzman Cortes, and Antonio López Epieyu, 89–114. Bogotá: Tercer Mundo, 1963.

Gutiérrez, Ruth Ester. "Prácticas sociales y control territorial en el Caribe colombiano: El caso del contrabando en la península de la Guajira, 1750–1800." *HISTORreLo: Revista de historia regional y local* 3, no. 6 (2011): 39–64.

Helg, Aline. *Liberty and Equality in Caribbean Colombia, 1770–1835*. Chapel Hill: University of North Carolina Press, 2004.

Hämäläinen, Pekka, and Samuel Truett. "On Borderlands." *Journal of American History* 98, no. 2 (2011): 338–361.

Hennessy, Alastair. *The Frontier in Latin American History*. Albuquerque: University of New Mexico Press, 1978.

Herrera, Marta. "La geografía de la guerra: Los chimila y el Estado colonial durante el siglo XVIII." In *Un caribe sin plantación: Memorias de la cátedra del Caribe*, edited by Alberto Abello Vives, 141–191. Barranquilla: Universidad Nacional-Sede Caribe, 2005.

Hill, Jonathan D., ed. *History, Power, and Identity: Ethnogenesis in the Americas, 1492–1992*. Iowa City: University of Iowa Press, 1996.

Hunter, Brooke. "Wheat, War, and the American Economy during the Age of Revolution." *William and Mary Quarterly* 62, no. 3 (2005): 505–526.

Julián, Antonio. *La perla de la América, provincia de Santa Marta: Reconocida, observada, y expuesta en discursos históricos*. Bogotá: Ministerio de Educación Nacional, 1951 [1787].

Klooster, Wim. *Revolutions in the Atlantic World: A Comparative History*. New York: New York University Press, 2009.

Kuethe, Alan. "The Pacification Campaign on the Riohacha Frontier, 1772–1779." *Hispanic American Historical Review* 50, no. 3 (1970): 467–481.

Kuethe, Alan. *Military Reform and Society in New Granada, 1773–1808*. Gainesville: University of Florida Press, 1978.

Lasso, Marixa. *Myths of Harmony: Race and Republicanism during the Age of Revolution, Colombia 1795–1831*. Pittsburgh, PA: University of Pittsburgh Press, 2007.

Loy, Jane M. "The Forgotten Comuneros: The 1781 Revolt in the Llanos of Casanare." *Hispanic American Hisorical Review* 61, no. 2 (1981): 235–257.

Lynch, John. *San Martín: Argentine Soldier, American Hero*. New Haven, CT: Yale University Press, 2009.

Lynch, John. *Simón Bolívar: A Life*. New Haven, CT: Yale University Press, 2007.

Matthew, Laura E., and Michael Oudjik, eds. *Indian Conquistadors: Indigenous Allies in the Conquest of Mexico*. Norman: University of Oklahoma Press, 2012.

McDonnell, Michael A. "Paths Not Yet Taken, Voices Not Yet Heard: Rethinking Atlantic History." In *Connected Worlds: History in Transnational Perspective*, edited by Anne Curthoys and Marilyn Lake, 46–62. Canberra: Australian National University Press, 2005.

McFarlane, Anthony, and Eduardo Posada Carbó. *Independence and Revolution in Spanish America: Perspectives and Problems*. London: ILAS, 1999.

McFarlane, Anthony. *Colombia before Independence: Economy, Society, and Politics under Bourbon Rule*. Cambridge: Cambridge University Press, 1993.

McFarlane, Anthony. *War and Independence in Spanish America*. London: Routledge, 2014.

Millett, Nathaniel. "Borderlands in the Atlantic World." *Atlantic Studies* 10, no. 2 (2013): 268–295.

Moreno, P. Josefina, and Alberto Tarazona, eds. *Materiales para el estudio de las relaciones inter-etnicas en la Guajira, siglo XVIII*. Caracas: Academia Nacional de la Historia, 1984.

Moreno, Petra Josepfina. "Guajiros-Cocinas: Hombres de historia (1500–1900)." PhD diss, Universidad Complutense de Madrid, 1984.

Múnera, Alfonso. *El fracaso de la nación: Región, clase, y raza en el Caribe colombiano, 1717–1821*, 2nd ed. Bogotá: Planeta, 2008 [1998].

Nabakov, Peter. *A Forest of Time: American Indian Ways of History*. Cambridge: Cambridge University Press, 2002.

Narvaez de la Torre, Antonio. *Escritos de dos economistas coloniales*, edited by Sergio Elías Ortiz, 17–120. Bogotá: Banco de la República, 1965 [1778–1803].

Olano, Margarita Restrepo. "Un ejemplo de relaciones simbióticas en la Guajira del siglo XVIII: Historia de una sublevación bajo el liderazgo del cacique Cecilio." *Revista Complutense de Historia de América* 39 (2013): 177–201.

Oliver, José R. "Reflexiones sobre los posibles orígenes del Wayu (guajiro)." In *La Guajira: De la memoria al porvenir*, edited by Gerardo Ardila, 81–127. Bogotá: Universidad Nacional de Colombia.

Pearce, Adrian. *British Trade with Spanish America, 1763–1808*. Liverpool: Liverpool University Press, 2007.

Pérez Morales, Edgardo. *El gran diablo hecho barco: Corsarios, esclavos, y revolución en Cartagena y el Gran Caribe, 1791–1817*. Bucaramanga: Universidad Industrial de Santander, 2012.

Phelan, John Leddy. *The People and the King: The Comunero Revolution in Colombia*. Madison: University of Wisconsin Press, 2011 [1978].

Pichón, Francisco D. *Geografía de la peninsula Guajira*. Tipografía Escofet: Santa Marta, 1947.

Picon, Francios René. *Pasteurs du Nouveau Monde: Adoption de l'elevage chez les Indiens guajiros*. Paris: Editions de la Maison des Sciences de L'Homme, 1983.

Polo Acuña, Jose Trinidad. *Indígenas, poderes y mediaciones en la guajira en la transición de la colonia a la república*. Bogotá: Universidad de los Andes, 2012.

Polo Acuña, José Trinidad, and Diana Carmona Nobles. "El mestizaje en una frontera del Caribe: El caso del pueblo de Boronata en la Guajira, 1696–1776." *Investigación & desarrollo* 21, no. 1 (2013): 130–155.

Price, Richard. *Alabi's World*. Baltimore, MD: Johns Hopkins University Press, 1990.

Price, Richard. *First-Time: The Historical Vision of an Afro-American People*. Baltimore, MD: Johns Hopkins University Press, 1983.

Radding, Cynthia. *Landscapes of Power and Identity: Comparative Histories in the Sonoran Desert and the Forests of Amazonia*. Durham, NC: Duke University Press, 2005.

Restall, Matthew, ed. *Beyond Black and Red: African-Native Relations in Colonial Latin America*. Albuquerque: University of New Mexico Press, 2005.

Restall, Matthew. *The Black Middle: Africans, Mayans, and Spaniards in Colonial Yucatan*. Palo Alto, CA: Stanford University Press, 2010.

Restrepo Tirado, Ernesto. *Historia de la provincia de Santa Marta*. Bogotá: Ministerio de Educación, 1953.

Rodríguez, Nelson. "El imperio contraataca: Las expediciones militares de Antonio Caballero y Góngora al Darién (1784–1790)." *Historia Crítica* 53 (2014): 201–223.

Rogers, Nicholas. "Caribbean Borderland: Empire, Ethnicity, and the Exotic on the Mosquito Coast." *Eighteenth-Century Life* 26, no. 3 (2002): 117–138.

de la Rosa, José Nicolas. *Floresta de la Santa Iglesia de catedral de la ciudad y provincia de Santa Marta*. Barranquilla: Publicaciones de la biblioteca departamental del Atlántico, 1945, [1741].

Rupert, Linda. *Creolization and Contraband: Curaçao in the Early Modern Atlantic World*. Athens: University of Georgia Press, 2012.

Rushforth, Brett. *Bonds of Alliance: Indigenous & Atlantic Slaveries in New France*. Chapel Hill: University of North Carolina Press, 2012.

Saether, Steinar. "Independence and the Re-Definition of Indianness around Santa Marta, Colombia, 1750–1850." *Journal of Latin American Studies* 37, no. 1 (2005): 55–80.

Saether, Steinar. *Identidades e independencia en Santa Marta y Riohacha, 1750–1850*. Bogotá: ICANH, 2005.

Salomon, Frank, and Stuart Schwartz. "New Peoples and New Kinds of People: Adaptation, Readjustment, and Ethnogenesis in South American Indigenous Societies." In *Cambridge History of the Native Peoples of the Americas*, Vol. III, Part 2, edited by Stuart Schwartz and Frank Salomon, 443–501. Cambridge: Cambridge University Press, 1999.

Saunt, Claudio. "Our Indians: European Empires and the History of the Native American South." In *The Atlantic in Global History, 1500–2000*, edited by Jorge Cañizares-Esguerra and Erik R. Seeman, 77–89. New York: Prentice-Hall, 2007.

Serulnikov, Sergio. *Revolution in the Andes: The Age of Tupac Amaru*. Durham, NC: Duke University Press, 2013.

Silvestre, Francisco. *Descripción del reino de Santa Fe de Bogotá 1789*. Bogotá: Biblioteca popular de Cultura Colombiana, 1950.

Simons, F. A. A. "An Exploration of the Goajira Peninsula, U.S. of Colombia." *Proceedings of the Royal Geographical Society and Monthly Record of Geography* 7, no. 12 (1885): 781–796.

Snyder, Christina. *Slavery in Indian Country: The Changing Face of Captivity in Early America*. Cambridge, MA: Harvard University Press, 2010.

Thomson, Sinclair. *We Alone Will Rule: Native Andean Politics in the Age of Insurgency*. Madison: University of Wisconsin Press, 2002.

Triana Varón, Gloria. "El Mestizaje." In *Indios y blancos en la Guajira*, edited by Ernesto Guhl, A. I. Staffe, Álvaro Camacho, Nora Segura, Virginia Gutierrez de Pineda, Gloria Triana Varon, Gregorio Hernandez de Alba, José Agustín de Barranquilla, Roberto Pineda Giraldo, Alvaro Guzman Cortes, and Antonio López Epieyu, 115–120. Bogotá: Tercer Mundo, 1963.

Van Young, Eric. *The Other Rebellion: Popular Violence, Ideology, and the Mexican Struggle for Independence*. Durham, NC: Duke University Press, 2001.

Walker, Charles. *The Tupac Amaru Rebellion*. Cambridge, MA: Belknap Press, 2014.

Warsh, Molly. "A Political Ecology in the Early Spanish Caribbean." *William and Mary Quarterly* 71, no. 4 (2014): 517–548.

Weber, David. *Bárbaros: Spaniards and Their Savages in the Age of Enlightenment*. New Haven, CT: Yale University Press, 2005.

Weber, David. *The Spanish Frontier in North America*. New Haven, CT: Yale University Press, 1994.

Weston, Julian A. *The Cactus Eaters*. London: H.F. & G. Witherby, 1937.

White, Richard. *The Middle Ground: Indians, Empires, and Republics in the Great Lakes Region, 1650–1815*. Cambridge: Cambridge University Press, 2011, [1990].

Whitehead, Neil L., ed. *Histories and Historicities in Amazonia*. Lincoln: University of Nebraska Press, 2003.

Wilbert, Johannes. *Survivors of El Dorado*. New York: Praeger, 1972.

Wim, Klooster. *Illicit Riches: Dutch Trade in the Caribbean, 1648–1795*. Leiden: KITLV Press, 1998.

Militarizing the Atlantic World: Army discipline, coerced labor, and Britain's commercial empire

Peter Way

History Department, University of Windsor, Windsor, ON, Canada

ABSTRACT

Historians of the Atlantic World have paid startlingly little attention to the main instruments European states deployed in their takeover of the region: their armies and navies. Conversely, few military historians have sought to re-think their own subject matter in terms of the many scholarly achievements of Atlanticists, being locked into the nationalist tropes embedded in studies of warfare. And rarely do scholars seek to recover the experience of the common soldier so as to relate them to the historical processes creating the modern world. As key players in the getting and keeping of Britain's Atlantic Empire, soldiers also played a central role in globalizing capitalism by acquiring new territories to be planted with slaves and indentured servants, producers of commodities, the lifeblood of commerce. Like these unfree laborers, soldiers also had masters more than willing to whip them to their duty, making them another form of coerced labor in the capitalist project. In early modern warfare getting enough men into the field proved key to success. Making men into good soldiers willing to suffer horrible wounds or death required the imposition of rigid discipline. And soldiers resisted that class discipline in many ways, from calculated ineptitude through insubordination and desertion to mutiny. In return, their officers brought the might of a legal system to bear. Military justice proved even bloodier than the civil justice system, which whipped, mutilated, and executed felons with abandon. The army in effect waged guerilla class war against its own men, maiming and killing many to coerce them to do their duty in a way that transcended indentured servitude and slavery. Studying the application of military discipline in such political economic terms while mapping it against the Atlantic shows how colonial expansion itself relied on force and not just the labor regimes it enabled.

Patrick Dunn could write Latin. That proved his undoing. Dunn, "bread a servt." in Dublin, claimed to be the nephew of a Protestant cleric in Ireland and a freemason. Yet 1756 and the outbreak of war with France found him in London in the grip of army recruiters empowered to take up those "able bodied Men as do not follow or exercise any lawful

Calling or Employment, or have not some lawful and sufficient Support." The Irishman affirmed his credentials to disprove he belonged to the rootless proletariat but to no avail, as the press consigned Dunn, along with 500 other men ensnared in Britain's metropolis, to the 35th Regiment safely stowed away on transport ships at Gravesend.[1] The conflict that became the Seven Years' War had erupted two years earlier in the American colonies, prompting Britain to begin committing troops across the Atlantic in unprecedented numbers for the purpose of, as George II informed Parliament in the King's Speech of November 1754, "promoting the trade of My good Subjects, and protecting those Possessions which make One great Source of Our Commerce and Wealth."[2] The struggle for supremacy, both commercial and military, would swirl round the Atlantic and near span the globe, catching men like Dunn in its slipstream.

The 35th Regiment arrived at New York in June 1756, soon moving inland to Albany then Fort William Henry, on Lake George's southern end marking the frontier with New France. John Campbell, 4th Earl of Loudoun and commander-in-chief of His Majesty's forces in North America, worried: "the prest Men, I dare not yet trust so near the enemy," not only due to their "raw" fighting abilities, but also as he feared they would abscond. In fact, six men deserted to the French in early September, among them a "watch maker," a "Taylor," and Dunn, who claimed to have been "unfortunately In veighgled [sic] away by some persons who gave yr. petitionr. such a potion of Liqr. that put yr. honrs. petitionr. out of his natural Senses."[3] Three days later, he surrendered at Fort Edward south of William Henry (clearly having headed for British settlements and not the French), begging Colonel Ralph Burton for a pardon, he "not understanding the affairs of the army or never heard the Articles of War nor was attested but quite Ignorant."[4]

Ignorant of the army Dunn may have been but once Burton discovered his knowledge of Latin the wheels of military justice began grinding to their inexorable end. Burton paired Dunn's bilingualism to his Irish ethnicity and surmised him a priest. The army banned Catholics at this time but winked at their enlistment when wars strained recruitment in an eighteenth-century variant of a don't-ask-don't-tell policy. But the specter of a hedgerow priest preaching to closeted Catholics in the ranks in a war against a Papist power proved too horrible, especially at that juncture in time. Only the month before, Irish Catholic deserters from British forces at Fort Oswego on Lake Ontario returned as guides with the French and Indian force that took the fort and massacred members of the garrison.[5] Amid heightened fears, Burton's suspicion became Loudoun's certainty that Dunn acted as both priest and ringleader to the deserters.[6] Pleading not guilty to the charge of desertion before a general court martial at Albany on 23 September, the Irishman reminded the court he had turned himself in, but for naught. The next day, he went to the gallows. Reverend John Ogilvie recorded: "Patrick Dunn of the 35th. Regt. was hang'd for Desertion," but true to his faith for the Protestant minister noted "he dy'd a strict Papist."[7]

Patrick Dunn's story reveals the army's assertion of absolute authority over soldiers' lives. Given that the army regularly executed and physically disabled its martial workers with the whip, the labor discipline within the military transcended that of indentured servitude and even slavery in its severity and regularity. In the army against his will, Dunn asserted his will by deserting, exposing himself to military law, which promptly dropped him from the gibbet of army discipline. At the time success in warfare depended upon fielding as many men as possible, yet there lay the rub. Making men into good soldiers willing to risk death or horrible wounds required the imposition of rigid discipline. And soldiers, like all other laborers, resisted that class discipline in many ways, from calculated ineptitude through insubordination and desertion to mutiny. But their officers, like the ruling class in civil society, brought the might of a legal system to bear. The British civil justice system whipped, mutilated, and executed felons with abandon but primarily to protect private property.[8] Military justice proved even bloodier, waging a war of terror against its own men, maiming and killing many to coerce all to do their duty. This is not to say that such violence alone enjoined soldiers to follow orders: the army adroitly exploited nationalistic, religious, gender, and racial rhetoric to secure their hearts and minds to the conflict; and the men themselves exhorted each other on as an aspect of unit loyalty or rank-and-file camaraderie. But physical punishment always served as the ultimate weapon of motivation and discipline, the threat of its deployment as much as the actual use having the desired effect on the soldiery.

The relevance to Atlantic history of Patrick Dunn's execution needs elaboration, as does the importance of military history. For an area of study centered on the European takeover of the Atlantic, its historians have paid startlingly little attention to the main instruments of its acquisition, the armies and navies of the various powers, and the centrality of warfare to the process. And in its desire for sweeping studies of historical phenomena, it sometimes abjures the trenchant empiricism of good social history, substituting discursive studies of the published written record, in this way neglecting such important subaltern figures as soldiers and sailors.[9] Conversely, few military historians have sought to re-think their own subject matter in terms of the scholarly achievements of Atlanticists. Many continue to treat armed conflict as an isolated phenomenon while being locked into the nationalist tropes embedded in traditional studies of warfare. Others have followed John Keegan's lead in recovering the experience of the common soldier and sailor; or mined the society half of the war & society dyad to break out of the claustrophobic studies of strategy, tactics, logistics, and army administration. More recently, military scholars have adopted approaches of the cultural turn to write across temporal and spatial boundaries. But they have proved less successful at positioning either the military or its combatants within the historical processes creating the modern world, in particular the spread of capitalism alongside that of empires.[10] This essay attempts such a reading of the British exemplar.

As warfare shifted to an imperial stage in the seventeenth century, commercial motivation came to the fore. Britain prioritized trade over the colonies themselves and valued the navy correspondingly as the mechanism for keeping the seas lanes of commerce open. Attaining the status of a fiscal-military state that waged war off the back of taxation and national debt, Britain pursued a series of wars with France. The conflict enhanced the importance of colonies in their own right as producers of wealth and combatants, so much so that they required a military presence and merited infusion of troops during wartime for their protection. As key players in the getting and keeping of Britain's Atlantic Empire, soldiers also played a central role in globalizing capitalism by acquiring new territories to be planted with slaves, indentured servants, and colonists, producers and consumers of commodities pumping the lifeblood of commerce. Like unfree laborers, soldiers also had masters more than willing to whip them to their duty, making them another form of coerced labor in the capitalist project. For Britain, this process climaxed in the Seven Years' War.[11] By studying the application of military discipline in such political economic terms while mapping it against the Atlantic, this study seeks to transcend a pornography of violence to show how colonial expansion itself relied on force and not just the labor regimes it enabled.

This paper addresses the British example in the era of the Seven Years' War but one can apply its deeper meaning more generally, in an effort to bring historical materialism back into the discussion. Historians speak of states constructing imperial policy meant to expand their power extraterritorially and of their concomitant ability to project military power to those areas. Students of the Atlantic (or broader) World conceive a more fluid globe where people, commodities, and ideas circulate with less attention to borders and barriers. An understanding of developing capitalism provides a matrix with which to integrate such imagined statist and transnationalist worlds. My first point, thus, is that we not lose sight of capitalism as a defining force in the creation of the Atlantic world, and capitalism understood as a developing world political economy that transcends sectors in the market or specific modes of exploitation. Capitalism operates at levels both interior and exterior to the state across polities, at core and periphery. My second point is that warfare played a central role within the development of capitalism, armies and navies functioning at once militarily and as engines of expropriation, subordination, and coercion in the colonial setting, where labor regimes built on exquisite exploitation flourished. State-sponsored warfare in the early modern through modern eras, while serving what-ever political or cultural objectives intended, also operated in the long term to protect, expand, and reinforce the capitalist market in labor and commodities. As such, warfare projected capitalism across time and space, providing multiple 'intersections,' places where expropriation occurred, labor relocated and reproduced, commodities were pro-duced, and ultimately capitalist social structure took root. At each of these intersections where metropolitan culture met local and regional cultures and communities, capital imposed or negotiated modes of expropriation and subordination typically anchored on models of difference such as race, ethnicity, and gender. It met with subaltern opposition and/or accommodation in varying measures but gradually systematized labor forms, pro-duction, and exchange. Thus, my final point is that this process of capital accumulation made for temporal and spatial variance can be studied contextually. But it comes with a qualification that leads us back to my first. For to lose sight of the driving historical forces in becoming fascinated by difference and contingency seduces one into primarily descriptive rather than explanatory renderings of history. Capitalism perpetuated number-less thefts in uncountable ways but nonetheless can best be understood as a singular destructive creation. This does not mean it alone drove imperialism, only that it played a significant role in the process, and in ways demonstrable from the documentary record by the historian.

This essay, by necessity, studies but one strand in such an historical complex, but argu-ably a quite important one: military discipline. In doing so, it weds transnational concep-tualization to specific qualitative evidence to make an argument that can but be sketched herein. The operation of military justice, particularly its punitive component of whipping, hanging, and shooting those convicted of crime, served as the *sine qua non* of war-making in the early modern era. Although varying in form and intensity from state to state, all armies found it necessary to deploy coercive discipline to insure their soldiers followed orders, in particular that sending them into battle. As such, the violence visited upon its own men served the interests of the state in going to war. But studying punishment, it should be remembered, focuses only on half the class struggle. Despite the severity of punishment they faced, soldiers consistently resisted the regime of control by actions running the gamut from noncompliance to outright disobedience on to desertion and mutiny. In fact, the extreme violence of military justice provides an apt measure of soldier resistance. Behind every show of force against its soldiers lay a challenge (real or imagined) to army authority.[12]

Military justice

Violent punishment pervaded eighteenth-century British society. More than jurispruden-tial abstraction, the law perpetuated a social order constructed by dominant groups, which wielded terror so as to protect their class interests. Douglas Hay argued that executions comprised "the climactic moment in a system of criminal law based on *terror*." Moreover, the law's exercise of majesty, justice and mercy also functioned as instruments of terror, giving the power of life and death to representatives of the propertied class, exercised upon whim as much as wisdom.[13] The charade of justice in civil society, however, pales before military justice, which applied corporal punishment more brutally and imposed capital punishment more liberally.

As long as armies have existed, they have relied in large part on physical force to insure discipline, the dependence only gradually waning in Western armies in the modern era. The role of the army during Cromwell's Protectorate and James II reign bred a fear of the military whereas the use of martial law in the Commonwealth to proscribe presumed enemies of the state, even within Parliament, sowed mistrust of another putative monarch with an army at his back, William of Orange. As part of the accord that led to his ascension to power, it adopted the Bill of Rights, which included the requirement of annual parliamentary legislation of the Mutiny Act for the maintenance of a standing army in peacetime. This act enabled the Crown to draft Articles of War and establish courts martial to oversee the operation of military justice but with oversight by elected representatives. The Mutiny Act of 1689 detached military from civil justice in the most fundamental way by treating soldiers as non-citizens, punishing them in a more summary fashion.[14] Contemporary commentators deemed military justice arbitrary and subversive of the rights of Britons. "For martial law, which is built upon no settled principles, but is entirely arbitrary in its decisions, is [...] in truth and reality no law," opined Blackstone. "The necessity of order and discipline in an army is the only thing which can give it countenance."[15] Given this arbitrariness, the operation of military justice requires interrogation.

The Mutiny Act established a broad array of offenses meriting capital punishment.[16] It identified non-capital offenses with far less specificity, however, characterizing them generally as "Immoralities, misbehaviour, or neglect of duty" subject to penalties of imprisonment and corporal punishment, being only limited by the provision not to harm life and limb, opening the door to abuses of power.[17] General courts martial tried all capital offenses whereas regimental courts martial tried minor offenses. Military courts differed from civil in a number of key ways. First, rather than a grand jury a court of enquiry composed of officers decided whether the alleged misconduct merited legal proceedings. Second, juries did not render the verdict in courts martial, this duty falling to the members of the court. Third, whereas in the civil court system, the police, jury, prosecutor and judge represented distinct interests, the members of a court martial handled all these functions. Fourth, the decisions of regimental courts martial were not subject to royal review, a commanding officer's authorization substituting. In short, courts martial protected the interests of the defendant less than in the civil justice system.[18]

The intended operation of courts and the 'justice' they actually produce can make for two different things, but British military justice proved every bit as punitive as the Mutiny Act and Articles of War promised. Arthur Gilbert examined over 1000 general courts-martial cases for the Seven Years' War. Of these, 19.2 percent resulted in acquittals, 24.3 percent in capital convictions, and 52.8 percent in lash convictions. The average number of lashes awarded was 742 but with 45.2 percent awarded 1000 lashes or more. Desertion constituted the most common crime committed by soldiers in the Seven Years' War, and those accused rarely won acquittal, only 9.8 percent. Furthermore, courts capitally convicted and sentenced to death approximately one third of men tried for desertion compared to 24.3 percent for all crimes as a whole.[19]

Calculating the number of lashes or conviction rate, however, cannot compute human suffering. Moreover, there exists a relativist tendency in the literature portraying the operation of military law, however harsh, as broadly reflective of contemporary criminal justice practices.[20] But this misses the point that such practices had become more punitive in the eighteenth century, and avoids the reality that capital and corporal punishments nonetheless terrified soldiers with their ferocity. Moreover, such a reading implicitly accepts the political economy of that system, naturalizes the law, and makes criminality justly punished deviance. No interrogation of the regime of crime and punishment occurs, nor recognition made of how it necessarily functioned as the creature of particular segments of society. Crimes do not arise as original sin; those holding the reins of power first have to criminalize the activity. From the military perspective, a new military discipline developed beginning in the late 1500s leading to professionally trained armies, but also to the army assuming property rights in its laborers with disobedience and desertion perceived as theft of labor owed.[21] The justice system in the military involved labor issues masquerading as military infractions, the Articles of War serving as a code of labor discipline.

Military justice functions first and foremost as a means of enforcing military discipline. But with the rise of standing professional armies and their increasing identification with the nation state, such discipline became increasingly complicit with the vested interests of the ruling class within the state. The Seven Years' War marked the point at which the capitalist class succeeded in an effective takeover of national policy in Britain, making warfare a means of achieving its ends of opening up the Atlantic World and beyond to exploitation by merchant capital.[22] Consequently, military justice and the discipline it enforced became a crucial mechanism for the violence that underwrote this expansion, making it of key importance to the history of the modern era and the phenomenon of imperialism.

Terror tactics

Military punishment involved a dramaturgy of terror. Not only did the scale of punishment exceeded social norms but courts martial occurred with a sickening regularity, rarely a week passing without public punishments. And whereas society's staged floggings intended more to shame than disable the criminal, corporal punishment in the army literally stripped the flesh from the felon. Military punishment also displayed a cruel personal face. The accused knew the officer-judges. The army made comrades of the convicted complicit in his degradation. Many of those who witnessed the carrying out of the sentence knew the recipient, and at times were forced to perform the punishments themselves, all the better to convey the message of the terrible act: break the rules, pay the pound of flesh. If, as Peter Linebaugh argued, "the Tyburn hangings were the central event in the urban contention between the classes," then the parade ground where punishment transpired marked the front line of class conflict within the military.[23]

The terror for soldiers began in the courtroom. General courts martial required a minimum of 12 commissioned officers, and a conviction on a capital offense required a two-thirds majority. The king in law figured as the prosecutor of all courts martial cases but the judge advocate represented his interests in court. Confronted by officers who had trained them to show absolute obedience and run through a gauntlet of bewildering procedures with no right to counsel as in civil courts, most defendants must have felt overwhelmed, especially given the stakes, violent corporal punishment or their lives. Upon reading of the charge, the defendant entered his plea. If not guilty, the judge advocate presented the evidence against, including witness testimony. The accused then could speak in his defense, and, at the end of proceedings, sum up his position, to which the prosecutor would respond.[24] Defendants could challenge court members and question the evidence brought against them, but few did so, not having the expertise. As in civil courts, support from a social superior could lessen the harshness of a penalty or even secure a not guilty verdict; conversely, such a witness could seal the accused's fate by blackening his character. Most defendants plead extenuating circumstances, called an officer as a character witness, and/or threw themselves on the mercy of the court.[25] Sentencing closed formal proceedings and punishment tended to follow swiftly except in the case of death penalties where the king or his designate reviewed the sentence. Even in such cases, death could soon follow if the right of review had been delegated far enough down the chain of command. Executions the day following the trial occurred regularly, as had that of Patrick Dunn, to achieve the most impact as exemplary punishment.

Regimental courts martial ran more informally, requiring only five commissioned officers as opposed to 12 for general courts martial. This group took evidence and rendered the verdict and sentence, which the commander could reduce or pardon but not impose a harsher one. Regimental courts left few records, although they tried the great majority of military offenses, thus obscuring the main experience of crime and punishment in the military.[26] The Mutiny Act also left vague the offenses subject to a regimental court and set no limits to corporal punishment short of harm to life and limb. The court also did not have to record the proceedings and send them to the Judge Advocate General to review, thus avoiding the possibility of dismissal of charges or reduction in sentence. As a result, these courts operated with little attention to civil legal practices. Officers took advantage of this flexibility to charge soldiers with lesser offenses so they could be tried "without regard for law, procedure, or even equity." The punishments ordered proved relatively mild in comparison to general courts martial, typically 200–300 lashes, and commanders regularly pardoned those convicted. Nonetheless, they regularly failed to operate fairly according to their foremost scholar.

Regimental Courts were a convenient "legal" device for punishing soldiers without being overly concerned with the niceties of English civil, or even military, law. It provided a blanket under which soldiers could be severely punished in what *seemed* like a court system, but was in reality only a dubious variation on [...] arbitrary "justice."[27]

Courts martial comprised only the formal mode of enforcing discipline whereas soldiers more regularly experienced summary punishment without benefit of legal process. Commanding officers regularly issued standing orders stipulating specific offenses and the punishment their contravention would bring. General Braddock's order book from 1755 proves instructive. Soldiers or camp followers discovered beyond the piquets faced being tied up, given 50 lashes and marched through camp to shame them. Drunken men risked 200 lashes without court martial and those giving liquor to the Indians 250. Any NCO or soldier found gaming would "immediately receive three hundred lashes without being brought to court martial, and all standers by or lookers on shall be deemed principals and punished as such." And finally, in a clear violation of the Mutiny Act if implemented, Braddock warned: "Any person whatsoever that is detected in stealing shall be immediately hanged witht [without] being brought to a Court Martial."[28] An incident at Quebec during the French siege of 1760 demonstrates that this could indeed happen. James Murray, the commanding officer, ordered a member of the garrison hanged "*in terrorem* without any trial" for breaking into storehouses for liquor, an act of "justice" meant to discourage others engaged in this activity.[29]

Officers also verbally reprimanded or publically humiliated the men, and reported them to the commander. They also imposed minor punishments such as standing extra guard, being sent to drill, or performing fatigue duties. They could impose fines for lost or damaged equipment caused by a soldier's misdeeds, to be paid for by stoppages to his pay.[30] Soldier punishments also included being sent to the "bread & water house" or immured in the black hole.[31] Summary punishment could involve "manual correction," applied by an officer or NCO with his hands or cane. For example, Peter Cloyne, a recent recruit of the 51st Regiment, went to get a drink when on a hot march in 1755, causing an officer to "beat him several times on the head, with a Gun, so that the Blood run down in Several places." He deserted the next day.[32]

Summary punishments may have accorded to established army customs, but it does not therefore make them benign.[33] Many constituted cruel assaults on the human body and soldiers experienced them as such, either viscerally as the victim or empathetically as enforced witnesses. The application of torture-like punishments persisted in the military despite their apparent elimination in the Articles of War, particularly as ordered by regimental courts martial. Riding the wooden horse involved making men straddle a wooden sawhorse structure, sometimes with the crossbar planed to an edge, with muskets or weights attached to the legs, which could lead to the dislocation of joints. A court martial tried two Massachusetts provincials in 1754, "for Curseing and Wising Damnation to them Selves and others threatening Mens Lives" because they had not received their pay, for example. It sentenced one to "Rid the Woodden horse: att which time the Regiment Were Mustered all In arms to Behold the Sight."[34] Running the gauntlet entailed making a soldier run between lines of men, sometimes more than a regiment, who beat him as he passed. A soldier at Lake George in May 1757, "Run the gandtelit through 30 men for sleeping upon gard which Cryed Lord god have mercy on me the B[l]ood flying every stroke this was a sorrowfull sight."[35] The practice of piqueting involved suspending an offender over a sharpened stake, which could lame the man. Caleb Rea, a doctor with the Massachusetts provincials in 1758, complained, "there is almost every Day more or less whiped or Piqueted or some other ways punished."[36] Soldiers could also be placed in irons, either as a summary punishment or for longer periods while awaiting court martial. Henry Bouquet put four deserters in chains at Fort Pitt in 1760, although his senior, Robert Monckton, advised "I should think they had best get a good Flogging for leaving their Command, & let them go about their business."[37]

Colonel James Prevost, a Swiss professional soldier recruited to lead a battalion in the new Royal American Regiment, garnered a particular reputation for cruelty in his introduction of Prussian-like punishment to the British forces. Prevost subjected a soldier to a punishment called "the Book" for getting drunk. He was tied by the hands and feet "and laid on his face in a Corner of the Guard Room with a Stick thrust thro' his Legs & Arms to prevent his being able to turn out of that Posture." Prevost ordered him to be kept like that from one evening to the next, but the officer of the guard untied him in the middle of the night or else "he would have been dead before Morning." Prevost denied knowledge of this "cruel practice" but Loudoun affirmed "I do know that it has been practised, & with very harsh Circumstances attending it, in your Battalion." He made clear to Prevost that the British Service forbid such "extraordinary Punishments."[38]

Where the "Book" proved too cruel, Loudoun and other officers felt no compulsion about flogging their men. Whipping comprised the signature British punishment.[39] In some ways, the lash's flaying of flesh more graphically captured the army's pretension to ownership of its soldiers than did hangings where the invisible spirit merely dissipated, as the message of the lash lived on as scars written in obscene cursive across victims' backs. Sentences of corporal punishment ranged from in the tens as awarded by regimental courts to as high as 2000 lashes for capital offenses.[40] Typically, drummers, their arms strengthened by their trade, wielded the whip on the victim, spread-eagled with hands tied to crossed halberds (poles topped by axe heads).[41] Meant as a public spectacle and performance of military labor discipline, whippings took place in front of the assembled ranks; often specifically before the victim's own company to insure the message struck home.[42] The provost martial might have orders to parade the man from regiment to regiment for each to witness a portion of his sentence administered.[43] Given the excessive number of lashes of some punishments, they could be applied in several doses over a number of days so that the soldier would be fit for service afterward.[44]

David Perry's account of a whipping at Halifax in 1762 provides insight into how harrowing an experience witnessing such punishment could be:

> Three men, for some trifling offense which I do not recollect, were tied up to be whipped. One of them was to receive eight hundred lashes, the other five hundred apiece. By the time they had received three hundred lashes, the flesh appeared to be entirely whipped from their shoulders, and they hung as mute and motionless as if they had long since been deprived of life. But this was not enough. The doctor stood by with a vial of sharp stuff, which he would ever and anon apply to their noses, and finding, by the pain it gave them, that some signs of life remained, he would tell them "d-mn you, you can bear it yet" – and then the whipping would commence again. It was the most cruel punishment I ever saw inflicted, or had ever conceived of before, – by far worse than death.[45]

Others, once given a taste of the lash, could not face the punishment. A soldier involved in the theft of £160 from a lieutenant of the 45th Regiment at Louisbourg in 1760 received a sentence of 1000 lashes. After suffering upwards of 300 strokes one day he hanged himself in the guardhouse before having to face the rest.[46] Some officers did not let death disrupt the remorseless exercise of justice, however. A light infantryman at Crown Point in 1759 was whipped to death, even receiving "25 lashes after he was Dead."[47]

Exemplary punishment

The whip may have defined military discipline but capital punishment constituted officers' ultimate weapon in the military class struggle. In the discretion exercised by judges in handing down capital punishment; in the choice of the mode of death; in designating audience and executioner; and in the discretion exercised through pardon, the army stage-managed executions to make real the puissance of military justice.[48]

Judges when handing down a capital sentence specified the means of execution, by firing squad or by hanging. Perishing by musketfire lent the illusion of a proper soldier's death and typically caused less suffering, whereas hanging evoked civilian criminality, an ignominious end. More "military" offenses like desertion could secure death by firing squad, whereas crimes against property like theft, or against the state such as treason, led to the gallows. A court at Crown Point in 1759, for example, sentenced a man convicted of robbery to hang in the hope it would "Intirrely put a Stop to that Infamous practice of Some Villains Robing their officers and Comrades."[49] But, as often as not, the decision rested on what message the army desired to send. Thus, General Jeffery Amherst in 1759 advised Colonel Thomas Gage that a light infantryman sentenced to death for desertion should "be hanged or shot as you imagine may tend most to strike a Terrour and hinder others from falling into that vice." And George Edwards, a deserter from the 17th Regiment, in August 1759 at Ticonderoga was ordered to be

> Hanged in his french Coat with a Lybel on his brest, Hang'd For Deserting to the French; he is to be Left Hanging all Day and at Retreat Beating is to be buried Deep under the Gallows and his french Coat with him.[50]

To personalize the terror, courts could order the company or regiment of the prisoner to attend the execution. Thus, when John Edwards and Thomas Davis of the 45th Regiment were executed at Louisbourg in December 1758, "ye 4 Regiments were Drawn up in a Square Rownd ye Parade & they were hang'd in ye Middle."[51] The attempt to evoke terror had its greatest effect when orders stipulated friends of the convicted should carry out the sentence. A court martial found Richard Studs of the 27th Regiment guilty of desertion from Lake George in July 1759, and sentenced him to be shot that same day by his comrades. An account of the execution by Lemuel Wood, a Massachusetts provincial soldier, conveys the pathos of such a punishment.

> … the Provost guard brought forth ye Prisoner and marched him Round before all ye Reglars Rigmt from thence to ye Place of Execution there was Drawn out of ye Regmt to which ye Prisenor Belonged 100 Plattons of 6 men Each ye Prisenor was brought and set befoer one of the Platones and kneeled Down upon his knees he Clinched his hand the Platton of 6 men Each of them fired him through ye Body ye other Plattoon then Came up instantly and fird him through ye head and Blowed his head all to Peaces they then Dug a grave by his Sid and tumbled him in and Covrd [sic] him up.[52]

The terror caused by such displays of military power Wood again captures several days later. A general court martial found Thomas Dayley of the 17th Regiment guilty of robbery and, "being a netoreous offender" for past crimes of theft, sentenced him to death. The next day he was brought to the same place where Studs was executed to be shot in the same manner, but

> he was very Lorth to Die they could not Perswad him to kneel down to be Shot they then tied him hand and foot but Could not make him Stand still they then took and tied [him] to an old Log and he hung Down under Sid ye Log they then fird and killed him.[53]

The utility of those executed did not die with them. As in civil society, displaying the dead miscreant's body graphically expressed the message of discipline. Thus, John Boyd of the 28th Regiment, found guilty of deserting a sentry post and fighting for the French against the British at Quebec, would hang in chains "on the very Spot where he appear'd in Arms against those Colours which he had sworn to Defend."[54]

How soldiers responded to the spectacle of execution is difficult to gauge. In civil executions the crowd could identify with either the state or the felon depending on the circumstances.[55] There are no instances of soldiers rescuing those about to be executed and only intimations of anger with the spectacle of punishment. Colonial soldiers unused to military discipline were charged with "Pulling up the wiping [sic] post & Carrying it of [sic]" at the camp by Fort Beauséjour in July 1755.[56] Also at times the army could not find a hangman from the soldiery to carry out a capital sentence.[57] And in May 1757, on Nut Island in New York harbor [present-day Governors Island], a mob of soldiers attacked the Provost Marshall, his guard, and the Executioner while in the execution of his duty, pelting them with rocks and dirt; the apparent cause of the attack, the crowd's mistaken belief that the Provost was drumming a woman out of the camp.[58]

Deterrence comprised the central purpose of the terror of both capital and corporal punishment, but the army's policy of crime prevention failed, particularly with regard to desertion. Desertion constituted the most common criminalized activity of soldiers, one that bedeviled all armies at this time. Rates of desertion typically ran quite high during wartime and necessitated near continuous mobilization to keep armies up to strength.[59] Men continued to take flight from the army despite the fierce punishment meted out. John Stanwix wrote from Carlisle, Pennsylvania in 1757, that desertion remained a problem though he had hung eight men from the Royal American Regiment. "I am apprehensive there will be no stoping of it without hanging every Deserter taken and condemned."[60]

Recognizing the limitations of terror, the military found it necessary to soften the iron fist with the glove of mercy. Granting pardons or partially remitting sentences acted to achieve this end. Ten convicted deserters marched to the gallows "under sentence of death" for a mass execution at Fort Ontario on Lake Ontario in July 1760. Nine received pardons on the spot, but the execution of a Connecticut provincial proceeded as "a sufficient example and warning to the following prisoners, who were under sentence of death, never to desert again, as likewise to put a stop to any more desertions in the army."[61] This but reiterated the ultimate purpose of this charade of death, to inspire mortal terror, as James Robertson, the commanding officer in Florida, made clear. A general court martial at St. Augustine in September 1763 condemned four deserters to death. "The other four equally undergo the fear but one alone suffers the pain of death," wrote Roberston, "four partys are prepared to shoot them, four Coffins are made, they are all to kneel in a row, blindfolded, but when one party fires, the others will be order'd to recover their arms." The regiment would then be told certain death would follow all future desertion.[62]

Such judicial discretion could also work to the opposite effect. John Rhode, a German from Frankfurt recruited by the 60th Regiment, deserted once in America and found himself before a general court martial at Fort Edward in New York in June 1757. Fearing the whip at the least, the "Young Lad about 21 Years of Age" fell on his knees and begged for mercy, promising "that if he is pardoned, he will for the future behave himself." The deaf court sentenced him to 1000 lashes, but later remitted the punishment. Rhode failed to live up to his word, however, for that September he, along with a number of other soldiers, faced the charge of stealing flour and clothing items from a sutler while on piquet duty. Found principally responsible, the court ordered Rhode to receive 2000 lashes and to be drummed out of the camp with a halter about his neck and a note of his crime pinned to his clothing. But he had his sentence changed to the death penalty upon review as "an old offender."[63]

The army stage-managed even the issuance of pardons in a way intended to unbalance clemency with fear in its scales of justice. As if to draw attention to the fact that mercy could not be counted upon by miscreants, the army sometimes left the decision of who would receive a pardon up to the Fates. In December 1759, in the midst of a cruel Quebec winter where the men suffered from poor provisions, William Davis of the 58th Regiment and Daniel Coleman of the 43rd stole a bag of bread from the King's Stores while on sentry duty. Sentenced to death, General James Murray ordered the two "shall cast Lots and do reprive him whose fortune Shall Favour." John Knox described the affair.

> The two men, who were condemned to die for robbery, have thrown dice for life, the Governor having been generously pleased to pardon one of them; eleven was the lucky number, which fell to the lot of a soldier of the forty-third regiment [...] the other poor fellow was instantly executed.[64]

Murray appears to have favored this stratagem, for when the deserters Patrick McGuire and James Savage of the Royal Americans received a death sentence at Quebec in March 1760, he ordered the two to cast lots. McGuire apparently won the game and the reprieve but fortune failed to continue favoring him, for, convicted of theft in July 1761, the army duly executed him.[65]

Military justice, by pairing brutal discipline to the randomness of death, meant to provoke terror, not principally in the principals (those convicted), but in the audience forced to watch their comrades' lives cast to the fortunes of class war. But exposure to terror can have lasting harmful psychological effects, particularly when ongoing. In fact this forms an object of guerilla warfare. In "asymmetrical" armed conflict where one side's numbers and/or resources are greatly outweighed by the enemy, it may adopt guerilla tactics as a means of unnerving the superior opponent. In the British army, where enlisted men greatly outnumbered officers, the latter deployed terror in the guise of military justice as a means of asserting control over the men. Only with this threat at hand, it was believed, could common soldiers be made to follow orders and go into battle. This meant, however, that public punishments occurred regularly, more frequently when including summary punishments.

The exact incidence of public punishment cannot be determined for a number of factors, the first being evidentiary. The relative lack of records for regimental courts martial and the fact that much punishment occurred on the spot without any documentation both obscures and underestimates punitive discipline. The scholar can but look at whatever cluster of cases the archives offer. A host of variables also bedevil any singular model of the routine: whether during peace- or wartime with the latter producing more intensive punishments; the size of garrison; if the miscreant served in a regular army as opposed to a provincial unit, the former being more rigid in the enforcement of discipline; or the personal qualities of one's officers, both commissioned and noncommissioned, among other factors. The well-documented general courts martial offer one solid measure. Gilbert examined 1146 general courts-martial cases for the period 1757–1763, near one-quarter of which produced capital convictions and just over half lash convictions averaging 742 strokes.[66] Placing such mandated punishments in a particular context conveys a sense of their commonality and the likely effect their repetition had on soldiers compelled to watch.

Patrick Dunn, sentenced to death at Albany on 22 September and hung the next day, figured as but one among many sent to their death by trial in the 1756 New York campaign, not to mention those others permanently disfigured by the whip. On 19 May 1756, a month before Dunn arrived in Albany, a general court martial had tried 15 soldiers of the 44th, 48th, and 50th regiments for the capital offense of desertion. Twelve received death penalties; the other three suffered 1000 lashes. On 11 June, a court martial sentenced five soldiers from the same three regiments for desertion, four to death and the other to 500 lashes. Sitting again the next day, it awarded 1000 lashes to another from the 44th for the same offense, whereas on the 14th, it ordered the execution of a soldier for taking flight from the 50th. Then on 25 June, another from the 48th likewise received the death penalty.[67] Upcountry at the beleaguered Fort Oswego, a general court martial sitting on 4 August, sentenced 5 men from the 50th and 51st regiments for desertion, one to 500 lashes, two to 1000, and two to death.[68] At Albany again on 31 August, a court martial dispensed 500 lashes to a soldier in the 44th for overstaying furlough 4 years, and two days later the death sentence to a comrade. On 20 September, a soldier in the 35th Regiment received only 500 lashes for inciting mutiny in consideration of his youth and inebriation at the time of the offense. A soldier of the 48th garnered 800 lashes for deserting but another from the 35th received the death penalty for desertion, Edward Jeffries, perhaps one of Dunn's fellow deserters.[69]

Lord Loudoun gloated shortly afterward that of the six from the 35th who deserted (Dunn among them), "two of them, after losing themselves in the Woods, and being Starving with Hunger, Surrendered to some of the Parties above; those I tried and hanged directly." The other four captured at Wood-Creek had "not yet come my length," presumably then to be measured for a length of rope. Such graphic displays, nonetheless, seemed to have had little effect. "The Situation of things here at present is bad," the general repined,

> the Provincials [colonial troops] extremely disheartened, Sickly and deserting, which last some of their Officers are in confinement for; no less than 40 went off at once; most of them we retook; but the numbers that go off in ones and two's are very great.[70]

Thus, the cycles of general courts martial continued apace. On 9 October at Fort Edward, five men from the 35th tried for desertion received death penalties. The court tried two from the 48th the next day for robbery and desertion, sending them to their maker. The courts continued to clear their dockets of cases from the campaign into mid-December at New York, trying four men from the 50th and 51st regiments for desertion, sentencing one to 500 lashes, another to 1000, and two to death.[71] It bears repeating that these instances only track capital cases, with sentences from regimental court martials and daily doses of beatings for infringing some standing order, or merely not marching properly, figuring more routinely. In short, soldiers proved no strangers to violence, not so much the infrequent engagements with enemies as the regular administration of military justice.

The Butcher's bill

From such accounting one can leap to a more speculative exercise, assessing the psychological trauma experienced by soldiers in the eighteenth century from the routine enforcement of military discipline.[72] Studies of psychological combat trauma have focused on the modern era when a combination of industrialized warfare and society cognizant of the psychological sphere produced both doctors and soldiers more inclined to admit the hidden damage of battle. They also concentrate narrowly on the combat experience. While those sources that have survived from the eighteenth-century soldier do not easily lend themselves to psychological analysis, the voluminous military records of the era do allow an engagement with the literature on combat's psychological impact; in this instance, trauma caused by the violence associated with military discipline rather than that of battle. Courts-martial records specify the types of punishments imposed and in what fashion, whereas scattered eyewitness accounts of punishments administered invoke the emotional toll. Pairing such information to what the medical profession now identifies as triggers of psychological trauma enables an informed assessment of the likely consequences of military justice. The diagnostics for Post Traumatic Stress Disorder (PTSD) offers one such measure.

The National Vietnam Veterans Readjustment Study (NVVRS) in the late 1980s identified four types of combat trauma that contribute to PTSD. They are (in descending order of importance): exposure to abusive violence; to deprivation; to combat; and exposure to loss of control and meaning. The American Psychiatric Association (APA) identifies five criteria in the official diagnostic for PTSD (with only the first being specific to combat PTSD). Someone with the disorder would have undergone "an event outside the range of usual human experience" that would be distressing to anyone such as a serious threat to his or her life, or that of close family members and friends; or seen someone who has been or is being severely injured or killed due to physical violence. The person: relives the traumatic event; engages in continuous avoidance of anything associated with the trauma or numbs their emotional response to such stimuli marked by detachment or pervading sense of doom; and experiences persistent alertness marked by such factors as difficulty sleeping, being quick to anger, and hypervigilance to danger. Symptoms last at least one month. Other social markers indicate combat PTSD: a propensity to violence and disproportionate incarceration in prison.[73]

British soldiers in the eighteenth century encountered the types of situations the NVVRS say led to the condition. They were exposed to abusive violence, both in combat and at the hands of their officers. They also, much more so than modern soldiers, had to live with insufficient food, clothing, shelter, and often pay. The criteria of the APA for PTSD also apply to Seven Years' War troops. Many saw acquaintances being severely injured or killed due to the physical violence of military discipline. Soldiers easily could have witnessed "an event outside the range of usual human experience" perpetrated against known individuals, such as 1000 lashes administered with a whip, or, even more damaging, been forced to execute their comrade by firing squad. Demonstrating that soldiers relived a particular traumatic event or experienced hypervigilance to danger proves more difficult, but their excessive alcohol use could function as a means of numbing their emotions and desertion could serve as an avoidance tactic of dealing with military justice. Much evidence also attests to their propensity to violence and a high level of criminality among veterans. While the argument that soldiers suffered psychological trauma from punishments is more intuited than proven, the nature of the punishments considered in light of a modern psychological understanding of the effect of violence on human beings suggests this as a logical conclusion.

Conclusion

Despite the very real violence the state perpetrated on its military workers in the name of discipline, soldiers regularly contested the legal order that held them in thrall. From shirking work through desertion up to the pinnacle of opposition, mutiny, soldiers sought to exert some control over their working lives, often with deadly consequences.[74] Rather than aberrations from legally defined norms, that is, simple criminal acts, such actions constituted an engagement with the military power structure and supporting legal system, part of a broader proletarian struggle with the emerging capitalist order. The army's role in this struggle must be taken into consideration, most straightforwardly in exposing living beings to physical danger, and more perniciously by subjecting them to an often brutal and arbitrary work regime policed by whips and capital punishment.

The fiscal-military state intended courts martial and the punishments they dispensed to maintain order in an institution, the army, which it sought to set outside civil society. Fielding an effective fighting force formed the army's central purpose, and the operation of military justice focused on this goal. The fact the system constituted a peculiar form of criminal justice geared to war-making should not blind us, however, to the fact that the enforcement of labor discipline among a particular class of workers largely comprised its main function. The army did not punish all soldiers but did expect them to abide by an exact discipline. Even that expectation broke down in practice, discipline becoming less precise as soldier recalcitrance and the military's insatiable need for manpower conspired to moderate the operation of military justice. In the place of an absolute economy of crime and penalty, the army settled on exemplary punishment to provoke terror in its men with the intention of promoting order. This enforcement regularly manifested itself in displays of physical violence perpetrated against soldiers, carried out before and sometimes by their peers. That common soldiers continued to desert and mutiny acquires its full importance only when realizing they knew firsthand that death by military justice could await them. Acts of resistance lose their meaning if the stakes on the table are not made clear.

Neither the role of the state nor the operation of the army can be taken at face value when engaging military history. Class permeated both state and military power structures in the eighteenth century and informed their operational goals, initiating a cycle of imperialistic warfare that saw much of the globe colonized by European powers for the purposes of extracting wealth and labor while expropriating land. This process accelerated the primitive accumulation of capital and formation of the capitalist mode of production, sparking much resistance in its wake. Yet state and military proved capable of containing such resistance usually by means of brutal force. In one such theater of class struggle, the army, this study reminds us that in recounting the history of the Atlantic proletariat we should not privilege Hydra's opposition to the rise of capitalism to the extent that Hercules becomes impotent. Hercules in myth as in history slayed the serpent in the end.

Britain in the eighteenth century became "the greatest state in Europe," in terms of "the external deployment of power," according to Lawrence Stone.[75] But the deployment of military power means nothing without an understanding of the ends to which a state deploys it. Typically conceived in terms of military fortune (who wins and why) or geopolitical gain (who gets what at the treaty table), warfare must also be understood in political economic and historically materialistic terms (what are the long-term outcomes and what interests within society profit as a result). In ways not always immediately apparent, the army in facilitating the expansion of the British Empire functioned as an instrument of capitalism at the moment in time it expanded globally. The state, the military, and merchant capital conspired in the historical development each for its own purposes. The labor of common soldiers played a key role in the process; labor the army coerced from volunteers and pressed men alike through its disciplinary regime.

A British empire of commerce predominated to the mid-eighteenth century, defended primarily by naval power, but with the Seven Years' War the empire became territorial in nature[76] and, consequently, the army emerged as central standard-bearer of British imperialism. State ownership of overseas lands, their resources and peoples, the defining feature of modern imperialism, required an international policing force, the military, to protect and maintain the ownership of such state commodities. The army's increasing significance to the imperial state and, tacitly, the interests of capital marks this watershed. Britain would acquire from France by the Treaty of Paris in 1763, Canada and Cape Breton in North America, as well as Tobago, Grenada, St. Vincent, and Dominica in the Caribbean. The lands claimed by Britain in 1763 now stretched from Labrador to Florida, and penetrated inland to Montreal, Fort Stanwix (New York), Pittsburgh, Charlottesville, Wachovia (South Carolina), and Mobile (West Florida), with frontier forts further west at Michilimackinac, Detroit, and Fort Chartres in the Illinois country.[77] But the war had spread over much of the globe and victory brought Britain immense gains further afield. At war's end, Britain retained Fort Louis on the Senegal River (captured in 1758) as a base for its African trade in slaves, ivory, and the gum Arabic used in silk production.[78] In the Indian subcontinent, Britain had expanded the role of the regular army alongside that of the East India Company, which secured a number of victories against the French, giving them control in Bengal, and setting the stage for the gradual assertion of total control over India.[79] From India, the British launched a successful campaign against Manila in the Philippines, Spain's base for the East India trade. With the peace Britain exchanged Manila and Havana with Spain for Florida, cementing their hold on eastern North America.[80]

The convergence of political, commercial, and military interests invites a reassessment of the meaning of this imperial expansion. The scale of ambition, investment, and geography marked a fundamental shift in the meaning of empire and the recognition that capital played the central role in the redefinition proves key to understanding that shift. Merchant capital had matured to the point that politicians not only recognized its centrality to national power but would also go to war to protect the profitable exchange of commodities. Simply, it had infiltrated the state and policymaking such that it drove decision-making over national security. It also helps to recognize the territorial expansion effected by the British Empire for what it amounted to, land theft on a massive scale. Just as at home in England, where economic interests abetted by politicians enclosed formerly common lands for conversion to commercial production; or in Scotland and Ireland where traditional peasant landholdings came under increasing pressure to "improve" and produce saleable commodities;[81] the British state initiated a cycle of "enclosures" of foreign territories through warfare and treaty-making that could then be opened to settlement and development. Imperialism in this era can be understood as enclosure writ globally. Like enclosure, it forms part of the long-term process of primitive accumulation but on a different scale spatially and temporally, and involving different players. The use of corporal and capital punishment not only underpinned military enterprise but, by so doing, also abetted the formation of Britain's Atlantic Empire and the spread of capitalism into new colonial territories.

Notes

1. Petition of Patrick Dunn "Desarter," [n.p.], [September 1756], Huntington Museum and Library, San Marino, CA. (Hereafter HML): Lord Loudoun Papers (Hereafter LO), 2483/44; Press Act cited in Middleton, "Recruitment of the British Army," 229; Loudoun to Daniel Webb. London, 27 March 1756, HML: LO, 974/21.
2. Simmons and Thomas, *Proceedings and Debates*, 1:1.
3. Petition of Patrick Dunn "Desarter," n.p., September 1756, HML: LO, 2483/44.
4. Ibid.; Petition of Patrick Dunn to Loudoun, [n.p], September 1756, HML: LO, 2484/44; Brumwell, "British Soldier in the Americas," 20; Maj. Henry Fletcher, A Return of a Detachment; Impressed Men; and Recruits of His Majesties Thirty Fifth regiment of Foot, Albany, 4 September 1756. HML: LO, 2774/44; Loudoun to Col. Ralph Burton. Albany, 17 September 1756. HML: LO, 1828/41; Loudoun to the Duke of Cumberland. Albany, 3 October 1756. HML: LO, 1968/44. A justice of the peace had to attest an army recruit to make enlistment official, and officers had to read the Articles of War to a soldier before he came under military law. See Great Britain, Parliament [An act for the better recruiting of His Majesty's Forces on the Continent of America; and for the Regulation of the Army ...], 25 March 1756. HML: LO, 2583/21.
5. Declaration of some Soldiers belonging to Shirley's Regiment, 21 August 1756, in O'Callaghan, ed., *Documents*, 7:126–127; Testimony of Claude Frederick Hutenac, John Noel, Joseph Guinegault, Peter Febure, Peter Pilly and Phillip Leforne, 21 August 1756. HML: LO, 1542/35; Chartrand, "Montcalm's Irish Soldiers," 1–2; Loudoun Memorandum Books, vol. 2, 8 May 1757, HML: Loudon Memo Books, 1717, Huntington Library; Way, "Soldiers of Misfortune," 49–88.
6. Burton to Loudoun. Fort Edward, 10 September 1756, HML: LO, 1756/39; Loudoun to Burton. Albany, 17 September 1756, HML: LO, 1828/41; Burton to Loudoun. [n.p.], 21 September 1756, HML: LO, 1867/42.
7. Court Martial Proceedings, Part 44. Judge Advocate General's Office, Series 71. The National Archives, Kew, London (hereafter TNA): War Office Papers (Hereafter WO) TNA: WO, 71/44/143–145; Loudoun, General Orders, Albany, 22 September 1756, HML: LO, 1538/35; Ogilvie, "Diary," 375.
8. Hay, "Property, Authority and the Criminal Law," 17–63; Linebaugh, *London Hanged*; and Linebaugh and Rediker, *Many-Headed Hydra*, 32.
9. Some notable exceptions: Rediker, *Devil and the Deep Blue Sea*; Frykman, "Mutiny on the Hermione," 159–187; Donoghue, *Fire under the Ashes*; Jennings, "Paths to Freedom," 121–141; Brunsman, *The Evil Necessity*; Campbell, *The Royal American Regiment*; McDonnell, *Masters of Empire*; and Hanna, *Pirate Nests*.

10. Keegan, *Face of Battle*; Parker, *Military Revolution*; Hansen, *Western Way of War*; Hansen, *Carnage and Culture*; Bourke. *Intimate History of Killing*; Lynn, *Battle*; Lynn, *Women, Armies, and Warfare*; Anderson and Cayton, *Dominion of War*; Lee, *Barbarians and Brothers*; and Harari, *Ultimate Experience*.

11. Baugh, "Great Britain's 'Blue-Water' Policy," 33–58; Baugh, "Maritime Strength and Atlantic Commerce," 185–223; Brewer, *Sinews of Power*. For a fuller exposition of this argument, see Way, "Class-Warfare," 65–87 and Way, "Black Service," 57–81.

12. Space precludes a discussion herein of this half of the dialectic that my earlier publications have addressed: Way, "Rebellion of the Regulars," 761–792; Way, "Soldiers of Misfortune," 49–88; and Way, "Class and the Common Soldier," 455–481.

13. Shepard, *Meaning of Manhood*, 130–135; Hay, "Property, Authority and the Criminal Law," 17–18, 25–49, 52–53; and Preyer, "Penal Measures."

14. Phillips, "To Cry "Home!"," 313–332; Collins, "Hidden in Plain Sight," 859–884; O'Connell, "Nature of British Military Law," 142–144; Samuel, *Historical Account*, 199; and Mutiny Act of 1689 reproduced in Winthrop, *Military Law*, 929.

15. Blackstone, *Commentaries*, 413.

16. Frey, "Courts and Cats," 7.

17. Mutiny Act cited in Samuel, *Historical Account*, 209–211, 224–228.

18. Tytler, *Military Law*, 176, 340–348; Gilbert, "Regimental Courts Martial," 50–66; Frey, "Courts and Cats," 6; and Brumwell, *Redcoats*, 103.

19. Gilbert made a comparison to the British navy, and found the lash average in that branch to be significantly lower, but the navy lash produced much more physical harm. Gilbert, "British Military Justice," table 1, 81–82.

20. "Seen in the context of the times," argued Sylvia Frey, "the army's reliance on harsh physical punishment was neither excessive nor untypical but reflected prevalent views on criminal law enforcement." Frey, "Courts and Cats," 7. Similarly, Glenn Steppler sees military justice as in line with civil justice but thinks soldiers broadly accepted the system. As they came from a society inured to physical punishment, "the common soldier was unlikely to feel that the army's use of corporal punishment was particularly cruel or unusual." Steppler, "Common Soldier," 181.

21. Childs, *Armies and Warfare*, 67–70 and Linebaugh and Rediker, *Many-Headed Hydra*, 32.

22. Lawrence Gipson, in his seminal multivolume imperial history, denominated this conflict the Great War for the Empire, an old theme that has re-surfaced in the last 20 years. P. J. Marshall espied "a sharp change of tempo" in British international trade and imperial expansion in the middle of the eighteenth century that "divides the period into two distinct phases," with the Seven Years' War as "the watershed." Britain's rulers invested Empire with new meaning in the war.

    > It was seen as vital to Britain's economic wellbeing, to her standing as a great power, and even to her national survival. British governments began to concern themselves with colonial issues and to commit resources to overseas war on an unprecedented scale.

    The British Empire thus began to assume its modern form with the Seven Years' War, "Britain's greatest imperial effort" in the eighteenth century as Kathleen Wilson put it, "the fulfillment and ultimate expression of mercantilist imperial aspirations." Gipson, *The British Empire Before the American Revolution*, vols. 6–8; Marshall, *Oxford History of the British Empire*, 2: 1, 4–8, 18, 20; Wilson, "Empire of Virtue," 144, 148. The argument that the war marks the conjoining of capitalism, state power, and militarism forms a central argument of the book-length study from which this essay derives.

23. Linebaugh, *London Hanged*, xix.

24. Tytler, *Military Law*, 206–208, 218–257, 313.

25. Frey, "Courts and Cats," 6; TNA: WO, 71/68/112–192.

26. Tytler, *Military Law*, 177, 179 and Steppler, "Common Soldier," 162–168.

27. Those convicted by a regimental court martial could appeal to a general court. In those appeals that went ahead the defendant could face additional punishment, with over 200

additional lashes often being added to the sentence for "frivolous" appeal. Gilbert, "Regimental Courts Martial," 57–66; TNA: WO, 71/40/41–42; TNA: WO, 71/40/42–43; TNA: WO, 71/40/7, 9; TNA: WO, 71/40/4–6, 8; TNA: WO, 71/40/6, 9; TNA: WO, 71/40/60–62; TNA: WO, 71/40/62–63; TNA: WO, 71/40/82–84; TNA: WO, 71/40/51–54; TNA: WO, 71/40/181–183; TNA: WO, 71/46/129–130.

28. Braddock's *Orderly Books*, 36–37, 38, 39, 40, 41, 49.
29. Knox, *Historical Journal*, 298 and Steppler, "Common Soldier," 153–154.
30. Steppler, "Common Soldier," 151–153, 155–160.
31. *Disney Orderly Book*, 10 October 1757; Otho Hamilton to Capt. John Hamilton and the Convention of Officers Mett at Lieut. Newtons. Placentia, Newfoundland, 18 September 1757, HML: LO, 4492/99.
32. TNA: WO, 71/44/237–238, 251.
33. Steppler, "Common Soldier," 161.
34. Frey, "Courts and Cats," 7; Gilbert, "Regimental Courts Martial," 54; and "Journal of Capt. Elezar Melvin's Company," 283. See also TNA: WO, 71/40/44–45; TNA: WO, 71/40/32–33; "Diary of John Thomas," 127; John Winslow Journal, 1 July 1755, vol. 1, 103; Ibid., 31 July 1755, 123; Ibid., 24 July 1755, 121; "Journal of John Cleaveland," 229.
35. *Luke Gridley's Diary*, 30. See also Timothy Nichols Diary, 18 August 1759.
36. Gilbert, "Regimental Courts Martial," 54; *Journal of Caleb Rea*, 36–37.
37. Bouquet to Monckton. Fort Pitt, 20 December 1760, in Stevens, Kent, and Leonard, eds., *Military Papers of Henry Bouquet*, mfm. reel 3, 174 (hereafter in form BP3/174); Monckton to Bouquet. New York, 26 January, 1761, BP3/191. See also John Armstrong to Bouquet. Carlisle, 26 August 1763, BP, 12/311.
38. Loudoun to H.R.H. [Cumberland]. New York, 25 April–3 June 1757, HML: LO, 3463/75; James Prevost to Capt. Cunninghame. Perth Amboy, 23 April 1757, HML: LO, 3435/74; [Loudoun] to Col. Prevost. New York, 25 April 1757, HML: LO, 3469/75.
39. Childs, *Armies and Warfare*, 68–70.
40. For example, Aaron Millforth, a private in the New York regiment, received an extreme sentence of 2000 lashes for desertion at Albany in June 1757, and Lazarus Berkeley of the Royal Americans, sentenced to 2000 lashes for desertion and robbery at Quebec in 1763, had his sentence remitted to 1000. TNA: WO, 71/65/322–326; TNA: WO, 71/48/306–308.
41. Brumwell, *Redcoats*, 101.
42. Michel Foucault noted that torture in the form of corporal punishment intended to mark the body of the victim as a sign of their crime, but also to provide a spectacle, an excess of violence underlining the power of the law, while exposing the victim to shame. Foucault, *Discipline and Punish*, 34.
43. A court sentenced William Antrobus of the New York troops and Robert Smith of the New Jersey provincials to 1000 lashes for desertion at Montreal in June 1760, further stipulating they be

   > marched by a guard from the provost to the parade at the mounting of the guards tomorrow morning, where they are each to receive two hundred lashes from the drummers of the garrison: then they are to be marched to camp and receive two hundred lashes from each of the three regiments of the New York troops, and two hundred from the New Jersey regiment. A mate of the Hospital will attend the punishment. (*Journals of William Hervey*, 70)

44. A general court martial convicted three men of theft of a keg of beer at Fort Cumberland during Braddock's expedition: "Conelly is to receive 900 lashes at 3 different times 300 lashes each time. Jas Fitzgerald and Jas Hughes are to receive 600 lashes each at two different times, 300 lashes each time." And at Halifax in 1757, a general court awarded James Granger of the 45th 1000 lashes for desertion, 500 to be given the next day and the rest when a surgeon deemed him fit. *Braddock's Orderly Books*, 34–35; *Disney Orderly Book*, 12 July 1757.
45. Perry, *Recollections of an Old Soldier*, 31–32.

46. Proctor, *Diary Kept at Louisburg*, 10.

47. Samuel Morris Journal, 2 September 1759.

48. "The public execution is to be understood not only as a judicial, but also as a political ritual," affirmed Foucault. "It belongs, even in minor cases, to the ceremonies by which power is manifested." Foucault, *Discipline and Punish*, 47–49, 57.

49. Orderly Book of David Holmes, 4 October 1759.

50. Amherst to Gage. New York, 24 January 1759, Jeffrey Amherst Papers, vol. 4, Clements Library; William Douglas Orderly Book, 3 August 1759.

51. "Diary of Nathaniel Knap," 23.

52. Studs claimed an Indian had scared him while on cattle guard, causing him to get lost in the woods. TNA: WO, 71/67/192–194; "Diaries Kept by Lemuel Wood," 73–74.

53. "Diaries Kept by Lemuel Wood," 144.

54. TNA: WO, 71/68/9–11.

55. Foucault, *Discipline and Punish*, 58.

56. John Winslow Journal, 24 July 1755, vol. 1, 121.

57. In August 1759 at Ticonderoga, failure to find a hangman to execute George Edwards, a deserter from the 17th Regiment, would result in the provost martial having to perform the deed himself. John Jones of the New York Independent Regiment was sentenced to die at Oswego in July 1760, but Amherst pardoned him on the condition that he serve as executioner for the Provost during the campaign. And at Crown Point in August 1761, "as a hangman Cannot be found," Alexander Mcclean of the 55th sentenced to death for desertion was "to be Shot to morrow at 1 Oclock after Noon by a Party of ye 55" on the meadow near their encampment. Amherst to Haldimand. Oswego, 29 July 1760, Library Archives Canada, Ottawa, Frederick Haldimand Papers; William Douglas Orderly Book, 3 August 1759; Orderly Book of Sarjeant John Grant, 2 August 1761.

58. TNA: WO, 71/44/391–394. The records leave unstated the actual duty being carried out at the time of the attack. Interestingly, two parties faced court martial as a result of this episode, the guards for not protecting the Marshall and one soldier for insulting the officer. The court found the guard party had done all in its power to offer protection and determined the offending soldier, although confessing to throwing a rock that hit a grenadier, not guilty of the charge.

59. Agostini, "Deserted His Majesty's Service," 960.

60. Stanwix to Loudoun. Carlisle, 25 October 1757. HML: LO, 4705/103.

61. *Journals of William Hervey*, 88, 91–92. See also Loudoun Memorandum Books, vol. 4, 6 October 1757; Loudoun, Warrant for the Execution of Rowland Brown and William Richards, with a pardon to Rowland Brown. New York, 16 October 1757. HML: LO, 4647/102.

62. James Robertson to Amherst. St. Augustine, 26 September 1763, Amherst Papers, vol. 4; Amherst to Lt. Col. Robinson. New York, 14 October 1763, Amherst Papers, vol. 1.

63. TNA: WO, 71/65/350–354; TNA: WO, 71/66/81–89, 91–92.

64. TNA: WO, 71/46/8–10, 13–14; Knox, *Historical Journal*, 2: 232.

65. TNA: WO, 71/68/28–29; TNA: WO, 71/70/272–274.

66. Gilbert, "British Military Justice," 82.

67. TNA: WO, 71/43/136–150; TNA: WO, 71/43/151–155; TNA: WO, 71/43/155–156; TNA: WO, 71/43/159–160; TNA: WO, 71/43/161–163.

68. TNA: WO, 71/44/4–9.

69. TNA: WO, 71/44/117–118; TNA: WO, 71/44/121–122; TNA: WO, 71/44/139–142.

70. [Loudoun] to Cumberland. Albany, 3 October 1756, HML: LO, 1968/44. Dunn's death spared him one thing. The next year the 35th Regiment formed part of the garrison at Fort William Henry famously massacred by a French and Indian force. Stewart, *The Service of British Regiments*, 182.

71. TNA: WO, 71/44/150–155; TNA: WO, 71/44/123–127.

72. Such an assessment proves no more speculative for the eighteenth-century soldier, given the limited numbers of first-person accounts, than for such questions as why men enlisted, what they thought of military life, or how they experienced combat.

73. Shay, *Achilles in Vietnam*, 121–124, 166–167, 195, 204.

74. See my "Rebellion of the Regulars," 761–792 and "Class and the Common Soldier," 455–481.
75. Stone, *An Imperial State at War*, 20–21.
76. Baugh, "'Blue–Water' Policy," 33–58; Baugh, "Maritime Strength," 185–223; and Marshall, *Oxford History*, 2: 1.
77. Hancock, *Citizens of the World*, 25–27, 216–217.
78. Anderson, *Crucible of War*, 306 and Steele, "The Anointed," 122.
79. Bayly, "British Military–Fiscal State," 325; Marshall, *Oxford History*, 2: x–xi, 8, 18; and Baugh, *Global Seven Years War*, 282–297, 462–483.
80. Ibid., 490, 515–517.
81. Neeson, *Commoners* and Mackillop, "More Fruitful Than the Soil," 77–83, 89–90.

Acknowledgements

I would like to thank Michael McDonnell for casting his critical eye over the various iterations of this paper, offering guidance and encouragement in equal measure, as well as the journal's academic editor, Manuel Barcia, and anonymous reviewers of the manuscript.

Disclosure statement

No potential conflict of interest was reported by the author.

References

Agostini, Thomas. "'Deserted His Majesty's Service': Military Runaways, The British-American Press, and the Problem of Desertion During the Seven Years' War." *Journal of Social History* 40, no. 4 (2007): 957–985.

Anderson, Fred. *Crucible of War: The Seven Years' War and the Fate of Empire in British North America, 1754–1766*. New York: Random House, 2000.

Anderson, Fred, and Andrew Cayton. *The Dominion of War: Empire and Liberty in North America, 1500–2000*. New York: Viking, 2005.

Baugh, Daniel A. "Maritime Strength and Atlantic Commerce: The Uses of 'a Grand Marine Empire." In *An Imperial State at War: Britain from 1689 to 1815*, edited by Lawrence Stone, 185–233. London: Routledge, 1994.

Baugh, Daniel A. "Great Britain's 'Blue-Water' Policy, 1689–1815." *International History Review* 10 (1998): 33–58.

Baugh, Daniel. *The Global Seven Years War, 1754–1763: Britain and France in a Great Power Contest*. Harlow, UK: Longman, 2011.

Bayly, Christopher A. "The British Military-Fiscal State and Indigenous Resistance: India 1750–1820." In *An Imperial State at War: Britain from 1689 to 1815*, edited by Lawrence Stone, 322–354. London: Routledge, 1994.

Blackstone, William. *Commentaries on the Laws of England in Four Books*. 1753. Vol. 1, edited by George Sharswood. Philadelphia: Lippincott, 1893.

Bourke, Joanna. *An Intimate History of Killing: Face-to-Face Killing in Twentieth-Century Warfare*. New York: Basic Books, 1999.

Brewer, John. *The Sinews of Power: War, Money and the English State, 1688–1783*, Orig. ed. 1989; rpt. ed. London: Routledge, 1994.

Brumwell, Stephen. "The British Soldier in the Americas, 1755–1763." D.Phil. thesis, University of Leeds, 1998.

Brumwell, Stephen. *Redcoats: The British Soldier and War in the Americas, 1755–1763*. Cambridge: Cambridge University Press, 2002.

Brunsman, Denver. *The Evil Necessity: British Naval Impressment in the Eighteenth-Century Atlantic World*. Charlottesville: University of Virginia Press, 2013.

Campbell, Alexander. *The Royal American Regiment: An Atlantic Microcosm*. Norman: University of Oklahoma Press, 2010.

Chartrand, René. "Montcalm's Irish Soldiers, 1756–1757." *Irish Sword: Journal of the Military History Society of Ireland* 26, no. 103 (2008): 1–2.

Childs, John. *Armies and Warfare in Europe 1648–1789*. New York: Holmes and Meier, 1982.

Collins, John M. "Hidden in Plain Sight: Martial Law and the Making of the High Courts of Justice, 1642–1660." *Journal of British Studies* 53, no. 4 (2014): 859–884.

Daniel Disney Orderly Book, 1747–1757. Manuscript Division, Library of Congress. Washington, DC. [hereafter LC]

De León, Fernando González. "'Doctors of the Military Discipline': Technical Expertise and the Paradigm of the Spanish Soldier in the Early Modern Period." *Sixteenth Century Journal* 27, no. 1 (1996): 61–85.

"Diaries Kept by Lemuel Wood, of Boxford; with an Introduction and Notes." Edited by Sidney Perley. Essex Institute, *Historical Collections*, 19 (January–March 1882), 61–74, and (April–June 1882), 143–152.

Diary Kept at Louisburg. 1759–1760, by Jonathan Proctor of Danvers from the Original in the Possession of the Peabody Museum, Salem. Salem, MA: The Essex Institute, 1934.

"Diary of John Thomas." Nova Scotia Historical Society. *Report and Collections* 1 (1879): 119–140.

Documents Relative to the Colonial History of the State of New York; Procured in Holland, England and France. Vol. 7. Edited by E. B. O'Callaghan. Albany: Weed, Parsons, 1856.

Donoghue, John. *Fire under the Ashes: An Atlantic History of the English Revolution*. Chicago: University of Chicago Press, 2013.

Foucault, Michel. *Discipline and Punish: The Birth of the Prison*. Translated by Alan Sheridan. New York: Pantheon Books, 1977.

Frederick Haldimand Papers, Sir Frederick Haldimand Fonds, MG 21, Library Archives Canada, Ottawa. http://heritage.canadiana.ca/view/oocihm.lac_mikan_105513.

Frey, Sylvia R. "Courts and Cats: British Military Justice in the Eighteenth Century." *Military Affairs* 43 (February 1979): 5–9.

Frykman, Niklas. "The Mutiny on the Hermione: Warfare, Revolution, and Treason in the Royal Navy." *Journal of Social History* 44, no. 1 (2010): 159–187.

Gilbert, Arthur N. "Why Men Deserted from the Eighteenth-Century English Army." *Armed Forces and Society* 6 (1980): 353–367.

Gilbert, Arthur N. "The Changing Face of British Military Justice, 1757–1783." *Military Affairs* 49 (April 1985): 80–84.

Gipson, Lawrence Henry. *The British Empire Before the American Revolution. Vol. 6. The Great War for the Empire: The Years of Defeat, 1754–1757*. New York: Knopf, 1946.

Gipson, Lawrence Henry. *The British Empire Before the American Revolution. Vol. 7. The Great War for the Empire: The Victorious Years, 1758–1760*. New York: Knopf, 1949.

Gipson, Lawrence Henry. *The British Empire Before the American Revolution. Vol. 8. The Great War for the Empire: The Culmination, 1760–1763*. New York: Knopf, 1954.

Haldimand Papers. Correspondence with General Sir. J. Amherst, 1758–1777. British Library Add. Mss. 21661, (B-1), microfilm collection, MG 21, held at Library Archives Canada, Ottawa. http://heritage.canadiana.ca/view/oocihm.lac_reel_h1428/100?r=0&s=2.

Hancock, David. *Citizens of the World: London Merchants and the Integration of the British Atlantic Community, 1753–1785*. Cambridge: Cambridge University Press, 1995.

Hanna, Mark. *Pirate Nests and the Rise of the British Empire, 1570–1740*. Chapel Hill: University of North Carolina Press, 2015.

Hansen, Victor D. *The Western Way of War: Infantry Battle in Classical Greece*. New York: Alfred A. Knopf, 1989.

Hansen, Victor D. *Carnage and Culture: Landmark Battles in the Rise to Western Power*. New York: Doubleday, 2001.

Harari, Yuval Noah. *The Ultimate Experience: Battlefield Revelations and the Making of Modern War Culture, 1450–2000*. Houndmills: Palgrave-Macmillan, 2008.

Hay, Douglas. "Property, Authority and the Criminal Law." In *Albion's Fatal Tree: Crime and Society in Eighteenth Century England*, edited by D. Hay, P. Linebaugh, J. G. Rule, E. P. Thompson, and C. Winslow, 17–63. New York: Pantheon, 1975.

Jeffrey Amherst Papers. *William L. Clements Library*. Ann Arbor: University of Michigan.

Jennings, Evelyn. "Paths to Freedom: Imperial Defense and Manumission in Havana, 1762–1800." In *Paths to Freedom: Manumission in the Atlantic World*, edited by Rosemary Brana-Shute and Randy Sparks, 121–141. Columbia: University of South Carolina Press, 2009.

John Winslow Journal, 1744–1757. Mfm. P–256. Massachusetts Historical Society, Boston.

"Journal of Capt. Elezar Melvin's Company, Shirleys's Expedition, 1754; Letter from John Barber in Shirley's Expedition of 1755; and Muster–Roll of Capt. Paul Brigham's Company, 1775–77." *New England Historical and Genealogical Register* 27 (1873): 281–286.

"Journal of Rev. John Cleaveland, June 14, 1758–October 25, 1758." *Bulletin of the Fort Ticonderoga Museum* 10, no. 3 (1959): 192–236.

Journals of the Hon. William Hervey in North America and Europe, from 1755–1814; with Order Books at Montreal, 1760–1763. Bury St. Edmund's: Paul & Mathew, 1906.

Judge Advocate General's Office. Court Martial Proceedings. Series 71, Parts 40, 44, 46, 48, 65–68, 70, War Office Papers, British National Archives, Kew, London.

Keegan, John. *The Face of Battle: A Study of Agincourt, Waterloo and the Somme*. New York: Viking Press, 1976.

Knox, John. *Historical Journal of the Campaigns in North-America, for the Years 1757, 1758, 1759, 1760*. 2 vols. London: W. Johnston, 1769.

Lee, Wayne E. *Barbarians and Brothers: Anglo-American Warfare, 1500–1865*. New York: Oxford University Press, 2011.

Lord Loudoun. *Memorandum Books. HM 1717*. San Marino, CA: Huntington Museum and Library.

Lord Loudoun Papers. LO. Huntington.

Linebaugh, Peter. *The London Hanged: Crime and Civil Society in the Eighteenth Century*. London: Penguin, 1993.

Linebaugh, Peter, and Marcus Rediker. *The Many-Headed Hydra: Sailors, Slaves, Commoners, and the Hidden History of the Revolutionary Atlantic*. London: Verso, 2000.

Luke Gridley's Diary of 1757 while in Service in the French and Indian War. Hartford, CT: Hartford Press, 1907.

Lynn, John A. *Battle: A History of Combat and Culture from Ancient Greece to Modern America*. Boulder, CO: Westview Press, 2003.

Lynn, John A., II. *Women, Armies, and Warfare in Early Modern Europe*. Cambridge: Cambridge University Press, 2008.

Mackillop, Andrew. *"More Fruitful than the Soil": Army, Empire and the Scottish Highlands, 1715–1815*. East Linton, UK: Tuckwell, 2000.

Major General Edward Braddock's Orderly Books, From February 26 to June 17, 1755. From the Originals, in the Congressional Library. Cumberland, MD: Will H. Lowdermilk, 1878.

Marshall, Peter J., ed. *The Oxford History of the British Empire. Vol. 2. The Eighteenth Century*. Oxford: Oxford University Press, 1998.

McDonnell, Michael A. *Masters of Empire: Great Lakes Indians and the Making of America*. New York: Hill and Wang, 2015.

Middleton, Richard. "The Recruitment of the British Army, 1755–1762." *Journal of the Society for Army Historical Research* 67 (1989): 226–238.

Neeson, Jeanette M. *Commoners: Common Right, Enclosure and Social Change in England, 1700–1820*. Cambridge: Cambridge University Press, 1996.

O'Connell, Daniel Patrick. "The Nature of British Military Law." *Military Law Review* 19 (1963), 141–156.

Orderly Book of David Holmes's [Company of the Third Connecticut Regiment]. 1758–1759. David Holmes Collection. Mfm. P–212. MHS.

Orderly Book of Sarjeant John Grant. HM 595. Huntington.

Parker, Geoffrey. *The Military Revolution: Military Innovation and the Rise of the West, 1500–1800*. Cambridge: Cambridge University Press, 1988.

Perry, David. *Recollections of an Old Soldier the Life of Captain David Perry, a Soldier of the French and Revolutionary Wars … Written by Himself*. Windsor, VT, 1822.

Phillips, Gervase. "To Cry 'Home! Home!:' Mutiny, Morale, and Indiscipline in Tudor Armies." *The Journal of Military History* 65 (April 2001): 313–332.

Preyer, Kathryn. "Penal Measures in the American Colonies: An Overview." *The American Journal of Legal History* 26, no. 4 (1982): 326–353.

Rediker, Marcus. *Between the Devil and the Deep Blue Sea: Merchant Seamen, Pirates and the Anglo-American Maritime World, 1700–1750*. Cambridge: Cambridge University Press, 1989.

Samuel, E. *An Historical Account of the British Army, and of the Law Military, as Declared by the Ancient and the Modern Statutes, and Articles of War for Its Government*. London: William Clowes, 1816.

Samuel Morris Journal. 1758–1759. Clements.

Shay, Jonathan. *Achilles in Vietnam: Combat Trauma and the Undoing of Character*. New York: Scribner, 1994.

Shepard, Alexandra. *The Meaning of Manhood in Early Modern England*. New York: Oxford University Press, 2003.

Simmons, Richard C., and Peter D. G. Thomas, eds. *Proceedings and Debates of the British Parliaments Respecting North America, 1754–83: Vol. 1 1754–1764*. London: Kraus, 1982.

Steele, Ian K. "The Anointed, the Appointed, and the Elected: Governance of the British Empire, 1689–1784." In *The Oxford History of the British Empire. Vol. 2. The Eighteenth Century*, edited by P. J. Marshall, 105–150. Oxford: Oxford University Press, 1998.

Steppler, Glenn A. "The Common Soldier in the Reign of George III, 1760–1793." D.Phil. thesis. Exeter College, Oxford University. 1984.

Stewart, Charles H. *The Service of British Regiments in Canada and North America: A Resume*. Ottawa: Department of National Defence Library, 1962.

Stone, Lawrence, ed. *An Imperial State at War: Britain from 1689 to 1815*. London: Routledge, 1994.

"The Diary of Nathaniel Knap of Newbury in the Province of Massachusetts Bay in New England." Written at the Second Siege of Louisburg in 1758. Society of the Colonial Wars in the Commonwealth of Massachusetts, *Proceedings*, no. 2 (1895): 1–42.

"The Diary of Reverend John Ogilvie 1750–1759." Edited by Milton W. Hamilton. *Bulletin of the Fort Ticonderoga Museum* 10, no. 5 (February 1961): 331–381.

The Journal of Dr. Caleb Rea. Edited by F. M. Ray. Salem: Essex Institute, 1881.

The Military Papers of Henry Bouquet: Brigadier General in America, Lieutenant-Colonel of the Royal American Brigade 1754–64 (Microfilm from British Library Additional Manuscripts 21631–21660). Edited by S. K. Stevens, Donald R. Kent, and Autumn L. Leonard. London: World Microfilms, 1978.

Timothy Nichols. Diary. 1759. Mfm. P–363. Reel 6. MHS.

Tytler, Alexander Fraser. *An Essay on Military Law, and the Practice of Courts Martial*. London: T. Egerton, 1806.

Way, Peter. "Rebellion of the Regulars: Working Soldiers and the Mutiny of 1763–1764." *William and Mary Quarterly*, 3rd Ser., 57, no. 4 (2000): 761–792.

Way, Peter. "Soldiers of Misfortune: New England Regulars and the Fall of Oswego, 1755–56." *Massachusetts Historical Review* 3 (2001): 49–88.

Way, Peter. "Class and the Common Soldier in the Seven Years' War." *Labor History* 44, no. 4 (2003): 455–481.

Way, Peter. "'Black Service … White Money': The Peculiar Institution of Military Labor in the British Army During the Seven Years' War." In *Workers Across the Americas: The Transnational Turn in Labor History*, edited by Leon Fink, 57–81. New York: Oxford, 2011.

Way, Peter. "Class-Warfare: Primitive Accumulation, Military Revolution and the British War-Worker." In *Beyond Marx: Theorising the Global Labour Relations of the Twenty-First Century*, edited by Marcel van der Linden and Karl Heinz Roth, 65–87. Leiden, The Netherlands: Brill, 2014.

William Douglas Orderly Book. 1759. Peter Force Papers (8D: 36, reel 37), LC.

Wilson, Kathleen. "Empire of Virtue: The Imperial Project and Hanoverian Culture c.1720–1785." In *An Imperial State at War: Britain from 1689 to 1815*, edited by Lawrence Stone, 128–164. London: Routledge, 1994.

Winthrop, William. *Military Law and Precedents*. 2nd ed. Washington, DC: Government Printing Office, 1920.

"The supreme power of the people": Local autonomy and radical democracy in the Batavian revolution (1795–1798)

Pepijn Brandon[a] and Karwan Fatah-Black[b]

[a]History Department, Vrije University, Amsterdam, Netherlands; [b]Institute for History, Leiden University, Leiden, Netherlands

ABSTRACT

The Batavian Revolution of 1795 that overthrew the old stadtholderly regime of the Dutch Republic was followed by a period of intense political conflict in which popular mobilization played a key role. Among revolutionary elites, the main dividing line between moderates and radicals occurred around questions concerning the reorganization of the state apparatus and the writing of a new constitution. A full rejection of the federative model of the state that had characterized the former Dutch Republic became central to the repertoire of the radical faction in the National Convention. However, instances of protest and rebellion from below, often supported by the radicals in the Convention, generally remained conspicuously local in focus. This clash between national ideals and highly localized realities remains one of the central paradoxes of the Batavian Revolution. The form in which this process unfolded was peculiar to the trajectory of the Batavian Revolution, which more than any of its counterparts became centered on constitutional issues. But severe tensions between programs for the rationalization of state bureaucracy along nationalizing lines and popular support for far-reaching local autonomy existed in each of the Atlantic Revolutions. In January 1797, radical democrats in Leiden attempted to find an organizational form to solve this problem. They called for a national gathering of representatives from local revolutionary clubs and neighborhood assemblies. The response by the moderate provincial and national authorities was remarkably swift, and the initiative was repressed before the meeting could take place. Examining the failure of this unique attempt to bridge the divide between local popular mobilization and national revolutionary programs, as well as the discussion that followed this failure, can help us understand the possibilities and limitations of Batavian radicalism.

Introduction

On 15 January 1797, in the midst of a growing political crisis engulfing the Batavian Republic that had been established in the Netherlands two years earlier, the regional government of the province of Holland took a remarkable step. Without the permission of the Batavian National Convention, and encroaching upon the jurisdiction of local authorities, provincial officers marched into the city of Leiden and arrested five well-known radical democrats. Among them were the leading Leiden radical publishers Willem van Lelyveld and Pieter Hendrik Trap. Their crime had been to sign a call for a "nation-wide assembly of neighborhood councils."[1] The aim of this gathering was to rally the lowest electoral organs, independently of the National Convention, in order to push the revolution in a more radical direction. The attempt led to panic among moderate politicians, who perhaps unsurprisingly backed the regional government of Holland's actions to quickly suppress the attempt. Rutger Jan Schimmelpenninck, a leading moderate who would later become head of state, led the charge. In a stormy meeting of the National Convention, he argued that if allowed, the nation-wide assembly of neighborhood councils would undercut the very system of indirect representation and create "a representative Body, that not just as *individual Citizens*, but with *authority* will pretend to sit in judgement of the interests of the Nation ... "[2] He therefore advocated stern measures to repress this attempt. Radicals at the local as well as the national level came to the defense of their Leiden associates. However, they did so not under the banner of their own program of direct democracy, but focused their protests on the violation by the Holland deputies of the local autonomy of the city of Leiden.

While the incident itself quickly sunk into oblivion, the brief uproar it created within radical circles with perfect clarity illustrates one of the key dilemmas faced by the Batavian revolution. Politically, the more radical leaders of the revolution advocated a far-reaching centralization of the state along national lines.[3] On the other hand, the rank and file that they sought to mobilize remained highly committed to the defense of local autonomy against any encroachment by centralizing authorities.[4] For radical leaders on the national as well as the local level, including the arrested publishers Trap and Lelyveld, the attempt at a "nation-wide convention of neighborhood councils" was aimed at strengthening the connections between the revolutionary leadership in the National Convention and local revolutionary politics. Instead, the complete failure of this attempt laid bare the fault lines along which the fragile alliance between state-modernizers and local popular mobilization would soon start unraveling.

R. R. Palmer was one of the first historians internationally to grant the Batavian Revolution its own distinct voice in the cacophony of the Age of Revolutions. While historians before him, including Dutch historians, had described the events surrounding the 1795 fall of the old regime primarily as an extension of French intervention, Palmer described the Batavian events as a "true revolution."[5] He pointed out the significant repercussions for the wider struggles in the Atlantic world, especially for the military conflict between France and Britain. He also noted the particular extent to which Batavian revolutionary politics became focused on constitutional issues, which was a result of the drawn-out crisis of the Dutch state that preceded it.[6] Study of the Batavian Revolution since then has affirmed the need to recognize that this revolution was driven by its own dynamic of popular contention and intra-elite struggles, rather than being simply an extension of French military power.[7]

The recognition of the revolutionary character of constitutional struggles and conflicts between radicals and moderates over the nature of popular sovereignty and democracy has greatly increased the relevance of the Dutch case for comparisons with similar events in the Atlantic World and beyond. This is particularly true for the far-reaching conflicts that arose over the deeply entrenched federalism of Dutch political life. Clashes between programs for the rationalization of state bureaucracy along nationalizing lines and existing traditions of far-reaching local autonomy were certainly not confined to the Netherlands. Although, as Pierre Serna has daringly suggested, all the Atlantic revolutions contained elements of a "War of Independence," at the national level these revolutions increasingly evolved into wars of subjugation of the regions to the center.[8]

This tension gave rise to explosive struggles for autonomy, mixed with battles over direct versus representative democracy. Sometimes resistance was mounted under the flag of a purer version of the original revolution, as happened when the former enslaved on Haiti raised the standard of liberty.[9] Sometimes it took more outwardly conservative forms, as in the War of the Vendée.[10] Most often it alternated between these two extremes. The Dutch colonies in the Atlantic world provided a third variant, in which struggles over the implementation of the revolution became connected to the rise of creole elites and their own agendas of preserving local autonomy in the face of increasing imperial competition and slave resistance.[11] In this wide variety of forms, the question of local autonomy versus an expanding, rationalizing national state had important effects for the relationship between revolutionary regimes and leaderships and local popular mobilizations. In this light, the Leiden events can be seen as a microscopic example of a much wider problem.

The Batavian context

The Batavian Revolution started in January 1795 with the overthrow of the stadtholderly regime that had ruled the Dutch Republic since 1747. The stadtholder and his family were forced into exile, the National Convention replaced the old States General, and the Batavian Republic became an ally of France in its war against Britain. Three years of popular rebellions and political conflict followed, culminating in 1798 in a coup and countercoup. The defining political issue in the newly established National Convention became whether the Batavian Republic replacing the *Ancien Régime* should be a loose federation of provinces as had been the tradition of the old Dutch Republic, or a national state. Federalism was deeply imbued in the structures of the state. The founding principle of the Dutch Republic laid down in the *Unie van Utrecht* at the time of the sixteenth-century Dutch Revolt had been the protection of the autonomy of the seven federated provinces against central rule. As a result representation in all the main organs of the state, from the States General to the five independent Admiralty Boards, and from finance to the management of the East and West India Companies, had remained painstakingly divided over the seven provinces. Social policy and jurisdiction largely remained the prerogative of the influential town-governments. Local protectionism remained a central plank of their economic outlook. However, under pressure of eighteenth-century military and economic setbacks, criticism of this elaborate state-structure mounted. Now, provincial privileges seemed to hinder growth and development.[12]

Some steps toward centralization were taken under the *Ancien Régime*. The last stadtholder William V was a remarkably central figure in the otherwise fragmented republic. Not only had his predecessor managed to make his position hereditary, he was also stadtholder of all the provinces, he chaired the Dutch East India Company and West India Company and actively intervened in the politics of the colonies. During his tenure there were two major waves of opposition, the failed Patriot Revolution of 1785–1787 and the successful Batavian Revolution of 1795. These movements fused Dutch traditions of constitutional thinking with the newly emerging political winds that blew across the Atlantic. Being directed against centralizing, semi-monarchical Orangist rule, the Patriot Revolution of 1785–1787 had called for a "restoration" of the old traditions of federative administration.[13] In doing so, it naturally took its inspiration from the American War of Independence, where revolutionaries in turn upheld the Dutch Republic as one of their own constitutional models.[14] The Patriots were able to take over several local governments until in 1787 the Prussian army invaded to restore the power of Willem V. This resulted in a purge of Patriots from the local governments and restored supporters of the House of Orange to positions of power.

The chances of the Orangists turned in 1793 when the Dutch Republic entered the war against revolutionary France. The French invaded the Netherlands in January 1795, chasing out Willem V and opening the second wave of constitutional experiments. In the meantime, under the influence of the French Revolution and the constitutions of 1791 and 1793 that had proclaimed the nation "one and indivisible," many of the former Patriots had changed their perspective on the desired outcome of their revolution. With few exceptions, the more radical revolutionary leaders now became ardent followers of the ideal of the centralized nation-state. The demand of a unitary state became the central plank of a program that henceforward became associated with state modernization, democratic opposition to local "aristocratic" ruling cliques, radicalism or even Jacobinism.[15] In a pamphlet written less than two years before the Batavian Revolution Bernardus Bosch, who after the revolution became one of the most radical representatives in the National Convention, summed up this program. Borrowing his terminology from French debates, he directly equated federalism with feudalism. "All the *provinces* have to form *but one union*; the gates of the cities, that close in the Citizen as in a cage have to be forever opened, as a token of general unification."[16] For Bosch and his fellow-radicals, national unification was almost synonymous with democracy. Local prerogatives were the powerbase of the old elites and the stadtholderly regime. A popular revolution would break them down.

Once the revolution unfolded, however, things proved to be not so simple. Although popular revolts accompanied the French invasion of 1795, the installation of the new regime was as much the result of large sections of the old elite accommodating to foreign occupation. The founding of an elected National Convention as a replacement of the old States General, consisting of delegations of the Provincial elites, was a great departure from the old federative model. However, from the provinces to the central state an influential layer of administrators remained in place that supported at best a very moderate course for state reform, leaving part of the old federative structure intact.[17] Frustrated radicals increasingly called for a purge of these "Orangists," "aristocrats" and "federalists," but lacked the powerbase to effect this. Meanwhile, popular protest did not unfold as the unified national revolution that the radicals had envisioned, but due to the completely fragmented nature of political life took the form of a loosely connected series of local uprisings. In this, they continued to resemble the pattern established by the Patriot revolution, that as Wayne te Brake noticed "was a localized revolution within a decentralized republic."[18] At the municipal level, regime-change was mostly enforced by heterogeneous coalitions of revolutionary clubs, moderate and radical veterans of the Patriot revolution, and sections of the lower classes.[19] They railed against the representatives of the old order that had nestled themselves in positions of power, but because their support base often remained rather small, they did not manage to oust them. Instead, next to the moderate official Batavian organs of power and often in opposition to them, local radical societies organized their own permanent structures of representation. One of these was the Citizens' Gathering in the *Marekerk* (a church) in Leiden, that would play an important part in the events leading up to January 1797. Similar institutions emerged elsewhere, under different names. In Amsterdam, a General Assembly of Neighborhood Councils became the seedbed of local radicalism.[20] In Friesland the *Hoofdvergadering* or Head Meeting fulfilled the same role.[21]

Through petitions, demonstrations and sometimes open riot, these institutions put pressure on local governments. Revolutionary societies and moderate municipal councils clashed over whether (male) suffrage should be universal or restricted for servants, the poor and other "dependents," over how to deal with the worsening state of the economy and its effect on living conditions, and over the desirability of "purges" of the supporters of the old Orangist regime from positions of power. Such conflicts led to particularly sharp outbursts of popular protest in Amsterdam. On 16 September 1795, armed and unarmed protestors stormed the Amsterdam City Hall to amplify their demands "to recognize the Batavian Clubs as official bodies, and to immediately decommission the civil servants of the old regime, and put sons of freedom in their place."[22] In May of the next year, the same issue led to an even more threatening armed revolt that lasted several days and centrally involved the city's artillery regiment. A French garrison had to be called in to quell the unrest.[23] Radicals also tried to gain influence through the neighborhood councils, the electoral bodies organized at the local level to facilitate the selection of representatives to the municipalities and later the National Convention. While there was an important difference between the revolutionary societies, representing a small minority of political activists, and these neighborhood councils that effectively formed the lowest rung of the new electoral system, the radicals consciously tried to blur this distinction. In 1798, leading radical Gerrit Paape misleadingly claimed that "[a]lthough the Societies do not literally form or represent the Batavian People, they were indeed seen as the people. For by the small change of calling themselves Neighborhood Councils, they became the sovereigns of the nation."[24]

By the end of Year II of the Batavian Revolution, this stalemate between vociferous local radical coalitions and a deadlock on constitutional reform in the National Assembly had reached crisis point. In the eyes of the radicals, the revolution remained unfinished. They blamed this on "aristocrats" who had dressed up as Batavian revolutionaries and had gained positions at all levels of the state. *Slymgasten*, "slimy fellows," was the term that the radicals introduced for this group. The influential newspaper *De Democraten* defined *slymgasten* as

> […] such persons, who in the execution of the affairs of this Revolution always lean towards the soft side; who [...] imagine themselves that this is the securest way, and therefore do not dare to deviate from it by a single step, unless they are being forced to do so by *the gravest emergency*, and even than can only do so while *shivering*.[25]

The only way to force such characters to take bolder action, was to make sure that they felt under direct pressure from the people. The radicals saw the Neighborhood Councils as the natural venue for organizing this pressure. A member of the Amsterdam society *Tot nut van het Vaderland* (For the benefit of the Fatherland), that in 1795 had taken the initiative for the establishment of the General Assembly of Neighborhood Councils, in the wooly language of the time proclaimed that "this Assembly is the access point between the People of Amsterdam and the Representation of that People, because in its turn it becomes the point of access to the Representation of the People of the Netherlands."[26] The same ideas would stimulate Leiden radicals to take the initiative for their Nation-wide Assembly of Neighborhood Councils.

Revolutionary Leiden

The course of the Batavian revolution in Leiden provides a good example of the ways in which radicals used popular mobilization around issues of democratic representation and local governance in order to push the revolutionary process further, as well as of the obstacles they faced in doing so. Already in 1795, the basic problems that gave rise to the failed attempt to form a National Convention of Neighborhood Councils were clearly laid out.[27]

Immediately after the French General Pichegru had led his troops across the Meuse in January 1795, Leiden radicals took action. Several days before French soldiers entered the city, they proclaimed the dawn of "Batavian Freedom." An estimated one thousand armed citizens participated in the overthrow of the old city government in the night of 18 and 19 January.[28] With a total urban population of 31,000, among whom were only 9,000 men of fighting age, this shows that the revolution was carried out with substantial popular par-ticipation.[29] An anonymous Orangist diarist noted that the crowd initially gathered at the Town hall. From there, they marched to the houses of members of the civil militia that they deemed untrustworthy in order to disarm them.[30] Already on the following day, the exist-ing radical societies of Leiden convened the General Citizens' Assembly in the Marekerk. This Assembly took the initiative in organizing elections for the neighborhood assemblies and installing a provisional municipal government.[31] The Citizens' Assembly remained in place, in order to guard the implementation of radical reforms. The lawyer Joost Roms-winckel opened the meeting. In his speech, he emphasized the need for citizens to main-tain vigilant control of the activities of the municipality, "which *without* your great influence, *without* your powerful support, *without* your unending assistance, will only lead to weak, insignificant measures."[32]

The speed and ease with which the old order in Leiden was overturned was a result of the strong roots of local opposition to the stadtholderly regime, going back even before the Patriot revolution of the mid-1780s. The decline of manufacturing industries that was a general feature of the Dutch economy of this period was felt with particular intensity in this formerly prosperous center of the Dutch textile production. Unemployment was exceptionally high, and about one quarter of the population at some point was dependent on poor relief.[33] Anti-Orangism had also penetrated the upper middle classes. Several of the curators and professors at the Leiden University had been known for their Patriot sym-pathies.[34] This longer history certainly had an influence on the formation of a Batavian radical leadership in the post-1795 period. The prominent Leiden Patriot Pieter Vreede, a democrat and abolitionist, became the main spokesperson of the radical wing of the National Convention. Both Willem van Lelyveld and Pieter Hendrik Trap, among those arrested in January 1797, came from families that were tied to the earlier opposition move-ment. Van Lelyveld came from a prominent regent family that included various known

Patriots.[35] Trap's mother had published the weekly *MOEI-AL* ("The Meddler"), containing blistering attacks on aristocratic government at the height of Orangist counter-revolution in 1790.[36]

These strong antecedents also help explain why the Leiden radicals from the very start viewed their local activities in the light of a nation-wide revolution. In the very first months of its activities, the newly formed Revolutionary Committee of Insurrection defined its task as to "help in the work of effecting the revolution to our Brothers, both in the vicinity of our city and in various cities and villages, yes, in other parts of the Republic."[37] Meanwhile, the Committee of Public Safety that convened on 19 January took concerted action within the town limits. Within two days, it elected a secretary, formed two armed companies, placed an officer of the old regime under house arrest, authorized the use of force in disarming the civil militia if the need arose, and ordered the city watchman to no longer blow the Orangist anthem on his trumpet.[38] The primary task of the Committee was a military one, but it also monitored the food supplies to the city population and garrisoned soldiers, market prices of basic goods, and conflicts between Leiden inhabitants and French soldiers.[39]

Initially, the committee also was responsible for snuffing out former functionaries of the Orangist regime, but responsibility for purging local government soon was transferred to a separate committee.[40] Like elsewhere, conflicts between radicals and moderates soon emerged. One of the first questions around which this happened was who would have the right to vote. Radicals such as Romswinckel argued for extending voting rights to servants and the poor. The argument for excluding them from the vote was that only 'independent" citizens – meaning people with property – could have a true stake in the future of the nation, and could be trusted not to deliver it back into the hands of tyranny. As counter-evidence, Romswinckel's radical colleague Meerburg asked for the inclusion in the debates of Bernardus Bosch' 1793 pamphlet.[41] As part of his argument for a thorough democratization that should lay the foundation for a new unified national state, the fierce abolitionist Bosch had argued that excluding servants from the vote was the equivalent of relegating them to a position of slavery.[42] Remarkably given the later course of Leiden events, this pamphlet also contained a warning that even universal suffrage would not suffice for keeping elected representatives on a clear revolutionary course. Therefore, Bosch proposed the erection of a separate, permanent assembly to control a future National Convention, "consisting mainly of neighborhood councilors or hundred-men, again elected by the people." Only such a permanent form of direct representation could ensure the "OPPERMAGT DES VOLKS," the supreme power of the people.[43]

However, on the issue of suffrage the radicals suffered a defeat. Women, men on poor relief and servants were all excluded from the vote, just as "bankrupts under guardianship, those who were dishonorably sentenced, prisoners and suspects."[44] Since about a quarter of the population at times was dependent on poor relief and servants formed one of the largest professional groups within the city, this meant that effectively a majority of the working class was disenfranchised.[45] A second proposal by the radicals to elect all officials at the municipal level directly from the Neighborhood Councils was also blocked.[46]

Radical attempts to influence the course of the revolution on the municipal level and the nature of local democracy were fueled by a stream of popular petitions, that also covered social and economic issues. Serious conflicts arose over the redistribution of offices and the punishment of former Orangist regents. The Citizens' Assembly in the

Marekerk more than once demanded firmer action. Already on 24 March 1795 it sent a proposal initiated by one of the radical societies to the municipality, demanding a freeze on all but the indispensable nominations of new officials until a general plan for the cleansing of local government from Orangist influence had been put into effect.[47] Similar requests were repeated well into 1797. But it was more militant protest that finally forced the moderates in the Municipality to give in. Public celebrations of another famous moment of popular struggle, the freeing of Leiden from a Spanish siege on 3 October 1583, set the stage. Probably under the influence of Leiden's main radical society, members of the armed militia attacked 70 houses of suspected Orangists. Now, after prevarications that had taken more than two years, a committee was formed to investigate the actions of former Orangist officials. The radical lawyer Romswinckel headed the investigation.

The failed nation-wide assembly of January 1797

Localized revolts combined with French invasion had been enough to replace the old order throughout the Republic. Reorganization of the organs of power at the level of the municipality demanded most of the attention of the radicals in this first period. But once the first National Convention replaced the old States General on 1 March 1796 democratic agitation became more and more focused on the deadlock that developed in national politics. The drafting of a new constitution fueled permanent conflict between radicals and moderates in the Convention that could not agree on the relationship between national, provincial and local organs of power. Meanwhile, revolutionary movements at the local level seemed to have hit a wall. The radical press fumed against "aristocrats" and "slimy fellows" sabotaging the process of reorganizing the state, but revolts in Amsterdam in November 1795 and April 1796 demanding wider popular representation and purges against former Orangists remained unsuccessful.[48] In Friesland the radicals held power at the provincial level, but were themselves confronted with popular protest against the failure to alleviate the economic hardship suffered by the lower classes, resulting in an uprising in the rural village Kollum early in 1797. To escape from the embarrassment that this caused for their democratic claims, radical administrators described these local rural riots as a Dutch Vendée.[49] Rumors of a planned British invasion and counter-revolutionary plots were rife. Already in 1796, the leading radicals in the National Convention Pieter Vreede, Bernardus Bosch and Johan Valckenaer called for popular armament against counter-revolution from within and from without. Significantly, they simultaneously sent round a call on Neighborhood Councils to put pressure on the National Convention and thus force the moderates to take concerted action. The majority in the National Convention responded immediately by sending their own call for restraint.[50]

The Leiden initiative to organize the nation-wide assembly should be seen against this background. On 21 December 1796 the Leiden General Citizens' Assembly sent a letter to a large number of Neighborhood Councils and revolutionary societies throughout the country.[51] The letter contained an invitation to elect delegates to a meeting that should take place on 18 or 19 January of the next year, the second anniversary of the revolution, in the old building of the Leiden civic militia. The aim of this gathering was "to form one Assembly of representatives in which the People, as it were, could speak with one mouth, [...] so that Growth and Prosperity could be advanced and established throughout the entire Republic, with united strength."[52] The proclamation was signed by three Leiden democrats, H. Boonacker, J. C. Harnisch and P. H. Trap.[53] It was not the first time that radicals organized a gathering of revolutionary clubs across municipal or provincial borders.[54] But this time, they consciously styled their initiative a meeting of elected representatives of the local organs of democracy. Implicit in their suggestion that through this assembly the people would speak with one mouth, was the idea that the National Convention was not the real representative of the popular voice. This challenged the foundational claims of the Batavian state, and thus was indeed a revolutionary step.

The Government of the Province of Holland discussed the call for the nation-wide assembly on 14 January. It took immediate action, without observing the common forms of consultation with national and local authorities. The next morning, the Leiden citizens Trap, Lelyveld, Van Lil, Van Tricht and Van Klaaveren were apprehended. Explaining this course of action some months after the events, an investigative commission of the Provincial Government stressed:

> [...] one should be willingly blind, when refusing to see that this letter [...] had as its aim to form an Assembly that very soon would have challenged this Government, yes, if it would have been possible would even have wrestled from it the power, entrusted to it by the People of Holland.[55]

Two days later, provincial authorities tried to arrest Trap's two co-signers of the proclamation Boonacker and Harnish in the same fashion. However, the bailiff did not find them at home. Instead, at the door of one of the two fugitives an unknown person yelled "a large number of rude and immodest qualifications" at them.[56] A later statement by the bailiff himself revealed that these "rude qualifications" had consisted of the charge "that his actions were in contradiction with the rights of Man, and violated Civil liberties."[57]

As soon as the president of the Leiden Municipality heard about the arrest, he called for an emergency meeting. Despite the differences in political outlook among the representatives, they condemned the actions of the provincial authorities. In their declaration, they foregrounded not the revolutionary aims of the proposed Assembly of Neighborhood Councils, but the infringement on local jurisdiction committed by the Provincial Government. They described the actions of the Province as:

> [...] an actual assault on the Security of this Community and a supremely criminal violation of the right of all Free Citizens, without prior knowledge of any member of the Municipal Government, Minister, or anyone else, let alone with proper consent of the Committee of Public Interest, or a competent judge; an act, so contemptuous to this Council, that it directly contradicts the lawful rights that not only this municipality, but the entire people has possessed since ancient times.[58]

The City Council decided on three points. First, it promised to do everything in its power to ensure the release of the five arrested citizens. Second, it promised full protection to H. Boonacker and J. C. Harnish. "The council will not allow that in the future any of the citizens of this Municipality will be stolen," except when the Leiden Committee of Public Interest had given its prior consent.[59] Finally, it made military preparations, in case the province would want to secure further arrests by sending troops. These measures were backed by popular mobilization, aimed at protecting the autonomy of the city against outside intrusion. The anonymous Orangist diarist that was previously cited, reported: "Early in the morning, one could hear that all those freshly converted patriotic citizens were up in arms and stood at the city gates."[60]

Representatives of the General Citizens' Assembly came to the meeting of the Municipality and presented a letter in which they complained about "the violated rights of Men and Citizens," and "requested resolute cooperation of our good representatives so that our five apprehended fellow-citizens can promptly return to the bosom of their fellow-citizens."[61] The representatives were not received cordially. Signifying the unwillingness of the majority within the municipality to be seen too much as the handmaidens of the radicals, the letter was not even taken into formal deliberation.[62] Instead, it installed an investigative committee that would judge the legality of the actions of the Province, as well as the proposed nation-wide assembly of Neighborhood Councils.[63]

The investigation did not last long. The following day, the commission – consisting of the moderates Van Santen and Akersloot – reported its recommendations, which reflected the position taken by the municipality. On the one hand, Van Santen and Akersloot insisted on the release of the Leiden citizens. The provincial authorities quickly heeded their request. On the other hand, they suggested that the Assembly of Neighborhood Councils should be prohibited. Without much discussion, the municipal government agreed to both points. It sent a new letter to the Provincial Government, in which it clearly adopted the dramatic style of the radicals:

> Now, when the aristocracy has been defeated and freedom has triumphed, you dare to undertake this action that supersedes those of our former tyrants in brazenness! Remember, fellow citizens, that all rule of terror is of such nature, that in order to remain standing, it needs more and more victims.[64]

But despite the harsh language, the moderates in municipal government had profited politically from the actions by the provincial authorities. Given the substantial support that the radicals could still muster among the city population, the Leiden moderates in all likelihood would not have had the power to suppress the Nation-wide Assembly of Neighborhood Councils itself. Thanks to the actions of the Provincial authorities, the threatening radical initiative had been sunk, while the municipal moderates could at the same time present themselves as the staunch defenders of civil liberties against "tyranny." Avoiding a direct confrontation with the influential Leiden General Citizens' Assembly, they had managed to steal the radicals' thunder by making the popular slogan of the "restauration of local autonomy" the only significant political demand following the arrests.

Resonance

The events that took place in Leiden were of national significance. On 16 January the National Convention heard its first report on the issue. Without delay, a commission was installed to judge on the political implications of the proposals of the Leiden radicals. The inclusion of the prominent representatives Van de Kasteele, Schimmelpenninck and Van Lennep in this commission shows how much weight the National Convention attached to this case. On the next day, Van Lennep presented their findings. They contained an unequivocal condemnation of the planned assembly, "for such a meeting already included in its name, that it was a representative assembly, which could create the most dangerous confusions and clashes."[65] Several of the radical representatives protested this claim. Like Bernardus Bosch and the Leiden radicals, they argued that an assembly elected directly from the neighborhood councils could be a necessary means to put pressure from below on the National Convention and prevent a relapse of the state into federalism and aristocratic government. "How disastrous would the situation be of a People, that is not allowed to meet in order to discuss its weightiest interests?," asked representative Nuhout van der Veen. And the leading Friesland radical C. L. van Beyma declared that the National Convention "would need the support from the People," suggesting that without popular backing, it lacked "courage and power."[66]

The moderate leader Schimmelpenninck retorted in kind. He repeated that the revolution was in safe hands with the elected representatives, and that interference from below could only lead to anarchy and confusion:

> It is about time to show the entire world that, on the one side, we will do everything in order to complete this Revolution with all our Republican energy, and will offer to the people a Constitution on the basis of the pure principles of a Popular Government through representation, but on the other side that we will counter with great resolution the principles of Anarchy and Demagoguery, in whatever lovely shape they might appear. [67]

Not to do so, Schimmelpenninck added, would result in civil war.[68]

The leading Leiden radical Pieter Vreede responded with equal intransigence. Unlike many of the other radicals in the Convention, he did not even attempt to prove that the Leiden proposal fell within the existing framework of legality. For "as long as the [new Batavian] Constitution is not accepted, we are still in Revolutionary times, and as a result, it is the Laws of Revolution, not constitutionality, according to which we should assess the actions of our fellow citizens."[69] Vreede continued to compare the Leiden initiative with the actions of Citizens' Assemblies that in 1785–1787 and 1795 had played such an important role in the struggle against the old order, thus indirectly comparing the moderates in the National Convention with the deposed Orangists. It was the lack of decisive action of the Convention that forced ordinary citizens to seek their own ways to push the revolution further.

> Oh, let us condemn ourselves, that we spur them on to such irregular actions! That the lukewarm ways in which all the powers that represent the People in positions of authority treat the interest of Freedom makes the People depressed and drives it to despair; that the open protection that almost everywhere is given to the supporters of the House of Orange, and the repression with which they face the patriots at last begins to exhaust the People's patience.[70]

After these words, the minutes of the session note that the applause from the public gallery was so loud that Pieter Vreede could no longer make himself heard. Confusion followed, in which some representatives demanded that the military empty the hall, under loud protest of others. After this intermission, the report of the commission was put to the vote. A majority of 78 representatives voted in favor, 24 voted against and 6 abstained. The next day, the French Ambassador to the Batavian Republic Noël wrote to Paris that the National Convention had taken resolute action in an incident that he deemed "assez important."[71] But the debates had also revealed the depth of the political differences in the Assembly that remained unresolved until a radical coup on 22 January 1798 ousted the moderates from the Assembly.

Despite the intensity of the debate, at this point the conflict did not move beyond verbal confrontation. One of the reasons for this was that although the Leiden radicals received much moral support for their actions, practical actions remained purely confined within the city limits. Messages of support were addressed to the Leiden municipal government, and focused completely on the issue of the violation of local autonomy. They conspicuously failed to mention the proposed Nation-wide Assembly of Neighborhood Councils that had been the cause of the political riot. It is remarkable that the first letter of support that came in, on 19 January was sent by the moderate Municipality of Delft and mainly expressed its joy that the provincial attack on local jurisdiction had been thwarted.[72] The Municipality of Zoetermeer sent a comparable message.[73] More importantly though, even the declarations sent to Leiden by radical associations from other parts of the country did not mention the proposal of Trap and the other radicals. The "Correspondence Commission of the Gathering of Representatives of Batavian Clubs and associated Popular Societies" wrote in a letter to the "sincere and courageous Council of the City of Leiden":

> We are touched – Yes! we would insult both your courage and our own feelings, if we would not express our emotions about your actions against the Holland Provincial Committee in the case of the citizens Lelyvelt & Trap; [...] We citizens of Amsterdam, members of Batavian clubs, do not only completely endorse your actions in this case, but affirm that our hearts beat for you at double speed.[74]

The Citizens' Society at Schiedam, the members of the "Assembly with the Slogan Courageous but Collected," the "Association of Exiled and Persecuted Patriots at Amsterdam" and the "Batavian Club-ists" all sent similarly worded messages to the Leiden Municipality – the Batavian Club-ists even sent two.[75] The Leiden General Citizens' Assembly in its proclamation did not include any criticism of the municipality's suppression of its own initiative.[76] Trap and Lelyvelt sent a small note expressing their gratefulness for the municipality's support for their release, again avoiding any mention of the cause of their arrest. They did however add their wish that "we soon may see the Altar of Freedom established on the Ruins of Aristocracy and Avarice."[77]

Aftermath

A little over a month after the Leiden events, an anonymous satirical pamphlet described the political fallout. Clearly marking the author as an adversary of the radicals, the pamphlet was dressed up as "a letter of a Jacobin revolutionary citizen to his friend."[78] The Leiden radicals were portrayed as cunning knaves who were only after their own interests. The call for the Nation-wide Assembly supposedly was a calculated attempt to provoke the "slimy fellows" of the Provincial Government. Compromising the moderates at the provincial level would open the way to execute the radical's sinister plans for a general purge. As the feigned Leiden Jacobin writes in his letter, the hidden intention of this scheme was to get all the radicals "a nice job in office."[79]

The Leiden affair had discredited the moderate Provincial Government. However, according to the anonymous author, this had been a close call: "if this would have gone wrong as well we could have rolled up our camp-beds, and our entire Revolutionary System would not have been worth as much as a single oilseed cake."[80] However, the "Jacobins" had been rescued by the blunders of their own adversaries:

> We were afraid like devils, I say, that nobody except us would open their mouths, and then it would have been over. But how lucky we were! We shouted, and the slimy fellows helped us

shout. They have made themselves truly useful. They shouted even louder than we did. The members of the Provincial Government will now be sent packing, and we sing Victory! Victory! Vive la République![81]

But the real radicals of 1797 did not feel so triumphant. More than anything, they saw the rising influence of the moderates in national politics, and feared that this would translate in the nature of the new constitution. In July, one leading proponent of the Nation-wide Assembly, Pieter Trap, published an important pamphlet in which a group of radical representatives, including Vreede, Van Beyma and Bosch, rejected the majority proposal for the new constitution. Among other points, they rejected the indirect system of elections of representatives in the National Convention.

> A People's Government is, in the truest meaning of the word, a Government, executed by the People itself. And a People's Government by representation is one, in which the People rules through its own Representatives. But how should we call such a People's Government by representation, if the People itself has been excluded from all influence over Government; when the People remains that old beast of burden, driven here and there by a handful, without any self-activity?[82]

If the possibility of self-activity was not provided through constitutional means, the only alternative for the people would be to make itself heard through "a revolutionary outburst of its physical power." According to the authors, such an act would be fully justified:

> [...] or would it be without example in these times, that the politicians would hold for revolt, what the good Citizen holds for nothing else than resistance against oppression? Should we commemorate here the recent events in Amsterdam, Leiden, and the things that happened to one hundred other individuals in almost all the Provinces?[83]

But the events in Leiden and the revolts in Amsterdam had not only shown the opposition of moderate municipal and provincial governments against attempts at influencing the course of the revolution through popular mobilization. They had also laid bare the structural inability of the radicals to force a breakthrough in national politics through actions from below. When their initiatives had been blocked by the Holland Provincial Government, radicals inside and outside Leiden had done little more than cheer their own moderate municipal government, while the moderates had successfully contained the popular response to the politically safe framework of the defense of local autonomy.

During the summer of 1797, the radicals achieved their most significant political victory. With a majority of 108,761 votes against 27,955, the Neighborhood Assemblies rejected a proposal for the new constitution that was supported by the moderates in the National Convention.[84] However, it remained hard to interpret what this tally meant for the balance of forces on the ground. The process that resulted in the new constitution had been so muddy and so compromised that large numbers of moderates did not support the draft. More importantly, although the rejection of the constitution blocked the way for a resolution of the existing crisis in favor of the moderates, it did not end the impasse in a direction supported by the radicals. Time and time again, attempts by the radicals to reform the state were stranded by their inability to mobilize their support base beyond local and provincial borders. By the summer of 1797 fatigue had set in among the popular movements and the radical faction in the National Assembly. Meanwhile, the French were turning to a more interventionist course toward their "sister republics." The coup in France of 18 Fructidor of year V (4 September 1797) seemed to open up a new road for the radical Batavians.[85] The combination of the appointment of the new French ambassador Charles-François Delacroix and support of the military commander Daendels provided the radicals in the National Assembly with the opportunity to take power. In important ways, the successful coup that a select group of radicals executed on 22 January 1798 signified a definitive breach between the democratic elements of Batavian radicalism on the one side, and their focus on rationalizing and unifying the state from above on the other. After the coup, the Neighborhood Councils were purged of supporters of the moderates, only to be relegated a mere secondary role in the process of reforming the state. Their task was confined to executing decisions taken by the new directorate. Increasingly distrustful of its own popular base, the radical regime, in which Pieter Vreede played a leading role, quelled local revolts and dismantled popular committees and revolutionary societies.[86]

Conclusion

The authoritarian turn of the radical leaders after 22 January 1798 has often led later historians to off-handedly dismiss their democratic pretensions of the years before.[87] However, to read the intentions of the radicals backwards in this way leads to conclusions that are one-sided at best, and more often are plainly mistaken about the complex interplay between revolutionary dynamics at the local and the national level. Instead, this article proposes to see the changing approach to the relationship between democracy and the struggle against federalism among leading Batavian radicals as the outcome of a very real clash between the ideal of radical and democratic unification on the one side, and the localized nature of radical popular mobilization on the other. This political problem reflected wider tensions between the sweeping success of the ideal of the national state as it was envisioned in the new French constitutions on the one hand, and on the other hand the strong traditions of revolt focused on the defense of local autonomy.

This article has suggested that the difficulties that radical Batavians experienced in advancing their ideals of a democratic national state at least in part resulted from the fact that among their own rank and file support base, patterns of mobilization remained highly localized. When faced with determined conservative resistance, the radicals themselves reframed their struggle in terms of the defense of ancient local rights. In this, they were not unique. The Leiden events form a microscopic example of the often contradictory relationship between popular struggles to defend local autonomy and the visions of a strong and unified state among revolutionary elites that, in different and often more significant forms emerged in all the key struggles of the Age of Revolutions. Pierre Serna has suggested that all revolutions contain important elements of a war of independence. However, seen from the height of the national state, the ultimate aim of revolutionizing the existing state apparatus was often the far-reaching subjection of formally autonomous regions or polities. Popular democratic movements took shape within this contradictory force-field.

The Leiden initiative of January 1797 was significant for what it represented, as well as for the relative ease with which it was swept aside. As the article has shown, the idea that popular assemblies elected directly through the lowest rungs of the electoral system could function as driving force for the revolution, was deeply seated in the radical interpretation of the nature of representative democracy itself. As such, it was connected to the attempts that started immediately after the installation of the Batavian Republic to extend (male) suffrage to the widest possible layer of people, and to counter the moderate and federalist wing of Batavian democracy at the local and the national level. During the first years of the revolution, radical societies, neighborhood councils and lower-class constituencies often coordinated their actions to further their demands. However, most of the time such coordination remained highly localized. The Leiden call for a nation-wide assembly was a serious attempt to muster these same forces on a supra-regional level, in order to change the course of the revolution itself. The ease with which the provincial authorities suppressed this attempt, as well as the success of moderates at the municipal level in diverting protest against this suppression in the direction of the politically more limited demand of the defense of local autonomy, lays bare one of the structural weaknesses of Batavian radicalism.

Notes

1. The text of the call for this meeting is included in *Dagverhaal*, Vol. IV, 486.
2. Ibid., 520.
3. For an overview of the political programs advanced by competing groups, see Van Sas, "Scenario's," and Poell, "Local Particularism."
4. For a detailed case-study of local revolutionary struggles that highlights this issue, see Prak, *Republikeinse veelheid*. A longer-term view on the complex relationship between local and national social movements in the Low Countries is provided in Boone and Prak "Rulers, Patricians and Burghers."
5. Palmer, *Age of Democratic Revolution* II, 179–180. The view that the Batavian Revolution was primarily a French export-product at that time was still deeply ingrained in Dutch national historiography, especially through the work of H.T. Colebrander, e.g., Colenbrander, *De Bataafsche Republiek*. The influential Dutch historian Pieter Geyl had argued before Palmer that the Batavian Revolution was homegrown, but he refused to extend this generosity to Batavian radicalism. Pieter Geyl, "De Bataafse revolutie," 106–127.
6. Palmer, *Age* II, 192. For a recent re-interpretation of the impact of the crisis of the old regime on revolutionary state-formation after 1795, see Brandon, *War*, Chapter 5.
7. An early attempt by C.H.E. de Wit to portray the Patriot and Batavian Revolutions of the 1780s and 1790s as a clash between "aristocracy and democracy" along a model derived directly from Palmer did not find many followers. De Wit, *De strijd*. For the new approaches that have emerged since then, see Grijzenhout, Van Sas and Velema, eds., *Het Bataafse experiment*.
8. Serna, "Every Revolution."
9. James, *Black Jacobins*.
10. Forrest, *Paris, the Provinces*, especially Chapter 8.
11. For example, see Klooster and Oostindie, *Curaçao*; Fatah-Black, "Patriot;" Van der Burg, "Cape of Good Hope."
12. Brandon, *War*, Chapter 5 and Poell, "Local Particularism."
13. Rutjes, *Gelijkheid*, 31.
14. Lucas, "Plakkaat van Verlatinghe." For American influence on the Patriots, also see Leeb, *Ideological Origins*, and Schama, *Patriots and liberators*.
15. For the concrete routes through which the French debates filtered into Batavian politics, see Rosendaal, *Bataven!*, Jourdan, *La Révolution Batave*, and Kubben, *Regeneration and Hegemony*.
16. Bosch, *Vrijhart*, 12.
17. Van Sas, *Metamorfose*,109–112; Rutjes, *Gelijkheid*, 36–39.
18. Te Brake, "Popular Politics," 201.
19. See Schama, *Patriots and Liberators*, 178, and Rosendaal, *Nederlandse Revolutie*, 97.

20. Poell, "Bataafs-Franse Tijd," 451.
21. Kuiper, *Revolutie ontrafeld*, 61.
22. Cited in Brugmans, *Amsterdam* V, 25.
23. Brugmans, *Amsterdam* V, 27 and Jourdan, "La république Batave," 413–415.
24. Paape, *Onverbloemde geschiedenis*, 200.
25. "Staatkundig woordenboek," *De Democraten*, no. 30, 15 December 1796.
26. *Nodige ophelderingen, ter Beantwoording der tegen bedenkingen, op het plan, ter oprichting van algemene wijk-vergaderingen in de stad Amsterdam. Voorgedragen in de burger-bijeenkomst, onder de spreuk: Tot nut van het vaderland* (1795), 10; Koninklijke Bibliotheek The Hague [hereafter KB], Knuttel Catalogus no. 18425.
27. A more detailed description of the course of Year One in Leiden is provided in Walle, "Revolutie in Leiden."
28. Blok, *Hollandsche stad*. Vol. IV, 386.
29. Ingekomen rapport van de commissie tot de telling en verdeling van het volk van Holland, 1796, GAL, SA II 501A, no. 898. Gemeente Archief Leiden [hereafter GAL], SA II 501A, no. 898.
30. Driessen, *Franschen Tijd*, 5.
31. The institution of neighborhood councils was not new, which explains why it proved such a natural step everywhere to convene them at the start of the revolution. However, pre-existing neighborhood organizations in no way had played the highly politicized role that the new neighborhood councils would play in the Batavian representative system. Walle, *Buurthouden*, 68–70 and 118–122.
32. Romswinckel, *Aanspraak*, 35.
33. De Vries and Van der Woude, *Nederland*, 339.
34. Van Maanen, "Leidse Patriotten," 251 and Blok, *Hollandsche Stad*, Vol. IV, 345.
35. Van Maanen, "Leidse Patriotten," 247.
36. Trap, "Patriot en stadsdrukker," 58.
37. Ingekomen stukken bij de provisionele raad 1795–1809, 19 January 1795–18 February 1795, GAL, SA II 501A, no. 586.
38. Notulen en bijlagen van het Committé van Algemeene Veiligheid, 1795, 19 January 1795, GAL, SA II 501A, no. 632.
39. Ingekomen stukken bij het Committé van Algemeene Veiligheid, 1795, GAL, SA II 501A, no. 688, and Minuten van uitgaande stukken van het Committé van Algemeene Veiligheid, met bijlagen, 1795, GAL, SA II 501A, no. 709.
40. Bijlagen bij de notulen van het Committé van Algmeene Veiligheid, 25 March – 26 May 1795, no. 6, GAL, SA II 501A, no. 667.
41. Notulen van een samengestelde commissie uit de raad en de burgerij ter organisatie van de grondvergaderingen, 1795. GAL, SA II 501A, no. 893, Annex 10.
42. Bosch, *Vrijhart*, 9–10.
43. Ibid., 28. Capitals in the original.
44. Blok, *Hollandsche Stad*, Vol. IV, 51.
45. A mid-eighteenth century survey counted 2,136 servants on a working population of 12,088. Of course many of them were women, who were excluded from voting all together. Diederiks, "Beroepsstructuur," 47.
46. Blok, *Hollandsche Stad*, Vol. IV, 49.
47. Ibid.
48. Jourdan, "Amsterdam en révolution," 23–30.
49. Kuiper, *Revolutie ontrafeld*, 256ff.
50. *Voorlichting aan de Grondvergaderingen, indien die moeten raadpleegen over het voorstel ter Nationale Vergadering gedaan, tot uitbreiding van derzelver magt* (Arnhem 1796), KB, Knuttel Catalogus no. 22700.
51. Blok, *Hollandsche Stad*, Volume IV, 55.
52. The integral text was read in the National Convention on 16 January 1797. *Dagverhaal*, Vol. IV, 486.
53. Ibid., 488.

54. Rosendaal, *Nederlandse Revolutie*, 98–99.
55. *Rapport der Personeele Commissie op het berigt van het Provintiaal Committé enz. mitsgaders het request van P.H. Trap c.s.* (The Hague 1797) 3; KB, Knuttel Catalogus no. 22930.
56. "Advis van den Advocaat Fiscaal en Procureur Generaal over Holland en Zeeland, in de zaken van P.H. Trap, G. van Klaveren Junior, J. van Trigt, J. van Lil en W. van Lelyveld," 21 January 1797, *Jaarboeken der Bataafsche Republiek* X, 163–164.
57. Ibid., 179.
58. Notulen van de Municipaliteit, Volume 1, 16 January 1797. GAL, SA II 501A, no. 552.
59. Ibid.
60. Driessen, *Franschen Tijd*, 21.
61. Notulen van de Municipaliteit, Volume 1, 17 January 1797, No. 46. GAL, SA II 501A, no. 552.
62. Ibid.
63. Ibid.
64. Ibid., 18 January 1797.
65. *Dagverhaal*, Vol. IV, 513.
66. Ibid., 517.
67. Ibid., 520.
68. Ibid.
69. Ibid., 520–521.
70. Ibid., 522.
71. Noël to Delacroix, 29 nivôse an V (18 January 1797), in: Colenbrander, *Gedenkstukken*, Vol. II, 88.
72. Notulen van de Municipaliteit, Volume 1, 19 January 1797. GAL, SA II 501A, no. 552.
73. Ibid., no. 65.
74. Ibid., no. 59.
75. Ibid., 31 January 1797 and 10 February 1797, no. 66.
76. Ibid., 7 February 1797, no. 72.
77. Ibid., no. 67.
78. *Vryheid, Gelykheid en Broederschap. Brief van een' Jacobynsch revolutionair burger, aan zynen vriend* (z.p. 1797), KB, Knuttel-catalogus nr. 22907.
79. Ibid., 2.
80. Ibid., 3.
81. Ibid., 5.
82. *Beoordeeling van het ontwerp van constitutie voor het Bataefsche volk enz., door eenige burgers, zynde repraesentanten van het volk van Nederland* (Leiden 1797) 3, KB, Knuttel Catalogus no. 22864.
83. Ibid., 5.
84. Schama, *Patriots and Liberators*, 269.
85. Jourdan, "La république Batave," 758.
86. Kuiper, *Revolutie ontrafeld*, 418, 430.
87. Geyl, "De Bataafse Revolutie," 122–123; Kuiper, *Revolutie Ontrafeld*, 508–509, 519.

Acknowledgements

This article is a translated and substantially revised version of an article previously published in *Tijdschrift Holland*: "'De Oppermagt des Volks': Radicale democraten in Leiden tussen nationaal ideaal en lokale werkelijkheid (1795–1797)." *Holland. Historisch Tijdschrift* 43:1 (2011), 3–23. We thank the editors of *Holland* for their permission to reprint parts of this article here. We would also like to thank Dennis Bos, Marjolein 't Hart, Michael A. McDonnell and the anonymous reviewers of *Atlantic Studies*, who commented on the previous and current version of this text.

Disclosure statement

No potential conflict of interest was reported by the authors.

References

Blok, P. J. *Geschiedenis eener Hollandsche stad*. Vol. IV. The Hague: Martinus Nijhoff, 1918.

Boone, Marc, and Maarten Prak. "Rulers, Patricians and Burghers: The Great and Little Traditions of Urban Revolt in the Low Countries." In *A Miracle Mirrored: The Dutch Republic in European Perspective*, edited by Karel Davids and Jan Lucassen, 99–134. Cambridge: Cambridge University Press, 1995.

Bosch, Bernardus. *Vrijhart aan het volk van Nederland over de ware constitutie*. 1793.

Brandon, Pepijn. *War, Capital, and the Dutch State (1588–1795)*. Leiden: Brill, 2015.

Colenbrander, H. T., ed. *Gedenkstukken tot de Algemeene Geschiedenis van Nederland van 1795 tot 1840*. Vol. II. The Hague: Martinus Nijhoff, 1906.

Dagverhaal der handelingen van de Nationaale Vergadering representeerende het volk van Nederland. Vol. IV. The Hague: Swart en Comp, 1796.

De Vries, Jan, and Ad van der Woude. *Nederland 1500–1815: De eerste ronde van moderne economische groei*. Amsterdam: Balans, 2005.

Diederiks, H. A. "Beroepsstructuur en sociale stratificatie in Leiden in het midden van de achttiende eeuw." In *Armoede en sociale spanning. Sociaal-historische studies over Leiden in de achttiende eeuw*, edited by H. A. Diederiks, D. J. Noordam and H. D. Tjalsma, 45–67. Hilversum: Verloren, 1985.

Driessen, Felix, ed. *Leiden in den Franschen Tijd: Handschrift uit de jaren 1794–1813*. Leiden: Ijdo, 1913.

Fatah-Black, Karwan. "The patriot coup d'etat in Curaçao, 1796." In *Curaçao in the Age of Revolutions, 1795–1800*, edited by Wim Klooster and Gert Oostindie, 123–140. Leiden: KITLV Press, 2011.

Forrest, Alan. *Paris, the Provinces and the French Revolution*. London: Arnold, 2004.

Geyl, Pieter. "De Bataafse Revolutie." In *Verzamelde Opstellen*, Vol. II, 106–127. Utrecht: Aula Boeken, 1978.

James, C. L. R. *The Black Jacobins: Toussaint L'Ouverture and the San Domingo Revolution, 1938*. New York: Vintage Books, 1989.

Jourdan, Annie. "Amsterdam en révolution, 1795–1798. Un Jacobinisme batave?" *Working Papers European Studies Amsterdam* no. 5 (2006): 23–30.

Jourdan, Annie. "La république Batave et le 18 Brumaire. La grande illusion." *Annales historiques de la Révolution française* no. 318 (1999): 755–772.

Jourdan, Annie. *La Révolution Batave: Entre la France et l'Amérique (1795–1806)*. Rennes: PUR, 2008.

Klooster, Wim, and Gert Oostindie, eds. *Curaçao in the Age of Revolutions, 1795–1800*. Leiden: KITLV Press, 2011.

Kubben, Raymond. *Regeneration and Hegemony: Franco-Batavian Relations in the Revolutionary Era, 1795–1803*. Leiden: Brill, 2011.

Kuiper, Jacques. *Een revolutie ontrafeld: Politiek in Friesland 1795–1798*. Franeker: Van Wijnen, 2002.

Leeb, Leonard I. *The ideological origins of the Batavian revolution: History and politics in the Dutch republic 1747–1800*. The Hague: Martinus Nijhoff, 1973.

Lucas, Stephen E. "The 'Plakkaat van Verlatinghe': A Neglected Model for the American Declaration of Independence." In *Connecting Cultures: The Netherlands in Five Centuries of Transatlantic Exchange*, edited by Rosemarijn Hoefte and Johanna C. Kardux, 189–207. Amsterdam: VU University Press, 1994.

Paape, Gerrit. *De onverbloemde geschiedenis van het Bataafsch Patriottismus*. Delft: M. Roelofswaart, 1798.

Palmer, R. R. *The Age of the Democratic Revolution: A Political History of Europe and America, 1760–1800*. Vol. 2. Princeton, NJ: Princeton University Press, 1964.

Poell, Thomas. "Het einde van een tijdperk: De Bataafs-Franse tijd 1795–1813." In *Geschiedenis van Amsterdam. Vol. II-2: Zelfbewuste Stadstaat, 1650–1813*, edited by Willem Frijhoff and Maarten Prak, 429–499. Amsterdam: SUN, 2004.

Poell, Thomas. "Local Particularism Challenged, 1795–1813." In *The Political Economy of the Dutch Republic*, edited by Oscar Gelderblom, 291–320. Farnham: Ashgate, 2009.

Prak, Maarten. *Republikeinse veelheid, democratische enkelvoud: Sociale verandering in het revolutie-tijdvlak, 's-Hertogenbosch 1770–1820*. Nijmegen: SUN, 1999.

Romswinckel, Joost. *Aanspraak gedaan (enz) aan Leydens en Neerlands inwooneren*. Leiden: Herdingh en du Mortier, 1795.

Rosendaal, Joost. *Bataven! Nederlandse vluchtelingen in Frankrijk 1787–1795*. Nijmegen: Van Tilt, 2003.

Rosendaal, Joost. *De Nederlandse Revolutie: Vrijheid, volk en vaderland 1783–1799*. Nijmegen: Van Tilt, 2005.

Rutjes, Mart. *Door gelijkheid gegrepen: Democratie, burgerschap en de staat in Nederland, 1795–1801*. Nijmegen: Van Tilt, 2012.

Schama, Simon. *Patriots and liberators. Revolution in the Netherlands, 1780–1813*. New York: Knopf, 1977.

Serna, Pierre. "Every Revolution Is a War of Independence." In *The French Revolution in Global Perspective*, edited by Suzanne Desan, Lynn Hunt and William Max Nelson, 165–182. Ithaca, NY: Cornell University Press, 2013.

Te Brake, Wayne. "Popular Politics and the Dutch Patriot Revolution." *Theory and Society* 14, no. 2 (1985): 199–222.

Trap, H. J. "Patriot en stadsdrukker: Een oprechte Leienaar tijdens de Bataafse Republiek." *Genealogische bijdragen Leiden en omgeving* 10, no. 3 (1995): 57–68.

Van Maanen, R. C. J. "Leidse Patriotten 1787–1795." *Holland: Regionaal-historisch tijdschrift* 19 (1987): 246–258.

Van Sas, N. C. F. *De metamorfose van Nederland: Van oude orde naar moderniteit, 1750–1850*. Amsterdam: Amsterdam University Press, 2004.

Van Sas, N. C. F. "Scenario's voor een onvoltooide revolutie, 1795–1798." *Bijdragen en Mededelingen Betreffende de Geschiedenis der Nederlanden* 104, no. 4 (1989): 622–637.

Walle, Kees. *Buurthouden. De geschiedenis van burengebruiken en buurtorganisaties in Leiden (14e-19e eeuw)*. Leiden: Gingko, 2005.

Walle, Kees. "Revolutie in Leiden. De twee omwentelingen van 1795." *Leids Jaarboekje* 84 (1992): 133–149.

Rethinking Africa in the Age of Revolution: The evolution of Jean-Baptiste-Léonard Durand's *Voyage au Sénégal*

Pernille Røge

Department of History, University of Pittsburgh, Pittsburgh, PA, USA

ABSTRACT

In the Age of Revolution, the idea that Europe should help a "savage" Africa attain civilization through colonization was on the rise. When explaining how such views came about, scholars have looked at the ways in which the production and reception of travel literature and natural histories of Africa shaped, and were shaped by, evolving ideas of race in eighteenth-century Europe. Though insightful, these studies ignore the impact of the encounter with Africa itself as well as the geopolitical context within which it took place. This article argues that the idea of a 'savage' Africa in need of civilization through colonization was linked to Europeans' inability to easily advance their commercial enterprises in Africa at a time when European colonization in the Americas was eroding. Through a study of Jean-Baptiste-Léonard Durand's activities in Senegal during his directorship of the French *Compagnie de la gomme du Sénégal* in the mid-1780s and of his published account of these experiences in the *Voyage au Sénégal* in 1802, the paper shows that Durand's struggle to negotiate French commercial interests in Senegal on his own terms, and his deep frustration with gum and slave merchants along the Senegal River, contributed to his subsequent depiction of Africans as "savage" and in need of civilizing. The paper also suggests that the changing geopolitical context in Europe and the Americas during the Age of Revolution further shaped Durand's call for the civilizing of Africa.

In 1802, the former director of the French *Compagnie de la gomme du Sénégal*, Jean-Baptiste-Léonard Durand, published a work entitled *Voyage au Sénégal*. The *œuvre* was a historical, political, and philosophical account of the region of Senegambia since its encounter with European powers based on the author's personal experiences in the region between 1785 and 1786. The book offered detailed descriptions of the region's flora and fauna, its river systems, its various populations, and their political cultures, religious practices, social hierarchies, and labor regimes. An accompanying volume carried striking illustrations of the peoples of Senegal and detailed maps of the region. Mixing travel literature and early nineteenth-century natural history, the *Voyage au Sénégal* also read as a burning call for the colonization and civilization of Africa. In the Preface,

Durand informed readers that Europe's maritime powers had directed their colonizing efforts towards the New World, neglecting to explore Africa – "the most fertile of regions."[1] Later he singled out what he saw as two laudable attempts to colonize Africa, namely the British "purely philanthropic" colony at Sierra Leone and a French colony at the mouth of the Benin River in present-day Nigeria.[2] Both colonies had failed due to Franco-British rivalry. Durand therefore urged European powers to leave their rivalries out of Africa. "Then, and only then," he concluded, "can we hope to free the Negroes (Nègres), hope to civilize them, to know and peacefully travel their country, and to found strong and happy colonies."[3]

Durand's emphasis on the need to civilize Africa through colonization echoed a growing discourse on imperial improvement in the Atlantic World during the Age of Revolution. Beginning in the second half of the eighteenth century, a rising critique of Europe's African slave trade and the plantation complex in the Caribbean became coupled with a neo-imperialist discourse that insisted on Europe's ability to help Africa become civilized.[4] This emerging narrative, as noted by William B. Cohen, was predicated on a view of African peoples as "savages" who Europeans had the responsibility to civilize.[5] In explaining how this view of "savage" Africa came about, historians have scrutinized the production and reception of eighteenth-century travel accounts on Africa in France and Europe.[6] From such studies, we know that Europeans who had frequented Africa often echoed preconceived ideas of Africa upon their return to Europe when narrating their experiences. To appear scientific in their approach, authors of travel accounts harmonized their story with pre-existing knowledge in order to persuade their readers of its veracity, a process referred to by Michel Foucault as "régime de véridiction."[7] David Diop, for instance, has demonstrated how the French botanist Michel Adanson who visited Senegal in the early 1750s depicted the Wolof as lazy in his Histoire naturelle du Sénégal (1757), thus conforming to the stereotypical view of Africans held by people in France.[8]

While illuminating, such insights stay focused on the published accounts and pay little attention to the actual encounter between African populations and authors of travel literature. Yet most authoritative publications on Africa emerging in France in the second half of the eighteenth century and first decades of the nineteenth century were published by people whose knowledge of Africa had been acquired through their service in the French colonial administration in Senegal. Their initial perceptions of Africa and its populations can therefore be gleaned from the considerable correspondence they maintained with the French Ministry of the Marine during their years of service.[9] Reading this archival trail against the published accounts is a fruitful endeavor. It points to intriguing ways in which authors came to modify their interpretations of African peoples. A "régime de véridiction" was surely at play, but two other factors were equally significant. One was the way in which the encounter itself shaped or altered an authors' ability to objectively describe Africans. Another was the rapidly changing geopolitical context of the Age of Revolutions, or "age of imperial revolutions" and "imperial reorganizations" as Jeremy Adelman has also called this period.[10] In the French context, the French and Haitian Revolutions profoundly shaped how Frenchmen thought about empire, slavery, and colonial opportunities in Africa and the Americas.

This article argues that the idea of a "savage" Africa in need of development and civilization was linked not only to modes of knowledge production in Europe but also to Europeans' inability to easily advance their commercial enterprises in Africa at a time when

European colonization in the Americas was eroding. Through an exploration of the discrepancies between what Durand narrated in his *Voyage au Sénégal* of 1802 and the archival records of his time in Senegal in the mid-1780s, the article suggests that Durand's encounter with the ethnic groups of the Trarza, Brakna, and Darmankour Moors, the Wolof, and the mixed-race population of Saint-Louis along with his struggle to advance the commercial interests of the *Compagnie de la gomme du Sénégal* on the Senegal River contributed to his later depictions of the peoples of Africa as "savages" and "barbaric" and in need of European civilization. Additionally, it highlights how a volatile transatlantic geopolitical context further encouraged a change in Durand's African discourse.

The establishment of the *Compagnie de la gomme du Sénégal*'s trade privileges

Durand's appointment to the directorship of the *Compagnie de la gomme du Sénégal* in 1785 came at a time when the French Crown was reasserting its power in West Africa. While Senegambia had been under French influence for over a century, the British had managed to capture Saint-Louis and Gorée from the *Compagnie des Indes* in the Seven Years' War. The French reoccupied these possessions during the American Revolution and Senegal was returned to France with the peace of 1783.[11] The semi-private *Compagnie de la Guyane française*, which had enjoyed an exclusive privilege to the slave trade at Gorée and its dependencies in the late 1770s and early 1780s, had been instrumental in engineering the French re-conquest but the process depleted its finances. In the wake of the territories' return, the Crown therefore decided to grant the company a nine-year monopoly in the trade in gum Arabic along the Senegal River under the new name of the *Compagnie de la gomme du Sénégal*.[12] Gum Arabic, used in the European textile industry in the manufacture of dyed fabrics and in the conditioning of silk materials, had for long been a sought after commodity in the region, seconded only by slaves.[13] After decades of costly competition for the trade, the Crown was eager to boost the trade in gum and willingly employed the *Compagnie de la gomme du Sénégal* to advance its interests.

It was into this complex landscape of rivalry and profits that Durand arrived in Senegal as the company's first director. Born in Userches in the department of Corrèze in 1742, Durand had been a lawyer for the *Parlement* of Bordeaux and a consul to Sardinia prior to his nomination to the directorship.[14] Nothing suggests that he had any previous knowledge, let alone experience, of West Africa and it is therefore unclear why the company offered him the position. What is certain is that Durand had accepted the job due to financial hardship and his affiliation with the *Compagnie de la Guyane française*.[15]

Leaving France from the port of Le Havre, Durand arrived at the island of Saint-Louis on 10 April 1785. This small and elongated island at the mouth of the Senegal River was the *chef lieu*, or headquarters, of the French Senegalese possessions. Over the years, a sizable population had come to inhabit the island in spite of its minute size.[16] Approximately 2500–3000 people lived on Saint-Louis in the 1750s, a number that had increased to 6000 by the mid-1780s. The inhabitants were composed of slaves and what one internal report described as "free mulattoes and negroes who are mostly catholic Christians."[17] Familiarity with commercial opportunities along the Senegal River made the Saint-Louis inhabitants important partners of European merchants seeking to trade in the region. The local mayor of Saint-Louis, a mulatto, enjoyed considerable authority among inhabitants. So did the many slave-owning women, the *signares*, who formed a central component of the local population and whose houses and services were woven into the very texture of the local French administration.[18] Well-versed in European cultural norms, the inhabitants of Saint-Louis were also accustomed to the cultures of the various ethnic groups of Senegal. Wolof, Fulbe, and Soninke people inhabited the south bank of the Senegal River. On the north bank lived the semi-nomadic Trarza and Brakna Moors whom Europeans often linked to the Berbers and Arabs of North Africa due to their lighter skin and practice of Islam.[19] The dominance of particularly the Trarza Moors had increased considerably during the British occupation of Saint-Louis at the expense of the Wolof, whose villages along the river were often pillaged for slaves by Moor soldiers.[20]

To establish the *Compagnie de la gomme du Sénégal*'s exclusive rights to the gum trade, Durand's immediate task was to obtain the cooperation of these local populations; particularly those on Saint-Louis and the "princes maures" (Durand's name for the leaders of the Trarza, Brakna, and Darmankour Moors) who came to the riverbanks to sell gum.

At that time, it would be hard to anticipate whether or not the island's population would be favorably inclined toward the *Compagnie de la gomme du Sénégal* and the introduction of monopoly trade. Monopoly trade was nothing new in the region. The French *Compagnie des Indes* had held a monopoly on the African trade up until the Seven Years' War. However, during the British occupation of the region, trade had opened to all British merchants.[21] Contemporaries believed that such measures had caused the price of gum to increase. Yet prices had more likely increased due to Trarza efforts to eliminate their interior competitors.[22] The British governor of Saint-Louis, Charles O'Hara, encouraged Trarza dominance in the hope that Trarza raids on neighboring populations might boost the British slave trade. O'Hara's behavior, however, had entirely alienated the local population on Saint-Louis.[23] To the population of Saint-Louis, a return of the French was therefore welcome. A reintroduction of monopoly trade might also be since it could mean more reliable business. Conversely, it could also mean less freedom to negotiate prices and conduct their business. Trarza and other gum merchants, however, might find it very inconvenient.

Upon his arrival, Durand first dealt with the inhabitants of Saint-Louis. He asked the French governor of Senegal to assemble the entire free population of the island at the governor's house. His plan was to give a speech announcing the arrival and exclusive rights of the *Compagnie de la gomme du Sénégal*. Durand gave a lengthy account of this meeting in the Preface to his *Voyage au Sénégal*. Admitting that he "based this on memory," he assured his readers that they could count on his accuracy (he even put the speeches in quotation marks).[24] In the *Voyage au Sénégal*, Durand explained that the French governor of Senegal, Louis Legardeur de Répentigny, had opened the meeting with a speech on the soaring prices of gum. The governor had insisted that increased competition had hugely benefitted Moor gum traders who had refrained from augmenting their gum supply. They had also started selling slaves that they drew from "their warfare with the negroes." To put a stop to this price inflation, the governor continued, the French government had granted an exclusive privilege to the company.[25] According to Durand, Répentigny had then proceeded to make several observations of the region's inhabitants: "The Moors and the Negroes of the interior never think of the future. Naturally lazy unless a momentary or personal reason excites them to work, or if they are not awoken by outside forces, they sleep and spend their lives doing nothing."[26] After quoting Répentigny, Durand then recalled his own speech, in which he allegedly said: "Monsieurs, I have nothing to add with regard to what the governor has just said [about the company's privilege] […] This measure has necessarily been put in place due to the avidity and insouciance of the Moors."[27] On behalf of the population of Saint-Louis, the mayor had then told Durand that the free population of the island (les habitans) respectfully accepted the King's decision, and agreed that "it is time to stop the harmful effects of competition, and to oppose the Moors' behavior. The privilege[d company] will restore all to its rightful place."[28] Durand concluded his recollections of the meeting, noting that les habitans of Saint-Louis seemed happy and satisfied with the announcement of the arrival of the company.

Répentigny's own report of this meeting, preserved in the archives of the French Ministry of Foreign Affairs, suggests that Durand's account of the event was not as accurate as he claimed. It states that it was Durand who informed the population that the French King had granted the Compagnie de la gomme du Sénégal a nine-year monopoly on the gum trade. Durand had explained this development by citing the Crown's hope that a reliable company with continued operations in the region might better serve the prosperity of the colony and the happiness of its population. Durand had promised the merchants of Saint-Louis that the company would supply them with all the merchandise they desired in exchange for "negroes, ivory and other objects."[29] According to Répentigny's report, the meeting had included no discussion of Moors, their alleged greed, or even any references to the "negroes" of the country.

Why, then, did Durand include this scathing view of Moors in his 1802 publication? One possible answer is that it reflected increasingly antagonistic feelings in France against Muslim North Africans due to the Directory and Napoleon's failure to successfully colonize Egypt.[30] But the pejorative descriptions might also have been the result of the difficulties Durand encountered once he started negotiating with the leaders of the Trarza, Brakna, and Darmankour. These suppliers, as well as other indigenous chiefs in the region, did not fall under the authority of the King of France. To maintain a presence in Senegambia, the French therefore relied on the goodwill of the local populations. In setting up small trade stations along the river, the Crown's representatives drew up treaties with local authorities to ensure favorable commercial conditions. Governor Répentigny, for instance, had re-established various forts along the river by drawing up new treaties or renewing old ones with princes and authorities of the Fulbe and with Joal, Salum, Barre, Portudal, and Baol.[31] To establish the trade of the Compagnie de la gomme du Sénégal, Durand had to draw up similar treaties with the main suppliers of gum. Doing so, however, had proved challenging.

The two main regional suppliers of gum in Senegal were the emirates of Trarza and Brakna. Both enjoyed substantial power in the region and were in no hurry to draw up treaties with Durand. According to a report by Governor Répentigny, Durand had reached out to the gum merchants but to no avail. Desperate and frustrated, Durand had therefore turned to Répentigny, who was under instruction to help the company establish favorable conditions for trade. The governor personally asked the head of the Darmankour (Semb), the King of the Trarza (Ely Koury), and the king of the Brakna (Ameth Moctar) to come to Saint-Louis to discuss terms of trade.[32] According to Répentigny, the three chiefs readily responded to the governor, whom they knew was the direct representative of the King of France. Accepting his invitation to come to Saint-

Louis, they expressed nothing but contempt for monopoly trade and roundly criticized the old *Compagnie des Indes*. The governor managed to reassure them that the new company should not be confused with the old one. He further appeased them by offering to have his own two translators and the mayor of Saint-Louis serve as witnesses during negotiations. Still according to Répentigny's report, it was only at this point Durand could start negotiations.

Durand first did so with the representatives of the Darmankour, then with Ameth Moctar, and finally with Ely Koury, but as the governor told the Minister of the Marine, Durand continued to face strong resistance from the gum merchants. Again, it is likely that the gum traders preferred to conduct trade with the direct representative of the French Crown, rather than with the director of a private company. For instance, negotiations with Ameth Moctar were stuck for days and Durand had to request the assistance of the governor once again. Répentigny finally managed to encourage Ameth Moctar to enter into a treaty with Durand.[33] It is also likely, however, that the gum traders were averse to the introduction of French monopoly trade in gum because it would reduce competition for their goods. Finally, Moor resistance to Durand may also have come from Durand's lack of training in negotiating with African populations. The newly arrived director seemed to have lacked the patience for any ceremonial aspects associated with establishing trade relations in Senegambia. In a letter to the Minister of Foreign Affairs, Durand pointed out that "I have negotiated with nomadic barbarians (*des barbares errans*) without prin[cipals] and without laws, and guarded against the company."[34] Happy with the ultimately positive results, he admitted it required "superhuman patience."[35]

Strangely, in the later account in the *Voyage au Sénégal* there is no mention of these difficulties. Durand offers long descriptions of the three chiefs, and of their manners, their gum trading, and family relations. Yet, in talking about establishing terms of trade, he merely states that "I have drawn up commercial treaties with these three peoples which can be found within the adjoining atlas of this work."[36] There was, in other words, no section on how the Trarza, Darmankour, and Brakna merchants had refused to negotiate with the company director, pushing Durand to despair before the negotiations' ultimately successful conclusion. This is puzzling since including this information might have granted Durand's pejorative language about the Moors in the Preface to the *Voyage au Sénégal* an air of authenticity. However, including it would also have exposed Durand's failure to negotiate with the gum traders without the repeated assistance of the French governor. Leaving it out may simply be a matter of Durand seeking to build up his own image as an authority on Africa to his literary audience.

The inland voyage from Saint-Louis to Galam

It was not only in descriptions involving Moor gum traders that one can find a discrepancy between the archival account and the *Voyage au Sénégal*; a similar disagreement appears in Durand's accounts of other ethnic groups in Senegal. This is clear from what was perhaps the most celebrated feature of his publication, namely the chapter that gave an account of a voyage made on land from Saint-Louis to Galam. Durand had planned to explore unknown parts of West Africa prior to his arrival in Senegal. As he told the Minister of the Marine before he left France, this was part of his wish to serve state interests in the region beyond the directorship of a semi-private company.[37] Galam was an important trade station for slaves on the Senegal River. The main route between Saint-Louis and Galam was by boat, but the passage could only take place during the high season (the rainy season from June to December) when the river was high. The rainy season was detrimental to Europeans and many died from dysentery and fever when visiting the region during these months. Travel between December and the end of May was less dangerous, but lack of water made the river hard to navigate. A route to Galam by land would make it possible to trade slaves at Galam all year round.

The result of Durand's exploration is fully developed in the *Voyage au Sénégal's* chapter XXI entitled "Voyage par terre, de l'île Saint-Louis, sur le Sénégal, à Galam." Durand had written a first draft of it in 1786 and asked the governor of Senegal to pass it on to the Ministry of the Marine.[38] According to the draft of 1786, Durand had not been able to undertake the voyage himself since his presence was needed at Saint-Louis. Sir Rubault, Durand's trusted employee, therefore made the voyage. He was accompanied by a "Maraboux Moor named Sidy-Carachi, two Negroes, and three camels."[39] To ensure that he obtained useful information Durand had asked Rubault to keep a journal during the trip. Although there is no archival trace of this journal, Durand claimed he had used Rubault's journal to write his own report about the trip to Galam in the *Voyage au Sénégal*. Reading the report of 1786 about Rubault's voyage alongside the narrative on the journey in the *Voyage au Sénégal*, both texts reveal Durand's eagerness to highlight opportunities for French expansion in Senegambia. There are, however, also important differences between them, especially in his descriptions of African populations.

Rubault's journey started in the Kingdom of Kajoor. At this time, France enjoyed friendly commercial relations with its ruler, the Damel. Rubault was therefore well received as he journeyed through the villages of the kingdom. At a village called D'hyam D'hyren he was even offered a place to sleep and a woman to cool him with a fan.[40] From Kajoor he moved into the zone dominated by the Darmankour, who occupied a large piece of land called the *Désert* where a considerable trade in gum Arabic took place (the Escale du Désert was one of the seasonal markets from which the French purchased gum).[41] In his description of this place, Rubault paid special attention to the ways in which land was cultivated. As Durand explained,

> Those who live here are cultivators. They have captive negroes who work the *Lougans* (Lougan is a terrain destined to be seeded like our fields in France), they obtain a large quantity of millet and cotton from this terrain, and they nourish cattle and sheep of which they have numerous flocks.[42]

Such information could be of immense value to the French colonial administration since it would convey the type of labor local slaves excelled at as well as a sense of what agricultural products could be cultivated locally.

On 18 January 1786, Rubault reached the Kingdom of Jolof. Travelling through various villages he came to D'hicarkor, capital and seat of the King. The King of Jolof, named Babakoury, received Rubault with great ceremony.[43] Rubault informed Babakoury that Durand wished to set up small settlements for trade in his Kingdom, a request the King approved. One week later Rubault continued his journey towards Galam. Reaching the end of the Kingdom of Jolof, the travelling party entered those of Barre or Mandingues (Durand was not sure which one and said that it was not the one normally referred to in travel literature), and Bambuk.[44] Durand conveyed to the Minister of the Marine that

Rubault had stressed the high level of development at Bambuk: "he traveled through a vast plain planted with superb trees and inhabited by people more civilized than those he had already seen, he says that property reigns among them as among whites."[45] Rubault also made a stop at Combalot, a territory that merited close attention since this area was well cultivated with indigo and worked "as in Europe."[46] Hereafter he travelled through regions that seemed less hospitable before arriving at Fort Joseph at Galam on 17 February.

Readers could thus learn about the well-cultivated land at Combalot and the civilized people of Bambuk who embraced property rights as in Europe. Both the draft narrating Rubault's voyage of 1786 and the *Voyage au Sénégal* includes these passages. However, in the *Voyage au Sénégal* Durand had added long commentaries after each encounter – comments ranging from explanations of food cultures to lists of what the locals cultivated to how much ivory or gum they traded. Interestingly, he also prefaced the chapter on Rubault's travels with a statement on the people Rubault had encountered:

> You will see that the greedy and sometimes demanding negroes have nonetheless welcomed my traveler affectionately, even with the most gentle care and most generous hospitality; that they have revealed their natural kindness, with the simplicity of the first age; that they con-veyed to him their desire, their need to learn, and revealed the efforts of a crude people striv-ing towards civilization; that they instantly demanded that we settle among them, that we lend them a helping hand to pull them out of the void and of the state of ignorance in which they live; that they are enlightened enough to sense this and wise enough to ask for help. You will see in the end all the advantages which will result from such relations.[47]

Durand's 1802 assertion that the indigenous populations Rubault encountered strove towards civilization starkly diverged from his own 1786 manuscript. Although some of the chiefs (such as Babakoury, King of the Jolof) had responded favorably to Rubault's request to create a trade station in their region, no one had of course expressed a wish to have the French settle to help them out of their so-called state of ignorance. Durand added this over a decade after, but why?

In both sources, Durand claimed that he was eager to advance French interests in Africa. In the earlier version, however, it was evident that he read French interests as an expansion for the sake of the slave trade, not because he wished to civilize Africans. It is possible to deduce as much from a comment made by Babakoury, as reported in the 1786 source, in response to Rubault's request to set up a trade station in his Kingdom. Babakoury had granted this wish but had emphasized that "in his kingdom, [slaves] were under his protection and that he would only sell wrong-doers and witches."[48] The King would not have expressed such reservations were it not for Rubault's interest in pur-chasing slaves.[49] We also know that once Rubault arrived at Galam he brought with him a large number of captives. Yet before he could transport them down-river to Durand at Saint-Louis the slaves revolted. The governor of Senegal mentioned the revolt in a letter to the Minister of the Marine, reporting that the company had lost 120 blacks and a lot of merchandise.[50]

What was not mentioned in the governor's report, nor in any of the correspondence between Durand and the administration, was that Rubault had lost his life in the uprising. The *Voyage au Sénégal*, however, described Rubault's death in painful detail. Durand told his readers that "[o]ne night, a fatal and cruel night, the slaves revolted and followed Rubault with furor [...] he was captured and massacred on the spot."[51] Durand did not go into any detail on the issue of Rubault's slave trading (he merely listed slaves as a commodity Rubault had purchased from different nations (over a thousand), together with a lot of gold, ivory, precious stones, and objects of natural history), but speculated instead whether or not "the slaves had been encouraged to rise up in revolt by enemies jealous of the successes of this voyage?."[52]

While the murder of Rubault went unmentioned in the archival record, it is peculiar that Durand chose to highlight it in the *Voyage au Sénégal* since his interests in French expansion in Africa had shifted from a focus on the slave trade to the civilization and colonization of Africa. Perhaps he included in the *Voyage au Sénégal* to warn readers of the dangers linked to the slave trade. France had abolished slavery in 1794 and had yet to reinstate slavery by the time of Durand's publication. The murder of Rubault may also have been included as part of Durand's efforts to depict Africa's populations as "savages." Moreover, despite his nuanced understanding of diverse African populations, Durand often lumped different ethnic groups into the single category of "Africans" in the *Voyage au Sénégal* and he repeatedly stressed "the ignorance, the barbarity, the misery and the deplorable state of the inhabitants of Africa."[53] Such simplistic categorization, of course, could only support the idea of a "savage" Africa in need of development. That Europe was in an ideal position to do so, moreover, was made explicit in the concluding section of the *Voyage au Sénégal*.

In the final part of the *Voyage au Sénégal*, Durand made some "general observation on the peoples of Africa" which reflect the extent to which his interest in promoting colonization in Africa was now predicated on a depiction of the local populations as infantile, savages, or barbaric. He first noted that he had visited all of the peoples of West Africa and "described them as truthfully as possible." He had not done so, he said, to "satisfy curiosities," but to "instruct" readers. He then noted that

> We do not know a more perfidious and more cruel race than that of the Moors [...] They oppress the negroes and make it their calling to persecute foreigners. The negroes, on the other hand, are naturally good, humane, and hospitable.[54]

Commenting then on the population of Saint-Louis and Gorée, who had been in contact with Europeans for centuries, he emphasized that these people were happier and more intelligent than any other people on the coast of Africa and "owe their civilization to Europeans…"[55] A more sustained contact between France and "savages" of Africa, in Durand's view, could have an equally positive outcome for the continent as a whole.

The shifting geopolitical context of the Age of Revolution and the publication of the *Voyage au Sénégal*

Between Durand's encounter with African populations in the mid-1780s and the publication of the *Voyage au Sénégal*, it was not only the memory of possible frustrations with ethnic groups along the Senegal River or a "régime de véridiction" in France that could have influenced his shifting perception of Africa and its people. The period from 1785 to 1802 was one of the most turbulent times in French and World history, where old colonial and political regimes were collapsing in Europe and in the Americas. The traditional role of Africa as a supplier of slaves to the American plantations was temporarily impeded by the commitment of French Revolutionaries to extend *liberté, égalité, et fraternité* to the French colonies in the Americas after the slave uprising on France's most valuable sugar colony, Saint-Domingue, in 1791.

The decree announcing the abolition of slavery in the French colonial empire in 1794, however, did not produce a universal acceptance of the Declaration of the Rights of Man and the Citizen. In the French colonies in the Caribbean, the abolition of slavery in colonies such as Guadeloupe and Saint-Domingue lead to what Laurent Dubois has called "Republican racism" which entailed a new kind of racial exclusion of former slaves due to their alleged incapacity to be full citizens.[56] While refraining from old-regime racial categories, Frenchmen now referred to African slaves arriving in Guadeloupe and then freed before sent to work in plantations as *cultivateurs* (cultivators).[57] In France, post-abolition racial equality existed alongside a new depiction of the African race as inherently violent and savage. This latter development, as Gilles Manceron has argued, was intimately attached to the slaves' massacre of white planters in Saint-Domingue.[58] In 1797, merchants from Bordeaux argued that abolition did not serve the freed population in Saint-Domingue since these new citizens were "born under the burning skies of Africa," uncivilized, and many of them "savages."[59] To some, this merely indicated that France should go to Africa and civilize its population through colonization. To others, it meant that France should reverse its decision to abolish slavery. With the coup of 18 Brumaire, the latter became a possibility. Napoleon's declaration of December 25, 1799 addressed to the "Brave Blacks on Saint-Domingue" maintained abolition but reintroduced "special laws" in the colonies.[60] With this, as Yves Benot has noted, the process towards the restoration of slavery in the French colonies had begun.[61] In 1802, slavery was reinstated. That year, a certain employee of the Ministry of the Marine and the colonies named Desclozière wrote a scathing critique of Africans in Saint-Domingue: "You, ferocious African, who momentarily triumph on the graves of your masters whom you have slaughtered freely, […] enter the political void nature has destined you for. Your atrocious pride announces only too well that servitude is your lot."[62]

Durand, who hoped to see France expand in Africa, would have to adjust his arguments in accordance with this rapidly shifting geopolitical context. Attention to Durand's efforts to publicize his knowledge on Senegal shows that he was clearly paying close attention to this volatile political situation. Durand had returned to France from Senegal in 1786 due to disagreements with the *Compagnie de la gomme de Sénégal*. Once back in Paris, he sought a meeting with the new Minister of the Marine, Comte de La Luzerne. He offered the Minister a copy of his account of the voyage into the interior with his notes and reflections which he claimed "present new knowledge on this part of the world and indicate not only ways to further such knowledge but also how to penetrate deeper into the interior."[63] Durand also conveyed to the Minister that the British were in the process of forming an association to explore Africa by going up the Senegal and Gambia Rivers. He now hoped that the Minister would ensure that the French made this trip ahead of the British thus "conserv[ing] not only the glory of the discovery which would be made for France but also all the advantages which would result from it."[64]

While Luzerne expressed interest in Durand's writings and wanted to hear more of his ideas on Africa, there is nothing in the archival sources to suggest they met.[65] Durand, moreover, had to shelve any interests he had in Africa once the Revolution began. He barely escaped the Terror due to his services to the Old Regime administration and had to go into hiding.[66] Meanwhile, the British group Durand was referring to, the African

Association founded by Joseph Banks in 1788, started exploring the interior of Africa and reporting on the geography, ethnography and natural history of the continent.[67] With support from the Association, the British explorer Mungo Park fully opened the exploration of the interior of West Africa when he reached the Niger River in 1796. These developments dashed Durand's dreams to render France the initial discoverer of the interior of West Africa though not his hopes of further exploring the continent and advancing French colonization in the region.

In the year VII of the first French Republic, Durand's name reappears within the sector of the Ministry of Foreign Affairs dealing with Africa. Durand was in the middle of editing a volume on a "voyage en Afrique" and requested permission to consult certain maps within the *dépôt de la marine* and examine papers within the colonial office (*bureau des colonies*). The Minister of the Marine and the Colonies, A. E. Bruix, granted Durand such permission on 12 Frimaire year VII.[68] Bruix told Durand to present himself to the *chef du dépôt des cartes et plans* to obtain access to the maps. With respect to Durand's interest in obtaining information from the colonial office, he was asked to write up a list of notes and questions which the head of the colonial office would then respond to upon authorization from Bruix.[69]

At this time, Bruix had pledged his support to France's second abolitionist society, the *Société des amis des noirs et des colonies*, which pushed for setting up slave-free colonies in Africa.[70] The Directory too was exploring the possibilities of building a colonial empire free of slaves in Senegal, on the Gold Coast, and in Egypt.[71] Durand might have known about these efforts and sought to bend his narrative of Senegambia in the direction of such desires. He would, at least, indicate in the *Voyage au Sénégal* how he thought France should go about these ventures.

Praising both the British attempt at Sierra Leone and the French attempt at the River Benin, he also offered a strong critique of the British one, pointing out where he thought this experiment had gone awry. In his view, it should not have relied on free black labor coming from outside of Africa. Instead, the British should have brought in local labor. As he said:

> I would have dealt with Africans as they are, meaning slaves, and I would have paid their masters the price of their day's work. I would have created gentle, humane, benevolent laws. I would have made them ready to work and attached to the land by means of the joy of property and cultivation. After having prepared them for the charms of liberty in this manner, I would have quickly bought them and accorded them their freedom. This approach, I am sure, would have provided me with a lot of cultivators (*cultivateurs*).[72]

Durand thus used the same word of *cultivateurs* used to describe the former slaves in the Caribbean.

Durand's information on how to approach colonization and civilization in Africa might have been interesting to Bruix and *Société des amis des noirs et des colonies*. However, it was not until the Directory had come to an end and Napoleon had been made first consul that Durand managed to publish his work. It was published only a few months prior to the reestablishment of slavery (made into law on 20 May 1802). As soon as it came out, it received a warm welcome. In the session of 26 Ventose year X (17 March 1802), a deputy called F. Delort presented Durand's publication to the *Corps Législatif*, the law-making body under the Consulate, stressing that Durand was a hero and an admirable compatriot. With respect to the book he emphasized its informative sections on commerce, monopoly trade and free trade, the slave trade, etc. and that "the work (*ouvrage*) by citizen Durand will be a fruitful mine of instructions on these high aims of public administration" since the author's account was based on "observable facts."[73] Durand's *Voyage au Sénégal* was soon translated into German as *Nachrichten von den Senegal-Ländern* in 1803 and into English as *A Voyage to Senegal* in 1805. Not only French speakers, but also German and English people could thus gain insights into the alleged characteristics of the people of Senegambia and Durand's civilizing hopes for "savage" Africa.

How Europeans came to think of Africa as "savage" and in need of "civilization" in the Age of Revolution was a complex and multifaceted process that hinged on developments in all of the continents around the Atlantic. In current scholarship on this process, however, the main focus has centered on Europe itself. The actual encounter with Africa as well as the larger geopolitical context, however, needs to be incorporated into the explanatory framework. Through an exploration of the historical context for the production of Durand's *Compagnie de la gomme de Sénégal*, this article shows that behind the idea of Africans as "savages" or "barbarians" rested a deep frustration with European colonial agents' inability to dominate and control commercial expansion in this region. In conjunction with such frustrations, the Age of Revolution altered the parameters of acceptable colonial expansion. The French and Haitian Revolutions were making centuries old forms of human exploitation unacceptable, including the enslavement of Africans. For a colonial agent such as Durand, who wished for France to advance its interests in Africa, illustrating how those ethnic groups formerly used in the slave trade were not only in need but also desirous of Europe's "civilizing" influence was politically and economically expedient. If Durand could show that the Moors who dominated trade in Senegal were a barbaric and crude race from which other ethnic groups needed rescuing, he might better persuade his audience. Tampering with the presentation of his experiences and recollections of his time in Senegal came at a cost, of course, but it was a price Senegambia and not Durand would come to pay.[74]

Notes

1. Durand, *Voyage au Sénégal*, iii. The title of the accompanying volume was *Illustrations de Atlas pour servir au voyage du Sénégal, ou Mémoires historiques, philosophiques et politiques sur les découvertes, les établissements et le commerce des européens dans les mers de l'Océan Atlantique, depuis le Cap-Blanc jusqu'à la rivière de Serra-Lionne inclusivement.* All translations in the paper are my own.
2. Durand, *Voyage au Sénégal*, 153. On the British settlement see Coleman, *Romantic Colonization and British Anti-Slavery*, and Braidwood, *Black Poor and White Philanthropists*. On the French experiment, spearheaded by Jean-François Landolphe, see Røge, "An Early Scramble for Africa."
3. Durand, *Voyage au Sénégal*, 171.
4. See, for instance, Brown, *Moral Capital*; Dorigny, "Intégration républicaine des colonies"; Manchuelle, "The 'Regeneration of Africa'"; Røge, "'La Clef de Commerce.'"
5. Cohen, *The French Encounter with Africans*, 174–180.
6. Excellent studies on the view of Africans in France have appeared in recent years. For the eighteenth century, see, for instance, Curran, *The Anatomy of Blackness*; Gallouët et al., eds., *L'Afrique du siècle des Lumières*; special volume on *L'Afrique*, in *Dix-huitième siècle* eds. Diop

et al.; Manchuelle, "The 'Regeneration of Africa." For general history which includes views of Africans in the eighteenth-century France, see Harvey, *French Enlightenment and Its Others*. These studies build on the pioneering work of Duchet, *Anthropologie et histoire au siècle des Lumières*; Cohen, *The French Encounter with Africans*; Curtin, *The Image of Africa*. On the development of racism in France see Liauzu, *La société française face au racisme*; Peabody and Stovall, *The Color of Liberty*.

7. Gallouët et al., eds., *L'Afrique du siècle des Lumières*, xv.

8. Diop, "La mise à l'épreuve d'un *régime de véridiction*," 15–29.

9. In 1767, Demanet, who worked as a man of the Church in Senegambia in the 1760s, published his *Nouvelle Histoire de l'Afrique Françoise* (Paris: Duchesne and Lacombe, 1767). In 1789, Lamiral, a merchant and resident of Saint-Louis from the 1770s, published *L'Affrique et le peuple affriquain* (Paris: Dessenne, 1789). Within the same period that Durand published his *Voyage*, three other colonial agents residing in Senegambia in the 1780s published their accounts of this region. These were Jean-Gabriel Pelletan, who succeeded Durand as director of the company. His publication was entitled *Mémoire sur la colonie française du Sénégal* (Paris: Vve Panckoucke,1800). Golbéry, who accompanied the new governor of Senegal, the Chevalier de Boufflers, in 1785, published his *Fragmens d'un voyage en Afrique* (2 vols. Paris: Treuttel et Würtz, 1802); Villeneuve, who also accompanied the Chevalier de Boufflers, published *L'Afrique, ou histoire, mœurs* (4 vols. Paris: Nepveu, 1814). While none of these authors have left as extensive a paper trail in the French National Archives as Durand, they too seem influenced by the Age of Revolution in their later accounts of Senegambia.

10. Adelman, "An Age of Imperial Revolutions," 320. For a general discussion, see also Armitage and Subrahmanyam, *The Age of Revolutions*, xxii.

11. On the French Administration in Senegal in the second half of the eighteenth century, see Jore, *Les établissements français*.

12. "Arrêt du Conseil d'État du Roi, Qui supprime le privilége exclusif de la traite des Noirs à Gorée & dépendances, & accorde en dédommagement, pour le terme, aux Concessionnaires, Intéressé & Administrateurs de la Compagnie de la Guyane françoise, celui de la traite de la Gomme seulement, dans la rivière du Sénégal & dépendances." 11 January 1784, Archives du Ministère des Affaires Étrangères (hereafter MAE): Archives Diplomatiques (hereafter AD), Mémoires et Documents Afrique (hereafter MDA), 11, pièce 202.

13. In the early 1700s, European rivalry over the Senegambian gum supply had caused several gum wars among the French, the British, and the Dutch. The Dutch were pushed out in 1727, but rivalry continued between France and Britain. Senegal's changing of hands in 1763 and again in 1783 was in large part due to the aim of these two powers to control the supply of gum to Europe. Barry, *Senegambia and the Atlantic Slave Trade*, 69–73.

14. Ersch, *La France littéraire*, 199.

15. Durand to the Minister of the Marine, the Marquis de Castries, Hotel de Bretagne sur St. André des Arts, 18 February 1785, Archives Nationales d'Outre-Mer, Aix-en-Provence, (hereafter ANOM): Col E164, Personal Dossier Durand.

16. For a description of the development of the inhabitants of Saint-Louis in this period, see Searing, "The Seven Years' War in West Africa."

17. "Mémoire du Roi pour server d'Instructions à Mons le Chev. De Boufflers marechal de Camp gouverneur du sénégal et dépendace." November 1785. ANOM: Col C6 18, ffs. 209–228. There were approximately 6000 people living on Saint-Louis in the mid-1780s, 700 Europeans, 2400 free blacks, and 2000 captives and a variable number of slaves. See also Jones, *The Métis of Senegal*, 30.

18. On the role of the Signares in general, and the position of mayor at Saint-Louis in particular, see Brooks, *Eurafricans in Western Africa*, 260.

19. Jones, *The Métis of Senegal*, 22. On local rivalries between these groups in the eighteenth century, see Curtin, *Economic Change in Precolonial Africa*, 121–127.

20. On the rise of the Moors with the British occupation of Saint-Louis between the Seven Years War and the American Revolution, see Barry, *The Kingdom of Waalo*, Chapter 7.

21. Brooks, *Eurafricans in Western Africa*, 259.

22. Dziennik, "'Till these Experiments be Made'," 1142.
23. Ibid., 1150. See also Newton, "Naval power and the Province of Senegambia," 139–141.
24. Durand, *Voyage au Sénégal*, xxvii.
25. Ibid., xxv.
26. Ibid.
27. Ibid., xxvi.
28. Ibid.
29. "Discours pronnoncé aux habitans de l'isle St. Louis au Sénégal par M. Durand Directeur Général de la Compagnie." Senegal, 15 April 1785. MAE: AD, Afrique, 11, Pièce 251. The company only had a monopoly for the trade in gum Arabic, and had to trade in slaves and ivory on an equal footing with independent French merchants. However, with its exclusive rights, it was likely that only few independent French merchants would frequent the region, and the company could therefore also expect to be able to trade a considerable amount of slaves and other goods drawn from the region.
30. On French views of the populations of North Africa, see Coller, *Arab France*; Said, *Orientalism*; and Thomson, *Barbary and Enlightenment*.
31. Castries to Répentigny. Versailles, 25 August 1785, ANOM: Col B188.
32. The Darmankour was the name used by Europeans at Saint-Louis to describe the Idaw al-Hajj communities. See Webb, "The Evolution of the Idaw al-Hajj Commercial Diaspora," 461.
33. Répentigny to Castries. Senegal, 30 May 1785, ANOM: Col C6 18, n. 161, f. 21. On rivalry between the Moor rulers in this period, see Barry, *The Kingdom of Waalo*, 137–139.
34. Durand to Castries. Senegal, 10 August 1785, MAE: AD, Afrique, 11, pièces 249.
35. Ibid. On the balance of power between European and African merchants, see Northrup, *Africa's Discovery of Europe*, 51.
36. Durand, *Voyage au Sénégal*, 266. According to Durand, the Trarzas traded mostly at Arguin and Portendick, but also came to the escale au Coq on the Senegal River and located approximately 25 *lieues* from Saint-Louis. The Marabou of Darmankour collected their gum from the forest of Lebiar, and sold it at the escale des Maraboux, 42 *lieues* from Saint-Louis. Hamet Mocktard of Bracknas obtained his gum from the forest of Afatack, and sold it at the escale du Terrier-Rouge close to Podor, approximately 60 *lieues* from Saint-Louis. Durand, *Voyage au Sénégal*, 265–266.
37. Durand to Castries. Senegal, 10 August 1785, ANOM: Col E164, Personal Dossier Durand. To whet the minister's appetite, he sent the minister two leopards, a Senegalese wolf, and a genette.
38. "Voyage du Sénégal à Galam par terre par M. Durand," Senegal, 13 June 1786, ANOM: Col C6 19, ffs. 76–121.
39. Ibid.
40. The names of villages and local rulers are given here as in Durand's accounts.
41. Webb, *Desert Frontier*, 119.
42. "Ceux qui s'y sont retirés sont cultivateurs, ils ont des captifs nègres qui font des Lougans (Lougan est un terrain destiné à être ensemencée comme nos champs en France) ils en retirent une très grande quantité de mill [millet] et de coton, ils nourrirent des bœufs et des moutons dont ils ont des troupeaux très nombreux." In "Voyage du Sénégal à Galam par terre par M. Durand," Senegal, 13 June 1786, ANOM: Col C6 19, f. 82.
43. There is a wonderful description of this encounter: "après l'avoir considéré quelque tems dans le silence, il lui demanda quelle etoit le sujet qui conduisoit un Blanc comme lui dans ses états ce qui n'était jamais arrivé. Je vais au Royaume de Galam lui répliqua le S. Rubault, je suis l'envoyé de M. Durand Directeur Général de la Compagnie, il m'a chargé spécialement de te voir, de te saluer de sa part et surtout de te faire connoitre l'extrême envie qu'il a de former quelque établissemens dans ton pays, c'est suffisant répondit le Roy, je suis charmé de te voir." Ibid.
44. There is no description of these kingdoms in the memorandum. In 1802, Durand stressed that they were not the kingdoms normally known by these names. Durand, *Voyage au Sénégal*, 291.

45. "...il parcourut une vaste plaine planté de superbes arbres et habitée par des gens plus civilisés que ceux qu'il avoit déjà vus, il dit que la propriété règne parmi eux comme chez les blancs." In "Voyage du Sénégal à Galam par terre par M. Durand," Senegal, 13 June 1786, ANOM: Col C6 19, ffs. 76–121.

46. In the region called D'youly (Wuuli), Rubault encountered a less hospitable people. In the village named Color, he was asked to pay for his lodging with some *pieces de guinée* and a man searched all of Rubault's belongings in the hope of finding European goods. Rubault went through a few more such inhospitable villages before he arrived at Fort Joseph.

47. Durand, *Voyage au Sénégal*, 271.

48. "Voyage du Sénégal à Galam par terre par M. Durand," Senegal, 13 June 1786, ANOM: Col C6 19, ffs. 76–121.

49. The sovereigns of Senegambia were increasingly hesitant to sell slaves to the French since they used most of them to advance local production. Searing, *West African Slavery and Atlantic Commerce,* 30.

50. Castries to Boufflers and D'Aigremont. Versailles, 30 March 1787, ANOM: B196.

51. Durand, *Voyage au Sénégal*, 341–343.

52. Ibid.

53. "l'ignorance, la barbarie, la misère et l'état déplorable des habitans de l'Afrique." Durand, *Voyage au Sénégal*, 164.

54. Ibid., 368.

55. Ibid., 369. On the complicated history between France and the francophone inhabitants of Gorée and Saint-Louis, see Aubert, ""Nègres ou mulâtres nous sommes tous Français.""

56. Dubois, "Inscribing Race," 96.

57. Ibid., 100.

58. Desclozières, *Les Égarements du négrophile*; quoted in Manceron, *Marianne et les colonies,* 72.

59. Dubois, *A Colony of Citizens*, 290.

60. Benot, *La démence coloniale*, 21.

61. Ibid. On the movement towards the restoration of slavery see also Pronier, "L'implicite et l'explicite."

62. Desclozières, *Les Égaremens du nigrophilisme*; quoted in Manceron, *Marianne et les colonies*, 72.

63. Durand to Luzerne. Paris Rue de deux portes St. Severin n. 6, 3 September 1788, ANOM: Col E164, Personal Dossier Durand.

64. "Vous n'ignorez pas, Monseigneur, le projèts des Anglois et leurs vues sur le vaste continens de l'Affrique. Iles se proposent de le parcourir, en remontant les fleuves de Sénégal et de Gambie. Il s'est formé pour cela une association considérable en Angleterre, et dans un voyage que je fis à Londre au mois de Mars dernier, on me fit des ouvertures qui m'instruisirent au moins du plan de l'entreprise. Il seroit peut-être aussi prudens qu'utile de les prévenir et de conserver à la France non seulement la gloire des découvertes qu'on va faire, mais encore et tous les autres avantages qui doivent en resulser." Durand to Luzerne. 3 September 1788. ANOM: Col E164, Personal Dossier Durand.

65. Luzerne to Durand. Versailles, 9 October 1788, Durand to Luzerne, 3 September 1788. ANOM: Col E164, Personal Dossier Durand.

66. Mathiez, "Danton and Durand."

67. Curtin, *The Image of Africa*, 17.

68. "Report," Paris, 12 Frimaire Year 7, ANOM: Col E164, Personal Dossier Durand.

69. Bruix to Durand. Paris, 12 Frimaire Year 7, ANOM: Col E164, Personal Dossier Durand.

70. As far as I am aware, there is no study dedicated to the *Société des amis des noirs et des colonies* apart from Gainot's introduction to the published notes of the society. See Dorigny and Gainot, *La Société des Amis des Noirs*, 307.

71. Lokke, "French Dreams of Colonial Empire under the Directory and Consulate."

72. "Je me serais servi des Africains, tels qu'ils sont, c'est-à-dire, esclaves, et j'aurais payé à leurs maîtres le prix de leurs journées; j'aurais fait pour eux des lois douces, humaines, bienfaisantes; je les aurais disposés au travail et attachés au sol par la jouissance de la propriété et de la culture. Après les avoir ainsi préparés aux charmes de la liberté, je me serais hâté de les

acheter et de la leur accorder. Cette marche, je n'en doute pas, m'eüt amené beaucoup de cultivateurs…" Durand, *Voyage au Sénégal*, 165.

73. "Discours prononcé par F. Delort, En présentant au Corps législatif, au nom du citoyen Durand, un livre ayant pour titre: *Voyage au Sénégal*," Séance du 26 ventôse an X, Paris: Impr. Nationale, Year XI.

74. On the change from the trans-Atlantic trading system to legitimate trade and French colonization, see Barry, *Senegambia and the Atlantic Slave Trade*, Parts III and IV.

Acknowledgements

The author would like to thank Michael A. McDonnell, Molly Warsh, Michel Gobat, Gregory E. O'Malley, and the participants of the conference on *The Future of Atlantic, Transnational, and World History* held at the University of Pittsburgh in May 2014 for their helpful comments on earlier versions of this essay. The author would also link to extend her sincere thanks to the two anonymous reviewers who offered encouraging and insightful comments at a later stage.

Disclosure statement

No potential conflict of interest was reported by the author.

References

Adelman, Jeremy. "An Age of Imperial Revolutions." *American Historical Review* 113, no. 2 (2008): 319–340.

Armitage, David and Sanjay Subrahmanyam, eds. *The Age of Revolutions in Global Context, c. 1760–1840*. Basingstoke: Palgrave Macmillan, 2010.

Aubert, Guillaume. "'Nègres ou mulâtres nous sommes tous Français': Race, genre et nation à Gorée et à Saint-Louis du Sénégal, fin XVIIe-fin XVIIIe siècle." In *Français? La nation en débat entre colonies et métropole, XVIe-XIXe siècle*, edited by Cécile Vidal, 125–147. Paris: Éditions de l'École des hautes études en sciences sociales, 2014.

Barry, Boubacar. *Senegambia and the Atlantic Slave Trade*. Cambridge: Cambridge University Press, 1998.

Barry, Boubacar. *The Kingdom of Waalo Senegal Before the Conquest*. New York: Diasporic Africa Press, 2012.

Benot, Yves. *La démence colonial sous Napoléon*. Paris: *La Découverte*, 2006.

Braidwood, Stephen J. *Black Poor and White Philanthropists: London's Blacks and the Foundation of the Sierra Leone Settlement, 1786–1791*. Liverpool: Liverpool University Press, 1994.

Brooks, George E. *Eurafricans in Western Africa Commerce, Social Status, Gender, and Religious Observance from the Sixteenth to the Eighteenth Century*. Athens: Ohio University Press, 2003.

Brown, Christopher Leslie. *Moral Capital Foundations of British Abolitionism*. Chapel Hill: The University of North Carolina Press, 2006.

Cohen, William B. *The French Encounter with Africans White Response to Blacks, 1530–1880*. (1980) Bloomington: Indiana University Press, 2003.

Coleman, Deirdre. *Romantic Colonization and British Anti-Slavery*. Cambridge: Cambridge University Press, 2005.

Coller, Ian. *Arab France Islam and the Making of Modern Europe, 1798–1831*. Berkeley: University of California Press, 2010.

Curran, Andrew S. *The Anatomy of Blackness Science & Slavery in an Age of Enlightenment*. Baltimore, MD: The Johns Hopkins University Press, 2011.

Curtin, Philip D. *The Image of Africa British Ideas and Action, 1780–1850*. Madison: University of Wisconsin Press, 1964.

Curtin, Philip D. *Economic Change in Precolonial Africa Senegambia in the Era of the Slave Trade*. Madison: University of Wisconsin Press, 1975.

Demanet, Abbé. *Nouvelle Histoire de l'Afrique Françoise*. Paris: Duchesne and Lacombe, 1767.

Desclozières, L. N. B. *Les Égaremens du nigrophilisme*. Paris: Chez Migneret, 1802.

Diop, David, Patrick Graille, and Izabella Zatorska, eds. *L'Afrique, Special issue Dix-huitième siècle 44*. Paris: La Découverte, 2012.

Diop, David. "La mise à l'épreuve d'un régime de véridiction sur 'la paresse et la négligence des nègres' dans le Voyage au Sénégal (1757) d'Adanson." In *L'Afrique du siècle des Lumières: savoirs et représentations*, edited by Catherine Gallouuët, David Diop, Michèle Bocquillon and Gérard Lahouati, 15–29. Oxford: SVEC, 2009.

Dorigny, Marcel. "Intégration républicaine des colonies et projets de colonisation de l'Afrique: civiliser pour émancier?" *Revue française d'histoire d'outre-mer* 87, no. 328–329 (2000): 89–105.

Dorigny, Marcel, and Bernard Gainot. *La Société des Amis des Noirs, 1788–1799 – Contribution à l'histoire de l'abolition de l'esclavage*. Paris: UNESCO, 1998.

Dubois, Laurent. "Inscribing Race in the Revolutionary French Antilles." In *The Color of Liberty Histories of Race in France*, edited by Sue Peabody and Tyler Stovall, 95–107. Durham, NC: Duke University Press, 2003.

Dubois, Laurent. *A Colony of Citizens: Revolution and Slave Emancipation in the French Caribbean, 1787–1804*. Chapel Hill: University of North Carolina Press, 2004.

Duchet, Michèle. *Anthropologie et histoire au siècle des Lumières (1971)*. Paris: Albin Michel, 1995.

Durand, Jean-Baptiste Léonard. *Voyage au Sénégal ou Mémoires historique, philosophiques et politique sur les découvertes, les établissemens et le commerce des européens dans les mers de l'Océan Atlantique: depuis le Cap-Blanc jusqu'à la rivière de Serre-Lionne inclusivement; suivis de la relation d'un voyage par terre de l'île Saint-Louis à Galam; et du texte arabe de trois traités de commerce faits par l'auteur avec les princes du pays*. 2 vols. Paris: H. Agasse, 1802.

Dziennik, Matthew P. "'Till these Experiments be Made': Senegambia and British Imperial Policy in the Eighteenth Century." *English Historical Review*, 130, no. 546 (2015): 1132–1161.

Ersch, Johann Samuel. *La France littéraire contenant les auteurs français de 1771 à 1796*. Hambourg: Hoffmann, 1806.

Gallouët, Catherine, David Diop, Michèle Bocquillon and Gérard Lahouati, eds. *L'Afrique du siècle des Lumières: saviors et representations*. Oxford: SVEC, 2009.

Golbéry, Sylvain Meinrad Xavier de. *Fragmens d'un voyage en Afrique: fait pendant les années 1785, 1786 et 1787, dans les contrées occidentales de ce continent, comprises entre le cap Blanc de Barbarie, par 20 degrés, 47 minutes, et le cap de Palmes, par 4 degrés, 30 minutes, latitude boréale*. 2 vols. Paris: Treuttel et Würtz, 1802.

Harvey, David Allen. *The French Enlightenment and Its Others: The Mandarin, the Savage, and the Invention of the Human Sciences*. New York: Palgrave Macmillan, 2012.

Jones, Hilary. *The Métis of Senegal Urban Life and Politics in French West Africa*. Bloomington: Indiana University Press, 2013.

Jore, Léonce. *Les établissements français sur la côte occidentale d'Afrique de 1758 à 1809*. Paris: G. P. Maison-Neuve et Larose, 1965.

Lamiral, M. *L'Affrique et le peuple affriquain*. Paris: Dessenne, 1789.

Liauzu, Claude. *La société française face au racisme. De la Révolution à nos jours*. Brussels: Complexe, 1999.

Lokke, Carl Ludwig. "French Dreams of Colonial Empire under the Directory and Consulate." *Journal of Modern History* 2 (1930): 237–250.

Manchuelle, François. "'The 'Regeneration of Africa': An Important and Ambiguous Concept in 18th and 19th Century French Thinking about Africa." *Cahiers d'Études Africaine* 36 (1996): 559–588.

Manceron, Gilles. *Marianne et les colonies Une introduction à l'histoire coloniale de France*. Paris: La Découverte, 2003.

Mathiez, Albert. "Danton and Durand." *Annales révolutionnaires* 11–12 (1919): 141–159.

Newton, Joshua D. "Naval power and the Province of Senegambia, 1758–1779." *Journal for Maritime Research* 15, no. 2 (2013): 129–147.

Northrup, David. *Africa's Discovery of Europe, 1450–1850*. Oxford: Oxford University Press, 2002.

Peabody, Sue, and Tyler Stovall. *The Color of Liberty: Histories of Race in France*. Durham, NC: Duke University Press, 2003.

Pelletan, Jean-Gabriel. *Mémoire sur la colonie française du Sénégal: avec quelques considérations historiques et politiques sur la traite des nègres*. Paris: Panckoucke, 1800.

Pronier, Thomas. "L'implicite et l'explicite dans la politique de Napoléon." In *Rétablissement de l'esclavage dans les colonies françaises Aux origines de Haïti*, edited by Yves Bénot and Marcel Dorigny, 51–67. Paris: Maisonneuve et Larose, 2003.

Røge, Pernille. "'La Clef de Commerce': The changing role of Africa in France's Atlantic empire ca. 1760–1797." *History of European Ideas* 34, no. 4 (2008): 431–443.

Røge, Pernille. "An Early Scramble for Africa: British, Danish and French Colonial Projects on the Coast of West Africa, 1780s and 1790s." In *The Routledge History of Western Empires*, edited by Robert Aldrich and Kirsten McKenzie, 72–86. New York: Routledge, 2013.

Said, Edward. *Orientalism*. New York: Vintage Books Edition, 1979.

Searing, James F. *West African Slavery and Atlantic Commerce: The Senegal River valley, 1700–1860*. Cambridge: Cambridge University Press, 1993.

Searing, James F. "The Seven Years' War in West Africa: The End of Company Rule and the Emergence of the Habitants." In *The Seven Years' War: Global Views*, edited by Mark H. Danley and Patrick J. Speelman, 263–291. Leiden: Brill Academic Publishers, 2012.

Thomson, Ann. *Barbary and Enlightenment. European Attitudes towards the Maghreb in the 18th Century*. Leyde: E.J. Brill, 1987.

Villeneuve, René Claude Géoffroy de. *L'Afrique, ou histoire, mœurs, usages et coutumes des africains*. 4 vols. Paris: Nepvey, 1814.

Webb, James L. A. Jr. *Desert Frontier Ecological and Economic Change along the Western Sahel, 1600–1850*. Madison: University of Wisconsin Press, 1995.

Webb, James L. A. Jr. "The Evolution of the Idaw al-Hajj Commercial Diaspora." *Cahiers d'études africaines* 35, no. 138–139 (1995): 455–475.

Sovereignty disavowed: the Tupac Amaru revolution in the Atlantic world

Sinclair Thomson

History Department, New York University, New York, NY, USA

ABSTRACT

While the Andean insurrection of the early 1780s, most often associated with the Inka leader Tupac Amaru II, was the most powerful challenge to Spanish rule in colonial Latin America, it is generally ignored in the Atlantic historiography of the Age of Revolution. This article reviews the reasons for this neglect and traces the problem back to the late eighteenth and early nineteenth centuries. It demonstrates for the first time that knowledge of the revolution in the Andes circulated widely throughout the Atlantic world in the early 1780s. It also provides evidence of a deep panic on the part of Spanish authorities, who feared that the anti-colonial revolution unfolding in British North America could find a counterpart in Spanish South America, especially with instigation by their British imperial rivals. It reveals Spanish attempts to prevent circulation of the news of the insurrection and the beginnings of a tradition that would reduce the meaning of the Andean revolution to an expression of race war. It argues more generally that this case of "silencing" (M. R. Trouillot) and "disavowal" (S. Fischer) in the Atlantic world reflected a repudiation of the radical principle of indigenous political sovereignty which underlay the Andean insurgencies. Rather than incorporate the Andean case into the existing paradigm of Atlantic revolutions, the article seeks to enrich the historiography of the Age of Revolution by showing that projects for indigenous territory and political authority, which challenged European and creole sovereignty in the Americas, deserve to be seen as integral to the epoch.

Cet événement est trop intéressant pour que nous ne réparions pas cet oubli.[1]
(1 May 1782, Le Cap, Saint-Domingue, *Affiches Américaines*)

Starting in the 1730s and 1740s, social turmoil spread and intensified around the southern Andes. In the countryside, economic conflicts involving indigenous communities led to seething political disputes and local clashes with authorities. In the late 1770s and early months of 1780, urban unrest and revolts flared up – especially in the cities of La Paz, Cochabamba, Arequipa, and Cuzco – against new Bourbon commercial restrictions and taxation. A wave of broader regional insurgencies against Spanish colonial rule began in late 1780 and would not fully subside until 1783. Together, the movements would later come to be known as the insurrection of Tupac Amaru, though in fact at the time they lacked any unified command.

The first insurgency began under the leadership of Tomás Katari in the district of Northern Potosí, near the famed Rich Mountain that had supplied massive quantities of silver bullion to the Spanish Crown. José Gabriel Condorcanqui Tupac Amaru, claiming royal Inka ancestry, headed the uprising in Cuzco, the fabled capital of the ancient monarchs of Peru. Julián Apaza who took the name Tupaj Katari commanded the insurgent forces on the high plateau south of Lake Titikaka, a thriving commercial territory with densely settled indigenous populations. Some of the foremost Andean cities – La Plata, Cuzco, Puno, La Paz – came under fierce siege, and their vast rural hinterlands fell under insurgent control. The combatants were mainly Quechua- and Aymara-speaking Indians, though a limited number of mestizos and creoles joined the uprisings, especially in the early phases.

The aspirations of the insurgents have been a matter of debate, but they clearly voiced anti-colonial aims and a range of claims to sovereignty. As Tomás Katari's brother Dámaso put it, indigenous peasants in northern Potosí anticipated becoming "the lords of their own lands and of the fruits they produce, in peace and tranquility."[2] This sentiment reflected a widespread imaginary on the part of Indian community members in the southern Andes who envisioned a new era in which they would exercise communal sovereignty over local territory and resources. Without renouncing the Spanish crown itself, Tomás Katari's denunciations of colonial misrule challenged the political and administrative hierarchy in northern Potosí and effectively carved out an alternative sphere of regional autonomy. Tupac Amaru likewise repudiated the abuses of regional Spanish authorities, and stood for the recovery of legitimate government in a land ruled by its own inhabitants. But in donning an Inka mantle, his personal, historical, and political significance resonated even more widely. He conducted himself in royal fashion and his followers treated him with corresponding reverence. Implicitly acknowledging the supremacy and political agenda of Tupac Amaru, Tupaj Katari titled himself Viceroy and called for the expulsion of Europeans from the Andes and the subordination of creoles to the new indigenous authorities. Out of these different projects for indigenous sovereignty which surfaced over the course of the colonial crisis and insurrection, it was Tupac Amaru's claim to restored Inka rule that would gain the most far-reaching and lasting notoriety.[3]

The outcome of the insurrection was by no means a foregone conclusion for contemporaries. But by the time the Spaniards reestablished effective military control in late 1781, tens of thousands of people on both sides of the conflict had perished, and Spanish hegemony had been irredeemably compromised. The movement constituted the most powerful threat to Spanish colonial government anywhere in the Americas prior to Latin American independence in the early nineteenth century. In his memoirs, Manuel de Godoy, the prime minister of Carlos IV (1788–1808), later asserted:

> No one ignores how close we were to losing, around the years 1781 and 1782, the entire Viceroyalty of Peru and part of the Viceroyalty of Río de la Plata when the standard of insurrection was raised by the famous Condorcanqui, better known by the name of Tupac-Amaru, answered and aided in the province of La Paz by the bloody Tupa-Catari.[4]

Missing the revolution

Despite the timing, magnitude, and attributes of the so-called Tupac Amaru rebellion, there has been little mention or memory of it in the historiography of the Age of Atlantic

Revolution. In the classic studies of the era by R. R. Palmer and E. J. Hobsbawm, the dramatic clash in the Andes disappeared from view altogether. Even in more recent books that incorporate Latin America and the Caribbean more fully to provide a broader Atlantic revolutionary frame, what Wim Klooster calls the "big revolt" earns a single paragraph.[5] In the recent boom in studies of Latin American independence, there has been an important tendency to go beyond national narratives and to reconsider the American processes in relation to developments in the Iberian metropole.[6] Yet here too the Andean experience is typically seen as outside the frame of reference for Hispanic American independence. Historians commonly assume that the case does not fit because of its timing (prior to the French Revolution or prior to the 1808 collapse of the Spanish monarchy following Napoleonic invasion of the Iberian peninsula) or because it had a supposedly premodern character.[7]

Was there in fact no connection between the developments in the Andes and the contemporaneous historical processes in North America, in France and Saint-Domingue, and in the rest of mainland Spanish America that are commonly associated with an Age of Revolution? The dramatic Andean episode occurred simultaneously with the war for independence that would lead to the creation of the USA and a few years before the storming of the Bastille. It threw into crisis Spanish rule over a large population in a vast territory for an extended period of time, and generated radical projects for emancipation, political autonomy, and decolonized social relations.[8] I will suggest that its neglect in the transnational historiography of revolution in this period, its absence in the grand narrative of the Age of Revolution derives less from a fact of history than an artifact of historical memory. We can begin by pondering general reasons for the historiographic invisibility, before turning to the historical dynamics in the late eighteenth to early nineteenth century that worked to produce it.

A first reason for the absence is that some historians, as noted above, believe that the 1780s movements fall outside the temporal scope of the Age of Revolution. Hobsbawm periodized the Age as essentially starting with 1789, and views the significance of North American independence as of a lesser historical order than that of the French revolution. Scholars of Latin America often classify the cases of Tupac Amaru, the 1781 Comunero uprising in New Granada (later Colombia), and the 1789 Tiradentes conspiracy in Brazil as part of a distinct political cycle. They were, in this view, essentially local reactions against Iberian reform, especially fiscal reform, whereas properly revolutionary movements would arise only in the aftermath of the French Revolution.

A distinct and more concrete problem emerges here, but one also related to historical timing. If the Andean revolution is not well known beyond the region, it can be attributed in part to the fact that it preceded, though not by much, the boom in print media that spread news around the Atlantic world at a much faster rate in the final years of the century. There were in fact a limited number of printing presses in colonial Spanish America and the gazette culture that would thrive after 1810 was still only emerging. The late-colonial *Gazeta de México*, for example, was launched in 1784, shortly after the insurrection in Peru. Once print culture exploded in Spanish America, news would travel far more quickly and widely.[9] Even so, there were early print sources, especially gazettes and shipping news, and information did travel by many vectors besides those of mechanized print media, through circuits of manuscript and oral transmission.[10]

Yet another possible explanation for the absence concerns geography. The Age of Revolution has often been conceived as a northern Atlantic phenomenon, one to which Iberia and Spanish America were marginal. For example, if Spain is seen as possessing an Enlightenment culture at all, it is often marked by its distinctions from Anglo-French varieties. Located on the far southern and western flank of South America, facing the Pacific, the Andes would then at best be seen as a peripheral zone within an already marginal geography. But such assumptions of spatial marginality have their drawbacks. The Andes were one of the two vice-regal Spanish power centers for most of the colonial period. The Andes, especially with their great mining center at Potosí in Upper Peru (today southern Bolivia), were the single greatest source of wealth for the greatest overseas empire during the early colonial era. The Andes were tied in economically, politically, culturally, and demographically to the development of the Iberian empire and to Europe's colonial and capitalist expansion in the early modern period.

By another reckoning, it is possible to argue that the Andean insurgencies actually did not constitute a "revolution" at all. Even many historians of the Andes, who have indeed been aware of the power of the movement in the early 1780s, have refrained from applying the term. Thus, for some, the episode should be thought of as a *jacquerie* situated within the political world of the *ancien régime*. Most have described it as a revolt, rebellion, or insurrection (in Spanish, *levantamiento*, *sublevación*, and *rebelión* are common designations). Peruvian historian Scarlett O'Phelan Godoy, the foremost scholar of the experience in the Andean historiography of the late twentieth century, employs the term Great Rebellion, which conveys the sense that this was indeed an uprising on a major scale though not a "revolution." Clearly, this raises problems concerning the definition of a revolution, but on the face of it, there is no clear-cut reason why the Andean mobilizations could not be a considered revolutionary movement.[11]

Along these same lines, we could ascribe the neglect of the Andean case to the "enormous condescension of posterity" shown toward history's so-called losers.[12] Spanish counter-insurgency ultimately put down the Andean revolution and its defeat surely goes far in explaining the lack of attention. For many historians, the inability of a revolutionary movement to seize or hold on to power would disqualify it from the rare ranks of true revolutions. But this would not be an entirely adequate explanation for the sidelining of the Andean case from broader Atlantic narratives. The Haitian Revolution too was ignored or trivialized by generations of historians, notwithstanding the fact that the emancipation movement there was successful in taking power and holding on to it despite formidable internal challenges and adverse international conditions.[13]

Beyond the timing, geography, and outcome, the deeper explanation for the historiographic neglect surely concerns the nature of the movement. We have to confront not only generic definitions of what constitutes a revolution, but the specific political content of the Andean project which appears to be at odds with the paradigm of modern, liberal, democratic, national, or enlightened revolution in conventional narratives. The Andean movement has long been depicted as backwards-looking and un-modern. The fact that Tupac Amaru sought to reestablish an Inka royal line suggests to some that his project was akin to old-regime monarchy. That it reasserted Inka authority has been taken to mean it was a nativist movement seeking to return to the pre-Columbian era. Others believe Tupac Amaru sought to restore an older and more legitimate Hapsburg colonial pact in the face of the Bourbon modernizing project.

All of these questions are significant and merit more sustained scrutiny than can be offered here. But the fact is that the Andean movement was not so closely linked to revolutionary developments in Europe as was the Haitian Revolution. Radical Enlightenment thought that we conventionally associate with the critique of *anciens régimes* did not circulate widely in the Andes in the 1770s, from what we know – there is no evidence that Tupac Amaru was reading the French *philosophes* or Tom Paine. There was no direct or clandestine intervention by foreign governments to destabilize or overthrow Spanish rule in the Andes in 1780–1783, so it again lacks the same degree of inter-imperial rivalry that characterized Saint-Domingue in the period. Ultimately, it is not possible to fit neatly Indian peasant insurgents and their leaders in the Andes into prevailing liberal or bourgeois notions of revolutionary Atlantic political culture or "modernity."[14]

There is, however, yet another reason for the invisibility of the Andean case. In his study of the long-term absence of the Haitian Revolution from historiographic and broader public awareness, Michel-Rolph Trouillot traced a "silencing" of the experience all the way back to the late eighteenth century. The initial prospect and the subsequent reality of a successful uprising by slaves themselves that abolished the institutions of slavery and established an independent nation founded on freedom from racialized bondage was, he argued, so improbable or so disturbing as to trigger powerful mechanisms of denial and trivialization. Sibylle Fischer elaborated on this same problem of the silence surrounding the Haitian revolution to demonstrate how the radical principle of revolutionary antislavery was so threatening to Caribbean elites that they felt compelled to "disavow" it.[15]

I believe a similar problem of silencing and disavowal has defined historiographic and broader public consciousness of the Andean revolution of the early 1780s. What was so disturbing to political and cultural elites in the Spanish empire was not only the vision of mobilized indigenous masses and the trauma of racialized violence, but the radical principle of indigenous political sovereignty that underlay the Andean insurgencies. In fact, I suggest that interpretations of the Andean experience as race war served precisely to conceal the dilemmas of sovereignty.

To open up and probe such concealed areas poses difficult methodological challenges. Trouillot trained our attention on the ways in which power relations shape the production of historical data, archives, narratives, and interpretations leading ultimately to the silencing of significant features of social experience in the past. Yet Ada Ferrer, analyzing the transformation of news and rumors in the revolutionary Caribbean, has reminded us that archival institutions contain contradictory traces of evidence reflecting different historical experiences, perceptions, and agendas. Thus, she points out, the inconsistencies between the complex documentary record and the simplifications of prevailing narratives can help us discern what was left out of the narrative and how the very phenomenon of silencing occurred. Fischer has creatively revealed how patterns of absence in historical discourse can be the negative sign of that which was disavowed. The concept of disavowal is especially helpful, in this sense, as it points to the otherwise occluded object in an expression of denial or negation.[16]

To justify any interpretation of the Andean revolution ultimately depends on how we construe the bulges and gaps in the existing historical evidence. It is a striking fact, and another possible explanation for historiographic invisibility, that the connections between the Andean revolution and the broader Atlantic world have never been investigated in any depth.[17] Historians have as yet failed to recognize that contemporaries around the Atlantic world had any meaningful awareness of the Andean upheavals, yet if there were a phenomenon of disavowal at work, it would have to be predicated on an awareness of that which contemporaries sought to deny. To demonstrate disavowal, we first have to establish a consciousness of the Andean revolution and of its meaning.

It is not my aim to inscribe the Andean revolution within the conventional narrative of the Age of Atlantic Revolution. Yet if we take seriously the simultaneity and radical features of the movement, reconsidering the Andean case can help us to reevaluate our notions of the Age of Revolution and of revolutionary Atlantic geography, and to reimagine that period in history and that world in new ways. Jeremy Adelman writes: "It was sovereignty of and within empires, monarchies, nations, and republics that was at stake during the great epoch of upheaval and struggle from the middle of the eighteenth to the middle of the nineteenth centuries."[18] What we learn by tracing the repercussions of revolution in the Andes is that the project for Indian political authority and sovereignty in the New World was another political current flowing through the revolutionary Atlantic. It was a prospect that deeply disturbed imperial authorities but also troubled many creole revolutionaries. Their efforts to suppress it or to downplay or distort its significance should also be seen as integral to the epoch of upheaval and struggle. Their efforts would also shape later historical narratives of the age.

South America and Spanish imperial panic

In the early 1780s, the perception of the Andean revolution in Europe and Spanish anxiety over colonial sovereignty in South America were indelibly marked by inter-imperial rivalry during the War for Independence in North America. France had taken the side of the colonies in order to weaken its British adversary. The North Americans had called on Spain to take a stand as well, but it was cautious, calculating its own interests. The Crown was wary of Portugal, an ally of England, and was waiting for the delivery of a major shipment of silver from the Americas. Yet Spain was still smarting from its earlier loss to England, especially during the Seven Years' War (1756–1763), and was only biding its time before taking the initiative. In the meanwhile, it provided clandestine resources for the American colonists' military campaigns. Finally in April 1779 Spain signed the Treaty of Aranjuez with France (with whom it shared dynastic relations through the Bourbon family), officially announcing its hostility toward England. Spain seized the moment to retake the island of Minorca and the region of Florida. Its strategy was to fortify its position in the Caribbean, and when England signed the peace treaty at Versailles in January 1783, Spain emerged a beneficiary.[19]

The Andean insurrection exploded in this complex moment of international armed conflict. Spain was very concerned by the prospect that England might initiate hostile actions in its territory. At the same time that it fomented anti-colonial revolution in North America, it feared that England might do the same in Spanish America. When the news of an uprising in Peru began to circulate, alarm spread among Spanish authorities in the Viceroyalties of Peru and Río de la Plata as well as in other American territories and at the highest strata of metropolitan government. In March 1781, the situation grew more complicated as the Comunero rebellion broke out in New Granada (today Colombia). In 1781, it seemed that a conflagration had consumed all of Peru, Upper Peru (today Bolivia), and New Granada, and the traditional heartland of Spanish South America seemed to lie in the balance.

The following letter reached New Granada from Lima in February 1781, and from there was sent on to Spain:

> The uprising of the cacique of Tinta, Joseph the 1st Tupamaro, has this city of Lima in consternation […] This causes great concern since they are domestic enemies, besides the English whom we have by sea [...] These Lima tribunals are indecisive and fearful that with such a battalion they could march with the aim of taking this city, which [they] will achieve without difficulty given its lack of defenses [...] It is assumed with reason that if they do not turn toward this city, they will proceed to conquer the provinces of Quito, Choco, Antioquia, and Popayán [in New Granada], if the ardent valor of the inhabitants there does not stop them [...] The cause that instills fear is the emulation that precedes this Indian.[20]

Mixed in with the letters and reports on Peru were others concerning the uprising that erupted in March 1781 in Socorro, New Granada, known as the Rebellion of the Comuneros. The information indicated that the Comuneros were inspired by the insurrection of Tupac Amaru. This movement, according to reports, was now spreading from Quito to Venezuela. In late September, letter-writers mentioned that the English had been seen off the coast and that the rebels were waiting for their assistance, at the same time that they looked with admiration on the struggles of the North American colonists.[21] Another private letter from late September rejected the reports that the movement in Peru had been defeated, and ridiculed the Spanish intendancy authorities for thinking that the people could be so credulous as to believe their assurances.[22]

England and France also had their eyes trained on the Spanish American territories and their diplomatic-intelligence services closely followed the news flowing from Peru and South America. In mid-1780, Jamaican Governor John Dalling expressed confidence in a plan to overturn the Spanish empire in the Americas. With blows struck against Veracruz and Nicaragua, it would be possible "to shake to the very center the enormous, wide extended and ill constructed fabric of Spanish dominion in America [...] At a future period it may be found that Peru may become as easy a prey."[23] In this initial moment, Dalling did not know a great deal about conditions in Peru. Tupac Amaru's movement had not yet begun, but there were already rumors circulating about the revolts in early 1780 against the customs-houses and commercial tax hikes in Arequipa, La Paz, and Cuzco. In October, still prior to the rise of Tupac Amaru, Dalling reported on the "extraordinary revolution" in Peru, and the Secretary of State for America, Lord George Germain, recommended communication with and military provisions for the Peruvian insurgents "to give a fatal wound to the Spanish government."[24] After Tupac Amaru asserted his leadership, British colonial and metropolitan authorities continued to scrutinize the anxious information forthcoming from the region, such as a cache of private and official Spanish correspondence dispatched from Venezuela and seized by the English corsair *Renown* in the Caribbean.[25]

Curbing the news of revolution

Even before Tupac Amaru had risen up in November 1780, the circulation of news about the customs-house and anti-fiscal revolts that had taken place in Arequipa and around the southern Andes earlier in the year was a sensitive point for Spanish officials. They immediately began to wrap the affair in "state-obscurity."[26] The news broke around the Atlantic world in September, when the *Glasgow Mercury* reported that a Spanish packet-boat carrying the first correspondence from Buenos Aires about the "revolutions" had been seized by an English privateer, the *Bellona*. Prior to its capture, the Spanish commander threw the public mail and official accounts overboard and "cautioned all aboard not to give the least information of the state of the country."[27] Nonetheless, some papers and letters were found aboard and the *Mercury* published the sensational news, which included word that the protestors were proclaiming an Inka king and that the Spanish crown faced the loss of America. Richard Cumberland, a British diplomat in Spain, reported in December 1780, that the news from Peru "fills Spain with most melancholy apprehensions; though I have heard many particulars, they are yet involved in too much state-obscurity for me to venture at reporting them."[28]

In the immediate aftermath of the uprising of Tupac Amaru, counter-insurgent Spanish authorities in Cuzco acted to suppress future knowledge of a movement they clearly saw as a challenge to the sovereignty of the Spanish Crown. They started with the meaning and memory of Amaru himself. In the minds of almost the entire "nation of Indians," declared Royal Inspector José Antonio de Areche in the death sentence, Amaru was "from the principal line of the Inkas, as he said himself, and therefore absolute and natural ruler of these dominions and their vassals."[29] Tupac Amaru was thus drawn and quartered, the symbolic punishment for a crime of lese-majesty committed against the sovereign power. Authorities sought to cut off his genealogical line, to destroy all traces of his home, fields, and property, and to eliminate all Inka symbolism in Cuzco society. After burning Amaru's body and casting the ashes into the air, a stone tablet detailing his "crimes" was to be left as the only record of him.[30]

Spanish officials beyond Peru also tried to silence news of Amaru's insurrection. In July 1781, a Venezuelan functionary in Maracaibo wrote in alarm to the Intendant about the strong popular support for Tupac Amaru, and cited the official efforts to play down the situation: "Your Lordship can infer the fatal nature of the times, and that they no longer allow for the dissimulation practiced until now; it is necessary to mix force with prudence."[31] British diplomats felt stymied in their efforts to learn more about conditions. The press reported that the Spanish ambassador at the court in Versailles had news of insurrections in Peru and Mexico, but "did all he could" to downplay the threat and indicate they had been quelled.[32] Even in 1783, a British official stationed in Spain complained:

> Late reports from different quarters mention the continuance and even the increase of the insurrection of South America, but the Spanish ministers are at such pains to throw a veil over the transactions of that continent, that it has not been in my power to obtain any particular or authentic information on the subject.[33]

In spite of the efforts to silence news of the events in Peru, word did indeed spread widely. Between 1780 and 1784, it traveled by land and by boat, carried by travelers and seamen, through personal and state correspondence as well as the maritime press and cosmopolitan gazette culture. The private and public communication was diffuse, and often confused. Word of the highland uprisings quickly reached Lima, capital of the powerful Viceroyalty of Peru, within whose jurisdiction Cuzco fell, and from there spread to Quito, New Granada, Venezuela, and the Caribbean. Buenos Aires to the south – which after 1776 governed Potosí, La Plata, La Paz, and the other provinces of Upper Peru – and Montevideo were other relay points for information to destinations further north in the Atlantic. Rio de Janeiro received travelers and correspondence bearing the latest reports and was another source for the news transmitted through Atlantic maritime circuits.[34] The "fatal news" that Tupac Amaru had proclaimed himself King in Cuzco stirred public awareness in Mexico City in February 1781, as we know from the diary of José Gómez, a common soldier and diarist of the life of the city.[35] In the Caribbean, a hub for information from around the region, Spanish officers in Havana and British officials in Kingston received news from Peru and passed it on to their metropolitan superiors. The *Royal Gazette* in Jamaica offered substantial press coverage, as might be expected given the hostilities between Britain and Spain, and news also cycled through points such as St. Johns and Martinique to North America. In Saint-Domingue, the news circulated publically, some of it rebounding back from France.[36] Local press reports proliferated in the USA, especially in the port cities up and down the eastern seaboard.[37] The Peruvian uprisings became the source of public fascination in the British press – via different transfer points including Kingston and New York – and were the cause of celebration.[38] The Spanish correspondence seized by British privateers, some of which was translated for the press, generated particular notoriety because of its deep tones of panic and gloom.[39] News out of Lisbon appeared in the *Royal Gazettes* of Jamaica and New York.[40] In Italy information evidently arrived not only through the Spanish press, but through the private networks of Jesuits exiled from Spanish America in 1767.[41] The news spread to Amsterdam and other sites in Central Europe, such as Prague, and further east to the Ottoman cities of Smyrna and Constantinople.[42]

In Spain itself, the first public news of turmoil in the Andes preceded the uprising of Tupac Amaru. In October 1780, the *Gazeta de Madrid* published an account written from London in late September on "the uprising (*sublevación*) in four or five provinces of Spanish America."[43] It was in fact the same story initially reported in the *Glasgow Mercury*. But this London account noted the British public was skeptical of the story, considering it quite possibly a government attempt to distract from widespread concerns about Britain's misfortunes in North America and to cause consternation among Britain's rivals. As the *Gazeta* was an official periodical of the Spanish government, the story was accompanied by an editorial note denying (falsely) the Bourbon tax increases and the establishment of new customs-houses and insisting that Indians in South America remained loyal and submissive. Shortly thereafter, the *Gazeta* reported from Lisbon that letters had arrived, from Buenos Aires via Rio de Janeiro, "clearing up the many rumors that have spread about the commotions" that had begun in the city of Arequipa.[44]

When news of the events involving Tupac Amaru reached Spain in late June 1781, it provoked a great public stir: "they spoke of nothing less than the total loss of that immense possession."[45] The Spanish court found itself obliged to respond to the profuse rumors, but the state's efforts to rechannel and recast the information also caused it to circulate further. As the Crown publically issued its version of events, this news was relayed from Madrid and Cádiz to the European press.

On 28 August, the press in Madrid reported the Crown's intervention in the public discussion: "The troubles arisen in Peru have been presented to the public from a point of view so false that the court has taken the decision to give an exact and authentic report."[46] The state's version provided an extended account of the origins of the affair, its early stages, and a profile of "the premier cacique Tupa-Aymaru," said to "descend from the royal family of the Incas, deprived of their throne in 1541 by the death of Atahualpa."[47]

There followed a fairly respectful evaluation:

> It concerned a powerful cacique, Tupac Aymaru, already rich himself, [who] found 50 thousand piasters in the home of the magistrate who perished by his orders, and 40 thousand in that of an official who escaped him. He has a great deal of valor and great talents. He was well brought up in the college of Cuzco, and beside the fact that he was supplied with various small cannon, he had raised the standard of the Inca, which could attract many people. Also, the establishment of the customs-house in Arequipa had caused discontent there; the mutineers had taken up arms, demolished it, and sacked the home of the customs official.[48]

To this point, the story was relatively detailed and without much intentional distortion.

Yet the account ended on a completely false note: "All of these alarming circumstances prompted taking the course of negotiation. Concessions have been made to that redoubtable cacique, and all the troubles have been pacified."[49] In fact, there had been no such negotiations or accord. The assertion that the conflict had been resolved was a clear bid to contain the rumors and indicate that the danger was past. But it demonstrates that the state was indeed genuinely preoccupied by the perceived danger, not only for its own political purposes abroad but for the public repercussions at home. In an uncharacteristic move, its concern to control the public news overrode its own prior policy of state secrecy.

In late September 1781, more news reached Cádiz. A boat from Buenos Aires brought word that the "revolt of Peru" had been extinguished and "Tupac-Amaro" taken prisoner.[50] The report in the Spanish press was apparently based on information released by the Viceroy in Buenos Aires. In this account, the leader was described as a "mestizo" whose parents' occupation was in hauling goods, though he was "truly of the race of caciques."[51] He was said to have used the same devices as Pugachov in Russia to seduce a "weak and credulous" people.[52] The report noted his deceptions and banditry:

> He said he was of the race of the Incas: his uncle and he wore the dress and other marks of sovereignty of the ancients sons of the sun. He assembled an army that was more considerable in number than redoubtable in valor, with which he had devastated several provinces and committed horrors and atrocities that give the lie to his celestial origin.[53]

The Spanish press report concluded:

> Such is the summary of the circumstances of this event, extracted from several letters from Buenos Aires. Any other account reported in the foreign public papers is a deception forged by the English, and merits no credence. One assumes that the court will give circumstantial details of all this agreeable news.[54]

It is important to note how much the tone toward Tupac Amaru and the insurrection had shifted. Rather than being wealthy and well educated, his family's business was said to be in the plebian sphere of transportation; while he was of cacique family, his claims to Inka descent were questionable; he manipulated an ingenuous population with his performances of sovereignty; lacking true military strength, he committed crimes and atrocities that betrayed his putatively divine status. After the impressive first announcement that Tupac Amaru was a true and illustrious Inka defending his people against injustice, he was now depicted as an impostor and brigand who merited no mercy. We can see in this critical shift the direct evidence and operations of disavowal – the reports now denied the Inka any legitimate claim to political sovereignty and reduced the movement to an expression of irrational, immoral, and "atrocious" violence.[55]

This expression of disavowal was evident in the account published in the *Gazeta de Madrid*. Reporting on the news and letters from Buenos Aires, it indicated that the colonial authorities had effectively put an end to the riots (*alborotos*), robberies, and atrocities provoked by "subjects of low extraction who in order to delude the gullible Indians pretended to be the descendants of ancient and noble caciques."[56] An editorial addition to the press report from Cádiz declared that the mutinous "caudillo" now in captivity was Joseph Condorcanqui Camino y Negeruela [*sic*], a mestizo muleteer posing as a cacique of the "distinguished family of the Tupac-Amaro who reside in Cuzco."[57]

These reports published in early October 1781 reflected an official effort to contain and control the information about events which would favor state interests and de-legitimize the Andean revolution in a context in which Spanish governors were clearly preoccupied with inter-imperial conflict. Any other version of affairs, allegedly, would constitute what today would be called "disinformation," that is, propaganda instigated by the English adversary. In fact the information arrived at a time when Spanish officials and the public were anxious about the rumor, circulating in the foreign press, that Commodore George Johnstone had embarked on an expedition to invade Buenos Aires and offer arms and support to the rebels in the districts of Peru and Río de la Plata.[58]

The reports about the pacification of the uprisings were themselves misleading. Tupac Amaru had indeed been executed in April 1781 in Cuzco (a fact still unknown in Spain in early October), but the fires of insurrection continued to burn in the Andean highlands. Only in mid-November 1781, when Tupaj Katari was executed in La Paz, did they begin to abate, and even then, the Inka leadership in Cuzco remained intact.

Two years later, in September 1783, a Londoner wrote in the press that the "repeated reports" of rebellion in South America, which had raised the hopes of Englishmen since 1780, had turned out to be effectively "illusions."[59] He drew the conclusion that the Spanish governors had been too vigilant and spoke of "the softness of the subjects born in climates that hardly favor sentiments of rebellion."[60] If there had been no more successful movement when the Spaniards were caught up in the war with England, he concluded, it was not going to emerge now. The moment of Spanish imperial crisis had apparently passed.

Even so, it seems that the chapter concerning insurrection in Peru was never definitively closed in Spain or beyond it. In late 1783, the news had reached Madrid from Buenos Aires and then Cádiz that "peace had been announced in all parts of the Spanish possessions."[61] But in early 1784, the issue of Peru arose again with reports from Chile, through Cádiz, of "new disturbances" involving Diego Tupal Amer [*sic*], described as "more proud and bold" than the "famous chief" Tupal Amer.[62] The report indicated that Chile had kept vessels at the ready ever since 1780, in case the English should attempt to invade. After this report, there was no subsequent news of final pacification in Peru.[63]

The authorities' scarcely suppressed anxiety over the events in Peru and their efforts to restore public confidence in the legitimacy of Spanish sovereignty are evident in a rather different cultural arena. In 1785, on the occasion of the birth of the two infants Carlos and Felipe to the royal family, and in celebration of the peace treaty with the British, the municipal government of Madrid held a literary competition. Besides the two award-winners for literary merit, it granted a special prize to the play *Atahualpa* written by

Cristóbal María Cortés y Vita in 1784. The play was part of the eighteenth-century vogue around Europe for theatrical accounts of the Inka during the sixteenth-century Spanish conquest in Peru. The *Royal Commentaries* of the Inka Garcilaso de la Vega, published in 1609, was the source for much of this historical imaginary. Voltaire's *Alzire* (1736) and Marmontel's *The Inkas, or the Destruction of Peru* (1777) generated widespread emulation, from England to Germany and Sweden. For the most part, this Inka theater followed the conventions of the Black Legend, which depicted native Americans as the innocent victims of Spanish cruelty and injustice. Cortés's *Atahualpa* breaks from this narrative as it frames Spanish intervention in Peru as disinterested and humane, and provides a justification for Spanish annexation of the territory. The play draws from Garcilaso, but turns Pizarro and Almagro into honorable men who try to help Huáscar, the rightful heir of Huayna Capac, to accede to the throne in the face of his iniquitous brother, the bastard Atahualpa. Atahualpa fears the fulfillment of prophecies that he will die with the arrival of "valiant and irresistible" men.[64] Atahualpa orders the death of Huáscar, but then during a revolt involving Indians and Spaniards, Atahualpa himself dies accidentally, from an arrow shot by an unknown Indian. Despite the Spaniards' noble attempt to preserve Inka sovereignty, both the Inka heirs are destroyed, and the Spaniards are forced to assume sovereign power in Peru.

The neoclassical tragedy clearly had a political-didactic purpose, evident in the fact that it received a special prize for being "worthy of publication" despite its poor literary quality.[65] According to literary critic Angel-Raimundo Fernández, the motive for the award was to "compensate for the situation in Spanish America."[66] Tupac Amaru's revolution had staked a claim to legitimate sovereignty in the Andes. The drama of Cristóbal María Cortes proclaimed, by contrast, that Spain had conquered legitimately, and that there was no legitimate heir to the Inka throne in Peru. Though Tupac Amaru and the Andean uprisings were never mentioned explicitly, we can read the play and its official stamp of approval in this critical conjuncture as an implicit disavowal of Inka sovereignty. In terms of the wider context, we can also read the play as an effort to compensate for the crisis in Spain itself. The jittery state of Spain and sense of a vulnerable sovereignty was generated as much by the shocking news arriving from Peru and South America as by the inter-imperial fray over the anti-colonial movement in North America.

Dissidents and dissonance

The news of the turbulence in Peru and South America not only alarmed Spanish officials and provoked self-interested designs on the part of Spain's imperial rivals at a time of revolution in North America. At least initially, they also stirred conspirators in the shadows of the empire beyond Peru, and kindled the revolutionary imagination beyond Spanish America. But the Andean revolution would gradually fade from view abroad, and when recognized, it increasingly took on darker tones of race war. Within Spanish America, even as resentment over colonial governance mounted, ambivalence or disavowal defined creole dissidents' relation to the past Indian-led insurrection.

In England, the news of the customs-house revolts and then the insurrection of Tupac Amaru proliferated beginning in the fall of 1780, and fed into longstanding popular hostilities toward the Spanish and the old discourse of the Black Legend. Radical intellectuals were clearly intrigued or inspired by the prospect of revolution in the exotic land of the

Inkas. Helen Maria Williams, a member of the Romantic literary scene in London whose political commitments would lead her to relocate to Paris after the revolution burst out on the continent, wrote an epic poem entitled "Peru" in 1784 whose climax invoked the insurrection of the Inka and the prospect of native Peruvian sovereignty:

> But, lo! where bursting desolation's night,
> A sudden ray of glory cheers my sight;
> From my fond eye the tear of rapture flows,
> My heart with pure delight exulting glows:
> A blooming chief of India's royal race,
> Whose soaring soul, its high descent can trace,
> The flag of freedom rears on Chili's plain,
> And leads to glorious strife his gen'rous train:
> And see Iberia bleeds! while vict'ry twines
> Her fairest blossoms round Peruvia's shrines;
> The gaping wounds of earth disclose no more
> The lucid silver, and the glowing ore;
> A brighter glory gilds the passing hour,
> While freedom breaks the rod of lawless power.[67]

The passage was accompanied by a note that announced:

> An Indian descended from the Inca's [sic] has lately obtained several victories over the Spaniards, the gold mines have been for some time shut up; and there is much reason to hope, that these injured nations may recover the liberty of which they have been so cruelly deprived.[68]

Less than a decade later, William Blake would also imagine the "soaring spirit" of revolution in the Americas as "sometimes a lion, stalking upon the mountains" in the Andes: "I see [...] in Mexico an Eagle, and a Lion in Peru."[69] His prophecy of anti-colonial emancipation drifted away from any concrete historical reference into fiery allegory, but it seems nearly certain that he knew of and took inspiration from the insurgent movements of the early 1780s, when he was a radical student in London.[70]

With time, public awareness of the Andean revolution in Europe would dissipate, reduced to the limited knowledge of historians and travelers to the region. The meaning of the episode was also increasingly associated with the specter of racial violence. Helen Maria Williams' friend Alexander von Humboldt (several of whose works Williams translated into English) would later speak about Tupac Amaru in more removed and damning terms. In 1811, Humboldt wrote that the Andean insurrection was little known in Europe, though his own stature would bring it to the attention of a widely flung readership. He had no doubt that the movement had posed a severe crisis to Spanish government: "The great revolt in 1781 very nearly deprived the king of Spain of all the mountainous part of Peru, at the period when Great Britain lost nearly all her colonies in the continent of America."[71] He also admitted his initial attraction toward the figure of Tupac Amaru, and collected primary documents on the uprising during his time in Peru in 1802. But he ultimately disputed Tupac Amaru's Indian identity (he was a mestizo bastard, the son of a monk, Humboldt declared) and questioned his motives (a desire for personal vengeance after being denied noble title). The German traveler asserted that Tupac Amaru's political project to "reestablish at Cuzco the ancient empire of the Inka" degenerated into "a war of extermination against everyone not of [the Indians'] own race."[72] As he put it in the narrative of his travels, translated by Helen Maria Williams in 1818, "A rising for independence became a cruel war between the different castes."[73]

Vicente Pazos Kanki, a pro-independence journalist and politician from Upper Peru who was himself of Indian background, disputed Humboldt's version. In his 1819 memorandum to Henry Clay, written while in New York and soliciting US support for the movement in South America, Pazos objected:

> The revolution of Tupac-Amaru [...] has been misrepresented by historians, and a great injustice has been done to the memory of that illustrious leader. Baron de Humboldt is incorrect in his biographical notice of Tupac-Amaru, having listened to the vulgar tales of the Spaniards, which he heard at Lima, in relation to his character.[74]

Pazos Kanki here defended the Andean revolution in the context of overt struggles for independence from Spain, but in truth it was not only Spanish loyalists who had developed a fraught or negative view of the movement by the 1810s. For South American creoles as well, the events associated with Tupac Amaru came to acquire very ambivalent historical significance. The uprisings in the Andes in 1780–1783 had initially set off chains of radical conspiracy that would span the Americas and Europe. Yet in the decades after 1783, as the prospects for independence waxed and waned, the meaning of revolution in the Andes would become double-edged even for Spanish American dissidents. There was not then any direct line from 1781 to creole independence. On the contrary, the Andean revolution often elicited silences and disavowal as many creole patriots stressed its connotations of race war rather than its implications of legitimate Inka sovereignty.[75]

The trajectory of the Jesuit agitator Juan José Godoy illustrates some of the more immediate Atlantic repercussions of the movement that shook the Andes. The shadowy underground world of Spanish American dissidents is difficult to discern, but the records of imperial espionage and surviving correspondence of the revolutionaries themselves offer important insights into their Atlantic networks. Godoy was a creole native of Mendoza, in the Andean region of Río de la Plata (today Argentina). At the time of the expulsion of the Jesuits from Latin America in 1767, he fled north to Chuquisaca (today Sucre, Bolivia) in Upper Peru. He was captured and eventually sent to Italy where many of his Jesuit brethren were exiled. When the news of revolution in Peru reached him, he apparently traveled to London in May 1781, in the hopes of meeting with British authorities about financing an expedition to overturn Spanish colonial government. In 1785, he suddenly disappeared from London where Spanish intelligence sources had him under surveillance. Spain's Minister of the Indies sent word to his viceroys to track down the fugitive and lure him to Spanish territory. The viceroy (and archbishop) of New Granada Antonio Caballero y Góngora sent a spy to Jamaica who successfully located Godoy in Charleston, South Carolina, in the company of a Cuban. He was found assailing Spanish government, propounding revolution in the Americas, and saying that Peru had already risen up. He was tricked into traveling to Cartagena where he was taken prisoner and interrogated by the Inquisition, including about whether he had spent time in Cuzco and had ties to the uprisings in South America. He was then sent as a prisoner to Cádiz, where he wound up in jail with other survivors of the Tupac Amaru and Comunero uprisings and where he died in 1788.[76]

But another trans-generational revolutionary trajectory – from Peruvian Jesuit Juan Pablo Viscardo y Guzmán to the Venezuelan Francisco de Miranda to the Liberator Simón Bolívar – reveals the longer-term process of ambivalence and disavowal. Viscardo was a creole from Arequipa, Peru, sent into exile in Italy in 1768 like Godoy. On hearing the news of insurrection in Peru, he immediately contacted British consular officials and in 1782 he headed to London to convince the Foreign Office that the time was ripe for an invasion that would trigger independence in South America. He would remain in London for two years, and then relocate there permanently in 1791. Until his death in 1798, he wrote with single-minded intention to bring about revolution in Spanish America, but a subtle shift took place in his outlook. In his initial enthusiasm, he celebrated the "great revolution that occurred in Peru" and he described Tupac Amaru in admiring terms and acknowledged him to be a descendant of the last Inka sovereign.[77] But by the 1790s, he adopted a more distanced tone toward what he called the Peruvian "disturbances" (*troubles* he put it in French) and elevated instead the case of the Comuneros in New Granada.[78] This seems paradoxical since Viscardo was an open advocate of separatism and the Comuneros' demands ostensibly presented a more reformist project, a less radical challenge to the Spanish Crown than did Tupac Amaru. But the Comunero movement gave the reassuring impression of a political project that was creole-led, orderly and rational, and marked by paternal harmony between the castes. In this period, Viscardo emphasized the "attachment and devotion" that Indians felt toward their creole superiors, and he used the relation of domestic service as a metaphor for the harmony that would exist between the races and classes after independence.[79] In his celebrated *Letter to Spanish Americans*, which would be circulated throughout the Americas after his death by Francisco de Miranda, Viscardo made no mention of Tupac Amaru and decried only the blood shed because of the Bourbon Minister of the Indies José de Gálvez's despotic taxation.[80]

Francisco de Miranda probably learned of the Peruvian insurrection in 1781 while serving under Juan Manuel de Cajigal y Monserrat, who was his patron and confidant. Together they fought in the Caribbean campaigns against the British, which included the taking of Pensacola and the Bahamas. Cajigal, after becoming Governor in Cuba, received the "happy news" of the capture and imminent execution of Tupac Amaru, along with accompanying documentation from Cuzco, from the Viceroy of New Granada in July 1781.[81] Miranda deserted in 1783, under persecution from Cajigal's superior Bernardo de Gálvez (the nephew of José de Gálvez) and perhaps encouraged by the sense that revolution was imminent in South America. He began his peripatetic life in North America and Europe, seeking to persuade foreign powers to support Spanish American independence, to recruit allies, and to train new cadre. He met and charmed luminaries wherever he went (including in Helen Maria Williams' salon in Paris), and during his lengthy time in London, he gained access to Viscardo's private archive and copied key documents from it.

In Miranda's own archive figures one document, known as the Letter of the Mantuanos and dated 24 February 1782, which historians have argued was probably fabricated by Miranda. In it, three of the leading creoles in Caracas, including Simón Bolívar's father, express their trepidation over the outcome of the revolts in Peru and Santa Fe de Bogotá, and call on Miranda to lead a movement for independence. The speculation is that Miranda concocted the letter to convince his foreign hosts that he was an important political player who had the backing of elites in Venezuela. In his meetings with Prime Minister Pitt in 1790–1791 and again in 1800, he provided documentation he had collected about the uprisings in Peru and New Granada. For Miranda, the Andean insurrection served as a basis for propaganda and negotiation in the imperial political context.[82]

Miranda also presented high-ranking US and British officials with fairly loose and fanciful plans for what government would look like in an independent and confederated South America. He sought to adopt a British model of constitutional monarchy to the New World setting, and believed it important to employ American terminology that would be comprehensible to the masses. The language he seized on was Andean – the two chiefs of the executive branch would be known as Inkas; the maximal representatives of the provincial assemblies would be *Curacas*, the Quechua term for indigenous governors; the ordinary legislators would be *Amautas*, the term for learned men in Inka society; the supreme military authority would be the *Hatunapa*, or "great captain."[83]

His rousing political proclamations were steeped in invocations of the preconquest and conquest history of South America. His address to the peoples of the "Colombian Continent (alias Hispano-America)" cited the proud deaths of Indians in Mexico, Peru, and Bogota during the conquest, and mentions the execution of Tupac Amaru I by Viceroy Toledo in the sixteenth century.[84] Concerning more recent history, he denounced Minister Gálvez and Royal Inspector Areche for their tyranny. He even explicitly mentioned the conflicts of the early 1780s. But here the historical references were exclusively to the Crown's betrayal of its promise to respect the settlement negotiated by the Comunero leaders at Zipaquirá in 1781. He generally acknowledged the natives and the descendants of conquistadors, side by side, as legitimate rulers in New World. But in his public proclamation, Tupac Amaru and the revolution in Peru in 1780–1781 were erased from contemporary history.[85]

In this, as in other spheres of activity, Simón Bolívar followed the trajectory of his mentor Miranda and then far surpassed him. While Bolívar did on occasion invoke the grandeur of the Inka past and contemporaries identified him as the "avenger of the Inkas," he did not indulge in pro-Inka public discourse like his contemporaries in Argentina. It is remarkable that the liberator of Peru, who visited Cuzco in triumph in 1825 and trod the same plaza where Tupac Amaru was so notoriously executed, never publicly acknowledged the leader of the 1781 insurrection.[86] He would have been even less inclined to invoke the memory of Tupaj Katari when he passed through La Paz or Tomás Katari when he reached Chuquisaca, the capital of the new nation named for him. This was not a case of ignorance or accidental oversight.

But Bolívar's obliviousness must also be seen in a wider Atlantic light. He grappled with the underlying problem in his famous "Jamaica Letter" of 6 September 1815, written while in exile in Kingston:

> We are neither Indians nor Europeans, but rather a middle species between the legitimate proprietors of the country and the Spanish usurpers; in sum, being ourselves Americans by birth, and our rights those of Europe, we have to dispute these rights with those from this country, and maintain ourselves in it against the invasion of the invaders; thus we find ourselves in the most extraordinary and complicated case.[87]

This startlingly frank passage contains an explicit admission that indigenous peoples could claim legitimate possession of the New World territory.[88] Independence raised the prospect of a restitution of sovereignty, and Indians were the rivals for the rights to dominion. In this "extraordinary and complicated case," the deeper problem was not that Tupac Amaru stood for a monarchist program and Bolívar for a republican one. Amaru could not be a precursor or an inspiration because he represented a threat to creoles' very right to rule.

Yet in a subsequent letter, written sometime after 28 September 1815 to the editor of the Jamaican *Royal Gazette*, Bolívar posed a counterpoint intended to defuse the anxiety over color and caste difference. Responding to the same presumption of racial antagonism in the Americas that had been raised by Humboldt, Bolívar began by addressing the concerns of European and US politicians that "caste difference" formed the main obstacle to independence.[89] If white Spanish Americans were the minority of the population, they were looked up to by their servants because of their superior intellect and benevolence:

> The Spanish colonist does not oppress his domestic with excessive labors; he treats him like a comrade; he educates him in the principles of morality and humanity, as Jesus's religion prescribes. As his gentleness is unlimited, he exercises it in its full amplitude with that benevolence which inspires a familial communication.[90]

Furthermore, he held, the abundance of territory and resources and the variety of colors of people would prevent open conflict or the attempt by one race to overwhelm the others. Indians in particular should not be a source of concern, he asserted, in a passage that utterly denied the experience of Indian insurrection in Peru:

> The Indian has a character so peaceful that he only desires repose and solitude; he does not aspire even to be the chief of his own tribe, much less dominate others. Fortunately, this kind of men is the one that least demands predominance; although its number exceeds that of the sum of other inhabitants. This part of the American population is a sort of barrier to contain the other parties; it does not pretend to authority, because it does not desire it nor does it consider itself capable of exercising it, contenting itself with its peace, its land, and its family. The Indian is the friend of all […][91]

He insisted, clearly negating his own concerns, on the fact of "perfect harmony" among the New World inhabitants and that this should calm the "fear of color":

> Thus, it seems we should count on the gentleness of much more than half the population, since the Indians and whites compose three-fifth of the total population, and if we add the mestizos who share the blood of both, the increase is more appreciable and the fear of color (*el temor de los colores*) diminishes as a result […]
> We are thus authorized to believe that all the children of Spanish America, of whatever color or condition they may be, profess a reciprocal fraternal affection that no manipulation is capable of altering […]
> Up until now, one admires the most perfect harmony among those who have been born on this soil […][92]

In his letter, Bolívar resorted to some of the same devices that Viscardo had used in his essays in the 1790s, including reference to the master–servant relationship to illustrate the fraternal harmony among the races. The genealogy from Viscardo to Bolívar was actually more a matter of political and rhetorical strategy than objective demographic and sociological analysis. In a trans-Atlantic frame of political diplomacy, they both sought to persuade the British that the creole minority enjoyed the loyal affection of the colored majority. With such an agenda, the Andean revolution of 1780 and its con-notations of racial violence and claims to Indian sovereignty would best be left in silence.

Reverberations and silences

Within one generation, the set of insurgencies in the southern Andes had triggered a range of responses around the Atlantic world. The Spanish state in a moment of imperial crisis deployed methods of silencing and public dissimulation, denigration of the rebel movements and affirmation of its own threatened sovereignty. As Spain was well aware, its recurrent adversary England followed Peruvian developments closely, contem-plating the possibilities for intervention in South America, but ultimately refraining from active support for nascent separatist forces in the region. The political imagination of rad-icals in Europe was briefly caught by the exotic circumstances of a pretender to the Inka throne returning to right the wrongs of Spanish conquest, a familiar theme of eighteenth-century theater and opera. But with time, men and women of European letters lost their initial sympathy for the insurrection, with some recalling it mainly as an instance of barbar-ous violence.

Of more lasting impact, a network of Spanish American dissidents was initially fired by the prospects of revolution in the Andes, and they corresponded and conspired around the Atlantic. But the meaning of the Andean revolution was double-edged for them, and for a significant number, their enthusiasm also waned with time. Ultimately many creole dissidents came to view the Andean movements in a similar way to that of their peninsular enemies: as instances of racial and caste warfare. The simultaneous Comunero movement in New Granada, in which Indians and plebians mobilized under creole leader-ship, represented for them a less threatening example of resistance to colonial despotism. For those who advocated republicanism, the notion of an Inka king posed yet another problem. But there was an even deeper level to Spanish American discomfort with the Andean revolution. Not only did it evoke memories of racial antagonism rather than patriotic unity against the Spanish. Not only did it stand for monarchism rather than a liberal or republican program. It meant the prospect of a nation under Indian rule. While nativist rhetoric and iconography could be attractive, Creole patriots were no less troubled by the real prospect of Indian sovereignty than were their metropolitan Spanish adversaries.

If the historiography about the Age of Revolution has rarely taken note of the revolution in the Andes, it is not because the region actually existed in isolation from the Atlantic pol-itical theater, for it did not. Rather, we can trace the production of silences in historical dis-course back to the Age of Revolution itself. It is not that Atlantic contemporaries were oblivious to the radical connotations of events in the southern Andes. It is precisely because they were aware of the profound upheaval and implications for change that there emerged such subtle and diverse expressions of disavowal. The repudiation of Indian sovereignty that marked the period would later shape the historical narratives about that era as a time of transition to political modernity. That so-called modernity would be defined in terms of Enlightenment notions of self-determination, representative democracy, and liberal individualism and citizenship. Such narratives would have no place for an anti-colonial emancipation movement in the Americas that drew upon alternative conceptions of self-determination, communal democracy, and native territorial rights, and that envisioned a society in which Indians ruled rather than served.

Notes

1. "This event is too interesting for us not to repair this neglect." The word *oubli* can be understood as oversight, neglect, omission, forgetting, or oblivion.
2. Serulnikov, *Revolution in the Andes*, 68.
3. The literature on these movements is abundant but for recent studies, which include fuller bibliographic treatments, see Thomson, *We Alone Will Rule*; Robins, *Genocide and Millenialism*; Serulnikov, *Subverting Colonial Authority* and *Revolution in the Andes*; and Walker, *Tupac Amaru Rebellion*.
4. Cited in Lewin, *Rebelión de Túpac Amaru*, 413.
5. Klooster, *Revolutions*, 127. Langley, *Americas*.
6. Note that there is debate as to whether or not Latin American independence should even be considered in the context of Atlantic revolution. See Breña, "Independencias americanas."
7. The Polish-Argentine scholar Boleslao Lewin's magisterial study of the Andean experience does indeed pursue the questions of Enlightenment thought, European imperial political context, and Atlantic networks of radical conspiracy that we associate with the Age of Revolution, yet his work has been overlooked in the historiography of Atlantic revolution.
8. Charles Walker believes that a mortality estimate of 100,000 may be reasonable for the Andes, where most of the violence took place from 1780 to 1781. This figure far exceeds estimates for the revolutionary war in North America between 1775 and 1783. Walker, *Tupac Amaru Rebellion*, 16.
9. Guerra, "Forms of Communication."
10. Scott, "The Common Wind"; Ferrer, "Noticias de Haití"; Soriano, "Rumors of Change."
11. Sergio Serulnikov's synthetic study *Revolution in the Andes* employs the language of revolution, as I have done in other work. As for late-eighteenth-century observers, they used many of the same terms to describe the movement as historians in the twentieth century, including the term revolution. Again, one can debate whether they understood the term revolution in a purportedly modern sense, but I believe that a debate over the modernity of the language would distract from the fact that they clearly saw the movement as a profound challenge to the constituted social and political order in the Andes.
12. Thompson, *Making of the English Working Class*, 12.
13. For another new reflection on the relationship between Tupac Amaru's insurgency and the Age of Revolution, which also considers the issues of geography and outcome and argues that the Andean movement did not pose a major threat to Atlantic power structures like the Haitian revolution, see Walker, "¿Revolución nor-atlántica?"
14. This is not to say that Andean peoples were un-modern or anti-modern either, but it is not my intention to enter into a discussion of who or what is or is not modern.
15. My thinking about this question has been influenced by the rich literature on the repercussions of the Haitian revolution. Besides Trouillot and Fischer, the work of Julius Scott, David Geggus, Ada Ferrer, and María Cristina Soriano has been especially stimulating.
16. Trouillot, *Silencing the Past*; Ferrer, "Talk about Haiti"; Fischer, *Modernity Disavowed*.
17. Again, the exception is Lewin. The converse phenomenon – specifically the reception of news about the French Revolution in Peru – has received attention. See the work of Rosas, *Del trono a la guillotina*.
18. Adelman, *Sovereignty and Revolution*, 2.
19. Despite its victory in Minorca, Spain failed to dislodge the English from Gibraltar. Spain had ceded Florida as part of a settlement after the English invasion of Havana in 1763, but it won the battle of Pensacola in May 1781, thereby recovering the eastern part of Florida. In the Treaty of Versailles, all of Florida was restored to Spain.

20. Caracas dispatches taken by the privateer "Renown," 1781; Noticias que vinieron en el correo de Lima que llegó el dia 1 de febrero de 1781 a Sta. Fe, f. 179. The National Archives, London (Hereafter TNA): Foreign Office (Hereafter FO), 95/7/2, ffs. 58–293, Spain and Spanish America, Supplementary correspondence.

21. Ibid., Documents 4, 6, 11.

22. Ibid., Document 7.

23. John Dalling, Governor of Jamaica, to Lord George Germain, Jamaica, no. 75, 23 June 1780, ffs. 64–70. See especially ffs. 65–65v. TNA: Colonial Office (Hereafter CO), 137/78.

24. John Dalling, Governor of Jamaica, "Report on Military Operations on the Mainland," Jamaica, no. 81, 25 October 1780, ffs. 48–48v.; "Draft Dispatch from Secretary of State to Dalling," 13 January 1781, ffs. 90v–91. TNA: CO, 137/79.

25. Caracas dispatches taken by the privateer "Renown," 1781, f. 179. TNA: FO, 95/7/2, ffs. 58–293, Spain and Spanish America, Supplementary correspondence.

26. Richard Cumberland, 1780, f. 267v. TNA: State Papers (Hereafter SP), 94/209.

27. *The Glasgow Mercury*: containing a report of the taking of the Spanish packet Cologn by the privateer Bellona, ffs. 417–417v. TNA: SP, 54/47/415.

28. Richard Cumberland, 1780, f. 267v. TNA: SP, 94/209. He added, "[Spain's] condition is grown so truly desperate that even peace in Europe could not save her from ruin in America."

29. For the death sentence by Areche, see Comisión Nacional del Bicentenario, *Colección Documental*, 268–277. An English excerpt is found in Stavig and Schmidt, eds., *Tupac Amaru and Catarista Rebellions*, 130–135 (see 130–131 for these quotes).

30. Ibid., 133.

31. Informe de Joaquín Alfaro, Administrador de rentas del Tabaco en la Provincia de Maracaibo, al Intendente de Ejército y Real Hacienda, Don José Avalos, Maracaibo, 24 de Julio de 1781, Archivo General de Indias, Seville: Caracas, 477. My thanks to Cristina Soriano for this reference.

32. The news dated from mid-July was published in the *Royal Gazette* of Jamaica, 27 October to 3 November 1781, Vol. 3, No. 133, 698.

33. Richard Cumberland, Robert Liston, and others, January 1781 to December 1783, f. 871, TNA: FO, 72/1.

34. See the Irish *Cork Evening Post* story of 29 August 1782, published in the *Royal Gazette* of New York, 19 October 1782, 3.

35. José Gómez, Diario de México, Mexico City, 1776–1789, f. 63 (153), Bancroft Library, Berkeley: MSS, M-M105. My thanks to William Taylor for the suggestion to review Gómez's diary.

36. It had been unclear whether Haitian leader Jean-Jacques Dessalines' invocations of the Inka in the war against France and at independence reflected an awareness of the uprising of Tupac Amaru. Bernard Camier and Laurent Dubois have convincingly argued that Dessalines' discourse could have drawn from Voltaire's work *Alzire* (1736), which played in Saint-Domingue theaters. See Camier and Dubois, "Voltaire and Dessalines." But an awareness of Tupac Amaru seems likely now that we know that the news of the Andean revolution was public in Saint-Domingue in the early 1780s. The evidence also points to a link between the theatrical and political worlds: coming soon after the news from Peru had arrived, the staging of *Alzire* in Le Cap and Port-au-Prince in 1783 involved a degree of enthusiasm (including purportedly authentic Inka costumes) unseen prior to that time. For the news in Saint-Domingue, see *Affiches Américaines*, 9 October 1781; 1 May 1782; 4 June 1783; 2 August 1783; 2 October 1784.

37. The press covered it from New Hampshire and Massachusetts down to South Carolina and Georgia, with New York a significant source of stories for other points. My thanks to Kathryn Callaghan for her research collaboration.

38. For news, letters, and opinions in the London press, see, for example, *Morning Chronicle and London Advertiser* (5 October 1780, 6 January 1781); *Morning Post and Daily Advertiser* (28 September, 3 October, 6 October, 17 November, 20 November 1780); *Lloyd's Evening Post* (4 October, 18–20 October 1780); *Whitehall Evening Post* (15 September 1780); *London Chronicle* (6 November 1781); *Morning Herald and Daily Advertiser* (7 January 1782). My thanks to Linton Melita for his research collaboration. For the Irish press, see, for example, the *Dublin Evening Post*, 8 November 1781. My thanks to Max Mishler for the Dublin references.

39. The captured Spanish warship *Diligencia* was the source of early information about a revolt said to be in five provinces of Peru, with Arequipa as the headquarters. The story appeared in the *Royal Gazette* of New York, 16 September 1780, 3. The *Glasgow Mercury* story with correspondence from Buenos Aires and Montevideo was a bigger sensation. See *The Glasgow Mercury*: containing a report of the taking of the Spanish packet Cologn by the privateer Bellona, ffs. 417–417v. TNA: SP, 54/47/415. See also the *Royal Gazette* from New York, 6 December 1780, 3. The privateer *Renown* captured letters from Peru, New Granada, and Venezuela. See the reports from Martinique in the *Pennsylvania Packet*, 29 November 1781; the story from the *Royal South Carolina Gazette* of 3 January 1782, published in the *Royal Gazette* of New York on 23 February 1782; and Caracas dispatches taken by the privateer "Renown," TNA: FO, 95/7/2, ffs. 58–293, Spain and Spanish America, Supplementary correspondence.

40. *Royal Gazette* of Jamaica, 17–24 November 1781, Vol. 3, No. 136, 794; *Royal Gazette* of New York, 19 January 1782, 3.

41. Juan Pablo Viscardo y Guzmán claimed to have received secret correspondence that included information from people who had known Tupac Amaru personally in Cuzco. See Viscardo y Guzmán, *Obra completa*, 5–6.

42. See for example, the *Gazette d'Amsterdam*, 3 October 1780; 29 June 1781; and 23 and 26 October 1781. The commentary in Prague, drawn from Viennese sources, speculated on the contrast between Spanish attempts to downplay the news and other reports, such as those of the British. One account asked, "Who is so impartial as to tell us what the situation is in Peru?" See Roedl, "Insurrección de Túpac Amaru." My thanks to Ana María Lorandi for this reference. For news from Smyrna, see the *Connecticut Journal* (out of New Haven), 8 September 1784, 2. For Constantinople, see the *United States Chronicle* (out of Providence, Rhode Island), 2 September 1784, 2.

43. *Gazeta de Madrid*, no. 85, 24 October 1780, 771–774.

44. *Gazeta de Madrid* no. 87, 31 October 1780, 794–795. Nearly a year later, a letter written in Cádiz said that word of the revolt in South America at this time had "raced rapidly from one end of Europe to the other." See *Gazette d'Amsterdam*, no. 52, 29 June 1781.

45. *Gazette d'Amsterdam*, no. 85, 23 October 1781. The correspondence from Madrid that reached Amsterdam is dated 18 September of that year. The Amsterdam paper remarked that the story was "singularly curious" for two reasons. It contained unusually intriguing information, which presumably included the fact that Tupac Amaru was a

> descendant of the imperial family of the Incas, which was thought to be extinct due to the death of Atabalipa [sic], the last emperor of Peru, strangled in 1541 by order of Don Diego Almagro, the companion of Francisco Pizarro, conqueror of that empire.

Also surprising was the "candid tone" of the official report. These quotes are from ibid. See also *Gazette d'Amsterdam*, no. 86, 26 October 1781.

46. *Gazette des Gazettes*, première quinzaine octobre 1781, 28.

47. Ibid., 29.

48. Ibid., 31.

49. Ibid.

50. *Gazette des gazettes*, seconde quinzaine novembre 1781, 23.

51. Ibid., 23–24.

52. Ibid., 24.

53. Ibid.

54. Ibid., 25. This account spread in English as well. See, for example, the *New Hampshire Gazette*, 9 March 1782, 2.

55. *Gazette des gazettes*, seconde quinzaine novembre 1781, 24.

56. *Gazeta de Madrid*, no. 81, 9 October 1781, 807.

57. Ibid.

58. Ibid., 806. An earlier account from April in London asserted that Johnstone was headed to Buenos Aires in the company of a shadowy ex-Jesuit who had been on the packet-boat seized by the *Bellona* in 1780. See *Gazeta de Madrid*, no. 37, 8 May 1781, 372. A previous

story from London in January 1780 had claimed that Admiral Edward Hugues was on his way from the East Indies to invade Spanish dominions along the Pacific Coast. *Gazeta de Madrid*, no. 11, 8 February 1780, 99–100.

59. *Gazette des Gazettes*, première quinzaine d'octobre 1783, 70.

60. Ibid.

61. The news of 29 December 1783 appeared in the *Gazette des Gazettes* in the first half of February 1784, 31. A similar report had arrived in Madrid in mid-1782: "The greatest tranquility reigns in all Peru and [Spain's] possessions in South America, where her troops have had the most advantageous success." *Gazette des Gazettes*, première quinzaine d'aout 1782, 28.

62. The reference is to Diego Cristobal Tupac Amaru, the cousin who took over the leadership of the movement after José Gabriel Tupac Amaru's capture. Charles Walker has shown how Spanish authorities considered Diego Cristobal's forces a profound threat until he was executed in July 1783. See Walker, *Tupac Amaru Rebellion*, 257.

63. *Gazette des Gazettes*, seconde quinzaine de juin de 1784, 36–37.

64. Fernández Cabezón and Vallejo González, "América en el teatro español," 111. They provide a synopsis of the play.

65. The award for *Atahualpa* was announced in the *Gazeta de Madrid*, no. 44, 1 June 1784, 474–475.

66. Fernández, "Dos dramaturgos navarros," 718.

67. Williams, *Poems*, sixth canto, lines 319–332.

68. Ibid., sixth canto, note 4. The poem elicited eulogistic sonnets from contemporaries, including her friend William Wordsworth. For literary treatments, see Kennedy, *Helen Maria Williams* and Cole Heinowitz, *Spanish America and British Romanticism*.

69. "America, a Prophecy" (1793), in Blake, *Complete Poetry and Prose*, 51–52.

70. Erdman, *Blake*, 251, 259.

71. Humboldt, *Political Essay*, vol. I, 200.

72. Humboldt, *Political Essay*, vol. I, 201; vol. IV, 244, 262.

73. Humboldt, *Personal Narrative*, vol. III, 438.

74. Pazos, *Letters*, 252.

75. I am unable here to explore more fully the impact of the Andean revolution on the independence process in Spanish America in the early nineteenth century. For more on this, including the contradictory implications of Tupac Amaru for Pazos Kanki and anticolonial revolutionaries in Argentina in the 1810s, see Thomson, "El reencabezamiento."

76. Lewin, *Rebelión de Túpac Amaru*, 219–222; Battlori, *El abate Viscardo*, 87–93; Donoso, *Persecusión, proceso y muerte*.

77. Viscardo y Guzmán, *Obra completa*, 5, 12.

78. "Ensayo histórico sobre los disturbios de América meridional en el año 1780," in ibid., 43–58.

79. "Esbozo político sobre la situación actual de América española," in ibid., 88.

80. For more on Viscardo y Guzman, see Thomson, "El reencabezamiento"; and D. A. Brading's introduction to Viscardo y Guzmán, *Letter to the Spanish Americans*.

81. Archivo General de la Nación, Mexico City, Correspondencia de Diversas Autoridades, vol. 21, exp. 27, ffs. 187–191. In *A Way in the World*, V. S. Naipaul imagines that Miranda heard of Tupac Amaru's execution while negotiating with British officers in Jamaica in 1781. In his telling, the news of the grisly execution of Tupac Amaru touched a nerve in Miranda and made the rebellious young man realize what his own fate would be if he challenged Spanish rule. It was in the back of his mind when he deserted, writes Naipaul.

82. Miranda, *América espera*, xxxv–xxxvi; Racine, *Francisco de Miranda*, 27–28; Boulton, "Miranda y la carta de los mantuanos," 1, 4.

83. Miranda, *América espera*, 286–289. Miranda drew here from the *Royal Commentaries of the Incas* by Peruvian chronicler Garcilaso de la Vega.

84. The reference to the "Colombian Continent" is found in Miranda, *América espera*, 263.

85. Ibid., 263–271.

86. He did refer to "Tupac-Amaru" in his 18 August 1815 letter to the *Royal Gazette* in Jamaica, but this was a reference to the sixteenth-century Inka leader executed by Viceroy Toledo, a story

that would have known to Bolívar through Garcilaso. See Sociedad Bolivariana, *Escritos del Libertador*, vol. 8, 54–68. I am grateful to Michael Zeuske for tracking down the reference. Bolívar's silence about Tupac Amaru is noteworthy since others on Bolívar's staff did acknowledge the Cuzco leader. See Miller, *Memoirs*, vol. 1, 16–19. Miller also cites General Daniel O'Leary's admiration for Tupac Amaru, in vol. 2, 225–226.

87. It is notable that the English translation of the letter, first published in the *Jamaica Quarterly Journal* in 1818, replaced the telling phrase "the legitimate proprietors of the country" (*legítimos proprietarios del país*) with "original natives." It is quite possible that Bolívar was himself responsible for this apparent example of disavowal since he was in close touch with the presumed translator General John Robertson during his exile in Jamaica. For a thorough treatment of the text and its various editions and translations, see Sociedad Bolivariana de Venezuela, *Escritos del Libertador*, vol. 8, 73–249.

88. Bolívar repeated this notion in his Angostura address of 15 February 1819: "Americans by birth and Europeans by rights, we find ourselves in the conflict of disputing with the Indians (*los naturales*) the titles of possession." See Sociedad Bolivariana, *Escritos del Libertador*, vol. 15.

89. Sociedad Bolivariana, *Escritos del Libertador*, vol. 8, 262.

90. Ibid., 262–263.

91. Ibid., 263.

92. Ibid., 264–265.

Acknowledgements

Numerous colleagues have given me leads and clues for this project over many years, a number of whom are cited in the notes. For their comments and editorial help, I am especially grateful to Ada Ferrer, Sibylle Fischer, Sergio Serulnikov, Michael A. McDonnell, Forrest Hylton, Manuel Barcia, and the two anonymous readers of this article. Special thanks go to Marcus Rediker and the organizers of the "Future of Atlantic, Transnational, and World History" conference, University of Pittsburgh, May 2014, where the paper was first presented. It also benefited from the comments of the participants in the Atlantic History Workshop, New York University, September 2014.

Disclosure statement

No potential conflict of interest was reported by the author.

References

Adelman, Jeremy. *Sovereignty and Revolution in the Iberian Atlantic*. Princeton, NJ: Princeton University Press, 2006.

Battlori, Miguel. *El abate Viscardo: Historia y mito de la intervención de los jesuitas en la independencia de Hispanoamérica*. Caracas: Instituto Panamericano de Geografía e Historia, 1953.

Blake, William. *The Complete Poetry and Prose of William Blake*. Revised edition by David Erdman. New York: Doubleday, 1988.

Boulton, Alfredo. "Miranda y la carta de los mantuanos." *El Tiempo*, May 15, 1960, Lecturas Dominicales.

Breña, Roberto. "Las independencias americanas, la revolución española y el enfoque atlántico." *Historia y Política* 24 (2010): 11–22.

Camier, Bernard, and Laurent Dubois. "Voltaire and Dessalines in the Theater of the Atlantic." Paper presented at the "Southern Intellectual History Circle Meeting," College of William and Mary, February 23–25, 2012.

Cole Heinowitz, Rebecca. *Spanish America and British Romanticism, 1777–1826: Rewriting Conquest*. Edinburgh, UK: Edinburgh University Press, 2010.

Comisión Nacional del Bicentenario de la Revolución Emancipadora de Túpac Amaru. *Colección Documental del Bicentenario de la Revolución Emancipadora de Túpac Amaru*. Tomo III, 1. Lima: P.L. Villanueva, 1981.

Donoso, Ricardo. *Persecusión, proceso y muerte de Juan José Godoy, reo de estado*. Buenos Aires: J.H. Matera, 1960.

Erdman, David. *Blake: Prophet Against Empire*. 3rd ed. Princeton, NJ: Princeton University Press, 1977.

Fernández, Angel-Raimundo. "Dos dramaturgos navarros en la transición del siglo XVIII al XIX." *Príncipe de Viana* 230 (2003): 715–736.

Fernández Cabezón, Rosalía, and Irene Vallejo González. "América en el teatro español del s. XVIII." *Teatro. Revista de Estudios Culturales/A Journal of Cultural Studies* 6–7 (1995): 107–112.

Ferrer, Ada. "Noticias de Haití en Cuba." *Revista de Indias* LXIII, no. 229 (2003): 675–694.

Ferrer, Ada. "Talk about Haiti: The Archive and the Atlantic's Haitian Revolution." In *Tree of Liberty: Cultural Legacies of the Haitian Revolution in the Atlantic World*, edited by Doris Garraway, 23–40. Charlottesville: University of Virginia Press, 2008.

Fischer, Sibylle. *Modernity Disavowed: Haiti and the Cultures of Slavery in the Age of Revolution*. Durham, NC: Duke University Press, 2004.

Guerra, Francois-Xavier. "Forms of Communication, Political Spaces, and Cultural Identities in the Creation of Spanish American Nations." In *Beyond Imagined Communities: Reading and Writing the Nation in Nineteenth-Century Latin America*, edited by Sara Castro-Klarén and John Charles Chasteen, 3–32. Washington, DC: Woodrow Wilson Center Press, 2003.

Humboldt, Alexander von. *Political Essay on New Spain* (1st ed., 1811). Vols. I, IV. Translated from the French by John Black. London: Longman, Hurst, Rees, Orme, and Brown, 1814.

Humboldt, Alexander von. *Personal Narrative of Travels to the Equinoctial Regions of the New World, During the Years 1799-1804*. Vol. III. Translated from the French by Helen Maria Williams. London: Longman, Hurst, Rees, Orme, and Brown, 1818.

Kennedy, Deborah. *Helen Maria Williams and the Age of Revolution*. Lewisburg, PA: Bucknell University Press, 2002.

Klooster, Wim. *Revolutions in the Atlantic World: A Comparative History*. New York: New York University Press, 2009.

Langley, Lester. *The Americas in the Age of Revolution: 1750–1850*. New Haven, CT: Yale University Press, 1998.

Lewin, Boleslao. *La rebelión de Túpac Amaru y los orígenes de la independencia de hispanoamérica* (1st ed., 1943). Expanded 3rd ed. Buenos Aires: Hachette, 1967.

Miller, John. *Memoirs of General Miller: In the Service of the Republic of Peru*. 2nd ed. 2 vols. London: Longman, Rees, Orme, Brown, and Green, 1828/1829.

Miranda, Francisco de. *América espera*. Caracas: Biblioteca Ayacucho, 1982.

Naipaul, V. S. *A Way in the World*. New York: Knopf, 1994.

Pazos, Vicente. *Letters on the United Provinces of South America, Addressed to the Hon. Henry Clay*. Translated by Platt Crosby. New York: J. Seymour, 1819.

Racine, Karen. *Francisco de Miranda: A Transatlantic Life in the Age of Revolution*. Wilmington, DE: SR Books, 2003.

Robins, Nicholas. *Genocide and Millenialism in Upper Peru: The Great Rebellion of 1780–1782*. Westport, CT: Praeger, 2002.

Roedl, Bohumir. "La insurrección de José Gabriel Túpac Amaru vista desde la Praga del año 1781." *Ibero-Americana Pragensia* XVIII (1984): 177–179.

Rosas Lauro, Claudia. *Del trono a la guillotina. El impacto de la Revolución Francesa en el Perú (1789–1808)*. Lima: IFEA, 2006.

Scott, Julius. "The Common Wind: Currents of Afro-American Communication in the Era of the Haitian Revolution." PhD diss., Duke University, 1986.

Serulnikov, Sergio. *The Revolution of Túpac Amaru*. Durham, NC: Duke University Press, 2013.

Sociedad Bolivariana de Venezuela. *Escritos del Libertador*. Vols. 8, 15. Caracas: Cuatricentenario de la Ciudad de Caracas, 1972/1982.

Soriano, María Cristina. "Rumors of Change: Repercussions of Caribbean Turmoil and Social Conflicts in Venezuela (1790–1810)." PhD diss., New York University, 2011.

Stavig, Ward, and Ella Schmidt, eds. *The Tupac Amaru and Catarista Rebellions: An Anthology of Sources*. Indianapolis, IN: Hackett, 2008.

Thompson, E. P. *The Making of the English Working Class*. 1st ed., 1963. New York: Vintage, 1966.

Thomson, Sinclair. *We Alone Will Rule: Native Andean Politics in the Age of Insurgency*. Madison: University of Wisconsin Press, 2002.

Thomson, Sinclair. "El reencabezamiento: Impactos, lecciones y memorias de la insurrección amarista/katarista en la independencia andina. (Los itinerarios de Juan Pablo Viscardo y Guzmán y Vicente Pazos Kanki)." In *De juntas, guerrillas, héroes y conmemoraciones*, edited by Rossana Barragán, 11–46. La Paz: Alcaldía de La Paz, 2010.

Trouillot, Michel-Rolph. *Silencing the Past: Power and the Production of History*. Boston: Beacon Press, 1995.

Viscardo y Guzmán, Juan Pablo. *Obra completa*. Lima: Banco del Crédito del Perú, 1988.

Viscardo y Guzmán, Juan Pablo. *Letter to the Spanish Americans: A Facsimile of the Second English edition (London, 1810)*. Introduction by D. A. Brading. Providence, RI: John Carter Brown Library, 2002.

Walker, Charles F. "La Rebelión de Túpac Amaru: ¿una revolución nor-atlántica?" Lecture, Universidad Diego Portales, Santiago, Chile, August 2014.

Walker, Charles F. *The Tupac Amaru Rebellion*. Cambridge, MA: Harvard University Press, 2014.

Williams, Helen Maria. *Poems*. Vol. 2. 2nd ed. London: T. Cadell, 1791.

Index

Adanson, M. 90
Adelman, J. 2, 90, 112
Africa 6–7, 17, 20, 60, 89–106
African Association 98–9
Africans 7, 20, 23, 30, 90, 94–5, 97–100
Age of Revolution 1–14; in Africa 89–106; in
    Batavia 70–88; and British commerce 45–69;
    and Guajiros 15–44; and Tupac Amaru
    movement 107–31
Alcoy, A. de 23–4
Altea, P. de 26
American Indians *see* Native Americans
American Psychiatric Association (APA) 58
American War of Independence 32–3, 73, 91,
    112
Americas 1–2, 4, 6–8, 16–17, 19; and Africa 90–1,
    97–8; and Batavian Revolution 73; and British
    commerce 46, 53, 55–6, 58, 60; and Guajiros
    29, 33; and Tupac Amaru movement 108–10,
    112–15, 117–24
Amherst, J. 54
Andes 1, 7–8, 33, 107–13, 115, 117–20, 122,
    124
anti-colonial movements 3, 8, 16, 108, 112,
    118–19, 124
Apaza, J. 108
Arébalo, A. 27–34
Areche, J.A. de 114, 122
Argentina 120, 122
Armas, J. de 20, 29
Articles of War 46, 49–50, 52
Asia 4
Assembly of Neighbourhood Councils 6, 75,
    78–80, 82, 84
Atahualpa, King 115, 117–18
Atlantic 3–8, 15–16, 18–21, 29–31, 33–4; and
    Africa 90, 100; Atlantic Revolutions 1–2, 17,
    32, 35, 71–2, 108–9, 112, 124; and Batavia 73;
    militarization 45–69; and Tupac Amaru
    movement 107–31
autonomy 6–7, 16, 27, 35, 70–88

Bahamas 121
banditry 20, 116

Banks, J. 99
Bastidas, R. de 18
Batavian National Convention 70–4, 76–80, 82
Batavian Republic 70, 72, 80
Batavian Revolution 6, 70–88
Bayly, C.A. 2, 4
Benot, Y. 98
Black Legend 118
Blackstone, W. 49
Blake, W. 119
Bolívar, S. 121–3
Bolivia 110, 112, 120
Boonacker, H. 78
Bosch, B. 73, 76–7, 80, 82
Bouquet, H. 53
Bourbon Reforms 18, 34, 107, 110, 112, 115,
    121
bourgeoisie 111
Boyd, J. 55
Brandon, P. 6, 70–88
Brazil 109
Britain 15, 33–4, 45–69, 71–2, 115, 119
British 15–16, 20–1, 24–8, 30–1, 35; and Africa
    90–2, 98–9; Army 45–69; and Batavian
    Revolution 77; Empire 60–1; and Tupac Amaru
    movement 112–15, 117, 120–3
Bruix, A.E. 99
bureaucracy 6, 72
Burton, R. 46

Caballero y Góngora, A. 120
Cajigal y Monserrat, J.M. de 121
Campbell, J. 46, 53, 57
Canada 8, 60
capital punishment 49–51, 53–8
capitalism 3–6, 8, 19, 29, 47–8, 50, 59–61, 110
Caporinche, T. 20–1, 23–4, 27–9, 34–5
Capuchins 16–18, 22–3, 25–7
Caribbean 15, 21–2, 35, 60, 90, 98–9, 109,
    111–15, 121
Catholics 17, 23–5, 46, 91
Charles III, King 16, 23–5, 34
Charles IV, King 108
Chile 117

Citizens' Gathering 74
citizenship 8, 124
civil society 47, 49, 55, 59
class structure 2, 47, 49–51, 54, 56, 59–60, 73, 75–7, 84, 121
Clay, H. 120
climate 21–2, 32
Clossey, L. 8
Cloyne, P. 52
coerced labor 5, 30, 45–69
Cohen, W.B. 90
Cold War 2
Coleman, D. 56
Colombia 4, 16, 21, 35, 109, 112, 122
colonialism 2–5, 7–8, 15–28, 32–5, 46–8; in Africa 90, 95, 97–100; and Batavia 72; and British commerce 55, 61; and Tupac Amaru movement 107–10, 112–13, 118–19, 123–4
colonization 6–7, 17, 20, 24–5, 59, 89–91, 93, 97–9
combat trauma 58–9
commerce 6–7, 24, 30, 33–4, 45–69, 89–91, 93–5, 100, 107–8, 113
common land 61
Compagnie de la gomme du Sénégal 6, 89, 91–4, 98, 100
Comunero movement 109, 112–13, 120–2, 124
constitutions 6, 35, 71, 73–4, 77, 80, 82–3, 122
contraband 18, 23–4
corporal punishment 49–51, 53, 55
corsairs 18, 113
Cortés y Vita, C.M. 118
courts martial 46, 49–59
creoles 2, 7, 16–17, 20, 23; and Batavian Revolution 72; and Guajiros 25, 27, 29, 33; and Tupac Amaru movement 108, 112, 118, 120–1, 123–4
Cromwell, O. 49
Cuba 121
Cubans 120
Cumberland, R. 114

Dalling, J. 113
Davis, T. 54
Davis, W. 56
Dayley, T. 54–5
Declaration of the Rights of Man 98
decolonization 6
Delacroix, C.-F. 83
democracy 1–3, 6, 8, 70–88, 110, 124–5
Diop, D. 90
disavowal 7, 111–12, 116–18, 124
discipline 5, 27, 35, 45–69
divide and rule strategy 16, 23
Drake, F. 18
Dubois, L. 98
Dunn, P. 45–7, 51, 57

Durand, J.-B.-L. 6–7, 89–106
Dutch 15–16, 20–1, 23, 25, 30–1, 35, 71–2, 75, 77
Dutch Revolt 72

East India Companies 60, 72
ecology 18–22
Edwards, G. 54
Edwards, J. 54
Egypt 93, 99
elites 2, 6, 8, 17, 19, 24, 71–3, 83, 111, 122
Encio, B. 26–7
enclosures 61
England 61, 110, 112–13, 117–18, 124
English 100, 113–14, 116–17
Enlightenment 110–11, 124
epidemics 19
ethno-genesis 15, 18–22
Europe 4–5, 7, 34, 59–60, 90–2, 96–7, 100, 110–12, 115, 118–22, 124
Europeans 4–7, 16–21, 23, 27–9, 47, 89–92, 95, 97, 100, 108, 122–4
evangelization 22–3, 25
explorers 5, 18, 22, 90, 94–5, 98–9

Fatah-Black, K. 6, 70–88
federalism 6, 71–3, 80, 83–4, 122
Fernández, A.-R. 118
Ferrer, A. 111
feudalism 73
Fischer, S. 7, 111
Folch de Cardona, J.S. 22
Foucault, M. 90
France 6, 15, 45, 47, 60, 71–3, 82–3, 90–5, 97–9, 109–10, 112–13, 115
freemasons 45
French 15–16, 20, 25, 30, 35; and Africa 89–95, 97–9; and Batavian Revolution 73–7, 80, 82–3; and British commerce 46, 52, 54–5, 60; and Tupac Amaru movement 111
French Revolution 7, 73, 90, 97–8, 109
Frykman, N. 5
further research 1

Gage, T. 54
Galluzo, J. 30–3
Gálvez, B. de 121
Gálvez, J. de 121–2
General Assembly of Neighbourhood Councils 74–5
George II, King 46
Germain, G. 113
Germans 56, 100
Germany 118
Gilbert, A. 50, 57
Global North/South 8
globalization 2–3, 8, 47
Godoy, J.J. 120–1
Godoy, M. de 108

Gold Coast 99
Gómez, J. 115
governance 75, 118
Guajira Peninsula 4, 7, 15–44
Guajiros 15–44
guerilla tactics 56
Guiror, M. 27, 30
Guyatt, N. 8

Haiti 2–3
Haitian Revolution 1, 7, 72, 90, 110–11
hangings 48, 51–5, 57
Hapsburgs 110
Harnisch, J.C. 78
Hay, D. 49
historical materialism 48, 60
Hobsbawm, E.J. 3, 109
Holland 15, 70–1, 78, 81–2
Humboldt, A. von 119–20, 123
Hunt, L. 2
hunter-gatherers 20, 22
Hylton, F. 3–5, 7–8, 15–44

ideology 34
imperialism 1–8, 15–16, 34, 45–69, 72, 90,
    112–13, 117–18, 120, 122, 124
indentured servants 3, 46–7
India 60
indigenous peoples 2–5, 7–8, 15–20, 33–5, 93,
    96, 107–8, 111, 122
industrial revolution 4
inequalities 3, 8
Inkas 108, 110, 114–19, 122, 124
Inquisition 120
Ireland 45, 61
Irish 45–6
Islam 92
Italy 115, 120–1

Jacinto, J. 16–17, 20–1, 23–5, 28–9, 31–3, 35
Jacobins 73, 81
Jamaica 115, 120, 122–3
James, C.L.R. 1, 3
James II, King 49
Jeffries, E. 57
Jesuits 23, 115, 120–1
Johnstone, G. 117
Julián, A. 23
justice 49–54, 56, 58–9

Katari, D. 108
Katari, Tomás 108, 122
Katari, Tupaj 108, 117, 122
Keegan, J. 47
kinship 4, 16–17, 19–21, 24, 26, 29, 32–3
Klooster, W. 109
Knott, S. 1–2
Knox, J. 56
Kuna 15, 19

Latin America 4, 108–9, 120
Leiden University 75
Linebaugh, P. 1, 3, 5, 7, 51
local autonomy 70–88
López Sierra, C. 16–18, 20–30, 34–5
López Sierra, D. 25
López Sierra, J. 23–4
López Sierra, Joseph Antonio 25–6
López Sierra, Joseph Francisco 27
Loudoun, Lord see Campbell, J.

McDonnell, M.A. 1–14
McGuire, P. 56
Majusare, P. 21, 23–5, 27–30, 34–5
Manceron, G. 98
matrilineal clans 20
Mendoza, G. de 16–17, 25–7, 120
mercantilism 15, 34
merchant capital 50, 60
merchants 7, 18, 23–4, 28–9, 31, 34, 91–4, 98
Messía de la Cerda, P. 25–7
mestizos 17, 25, 108, 116–17, 119, 123
Mexico 114–15, 119, 122
Middle East 4
military 5, 15–17, 20, 22, 25; and Batavian
    Revolution 71–2, 78, 80, 83; and British
    commerce 45–69; and Guajiros 27, 32, 34–5;
    and Tupac Amaru movement 108, 113, 116,
    122
Miranda, F. de 121–2
missionaries 16–18, 20–6, 28, 30, 32–5
mixed-race peoples 16–17, 20, 23, 26–7, 91
Monckton, R. 53
monopolies 15, 24, 34, 91–4, 100
Moors 92–5, 97, 100
Moskito 15, 19
mulatos 17, 20, 25, 29, 91
Murray, J. 52, 56
Muslims 93
mutinies 5–6, 47, 49, 51–2, 57, 59

Napoleon, Emperor 93, 98–9, 109
National Vietnam Veterans Readjustment
    Study (NVVRS) 58
nationalism 1–2, 6, 47
Nationwide Assembly of Neighbourhood
    Councils 75, 79–80, 82, 84
Native Americans 1–2, 4, 7–8, 16, 23; and
    British commerce 46, 52; and Guajira
    Peninsula 25, 27, 29–30, 32–3, 35; and
    Tupac Amaru movement 108, 111–15,
    117–25
navies 5, 24, 47–8, 60
Neighbourhood Councils 6, 75, 78–80, 82, 84
neo-liberalism 2
Netherlands 70, 73, 75
New Granada 4, 16–17, 27, 109, 112–14, 120–2,
    124
New World 90, 112, 122–3

Nicaragua 19, 113
Nigeria 90
North Africa 92–3
North America 4–5, 17, 46, 60, 109, 112–13, 115, 118, 121

Ogilvie, J. 46
O'Hara, C. 92
Ojeda, A. de 18
O'Phelan Godoy, S. 110
Orange, House of 49, 73–8, 80
Ottoman Empire 115

Paape, G. 74
Pacific 110
Paine, T. 1, 111
Palmer, R.R. 1–3, 6, 71, 109
Paredes, A. 16–17, 21, 24–35
Park, M. 99
Parliament 46, 49
pastoralism 19–20
Patriot Revolution 72–3, 75–6
Pazos Kanki, V. 120
Pérez, J.A. 30, 32
Perry, D. 53
Peru 108, 110, 112–24
Pestaña y Chumacero, X. de 23
Philippines 60
Phillip V, King 22
Piche, S. 30
piqueting 52–3, 56
Pitt, W. 122
Pittsburgh University 2
plebians 116, 124
political economy 47–8, 50, 60–1
Portugal 112
Post Traumatic Stress Disorder (PTSD) 58
postcolonialism 3
Prevost, J. 53
privateers 18, 114–15
proletariat 46, 59–60
property rights 16–17, 19–21, 24, 28, 47, 49–50, 54, 76, 96
Protectorate 49
Protestants 1, 45–6
Prussians 53, 73

race wars 7, 111, 118–20, 124
radical democracy 70–88
Rea, C. 52–3
Rediker, M. 1, 3, 5, 7
Répentigny, L.L. de 92–4
Rhode, J. 56
Robertson, J. 55
Røge, P. 3, 6, 8, 89–106
Romanticism 119
Romswinckel, J. 75–7
Royal American Regiment 53, 55–6
royalism 18

Rubault, J. 95–7
Ruíz de Noriega, B. 20, 24, 29
Russia 116
rustling 24

Saint-Domingue 98, 109, 111, 115
Sardinia 91
Savage, J. 56
Schimmelpenninck, R.J. 71, 80
Scotland 61
seasons 21
Senegal 6–7, 60, 89–93, 95, 97–100
Senegambia 89, 91, 93–5, 99–100
Serna, P. 6, 72, 83
settlers 16–19, 21, 23–9, 32–5
Seven Years' War 46–8, 50, 58, 60, 91–2, 112
shootings 48, 54–5, 59
Sierra, F. 25
Sierra Leone 90, 99
silencing 1, 3, 5–8, 107, 111, 114, 120, 124
slavery 1–3, 6–7, 18–20, 23–6, 30, 46–7, 60, 72, 76, 90–2, 95–100, 111
smuggling 21, 26
socialism 2
Société des amis noirs et des colonies 99
South America 17, 110, 112–15, 117–18, 120–2, 124
South Asia 4
sovereignty 2, 7–8, 15, 18–19, 26, 30, 33–5, 71, 107–31
Spain 15–17, 23, 33, 60, 110, 112–15, 117–20, 124
Spanish 4, 7, 15–35, 77, 107–24
Stanwix, J. 55
state 6, 17, 34, 48, 50; and Africa 94; and Batavian Revolution 71–3, 76–7, 83; and British commerce 54–5, 59–61; and Tupac Amaru movement 113, 124
Stone, L. 60
Studs, R. 54–5
suffrage 74, 76, 84
Sweden 118
Swiss 53

taxation 18, 24, 34, 47, 107, 113, 115, 121
Te Brake, W. 73
Thomson, S. 3, 7–8, 107–31
Tierra Firme 15, 18, 21
tobacco 20, 29
trade 6–7, 15–21, 23–8, 30–1, 33–4, 47, 90–5, 97, 100
Trap, P.H. 71, 75–6, 78, 81–2
Trouillot, M.-R. 1, 3, 5, 7–8, 111
Tupac Amaru, J.G.C. 107–31

Unie van Utrecht 72
United Kingdom (UK) 8
United States (US) 6, 8, 19, 109, 115, 120, 122–3

Valckenaer, J. 77
Van Beyma, C.L. 80, 82
Van der Veen, N. 80
Van Lelyveld, W. 71, 75, 78, 81
Velasco de Amoscótegui, L. de 22
Venezuela 4, 16, 18, 20–1, 34–5, 113–14, 121–2
Vespucci, A. 18
violence 2, 5, 7, 17, 25; and Africa 98; and British commerce 47–51, 58–9; and Guajiros 31, 34–5; and Tupac Amaru movement 111, 117, 119, 124
Viscardo y Guzmán, J.J.P. 121, 123
Voltaire 118
Voyage au Sénégal 6, 89–106
Vreede, P. 75, 77, 80, 82–3

Wahhabis 1
War of Jenkin's Ear 34

War of the Vendée 72, 77
wars 15, 18, 26, 32–4, 45–50; and Africa 91–2; and Batavian Revolution 72–3, 77, 83; and British commerce 52, 55, 57–61; race 7, 111, 118–20, 124; and Tupac Amaru movement 109, 112, 117
Wars of Independence 18, 32–3, 72–3, 83, 91, 109, 112, 120
Way, P. 3, 5, 8, 45–69
West Africa 7, 91, 94, 97, 99
West India Company 72
whippings 48, 50–4, 56–9
Williams, H.M. 119–21
Windward Islands 21
Wood, L. 54

zambos 17, 20, 25, 29–30, 32